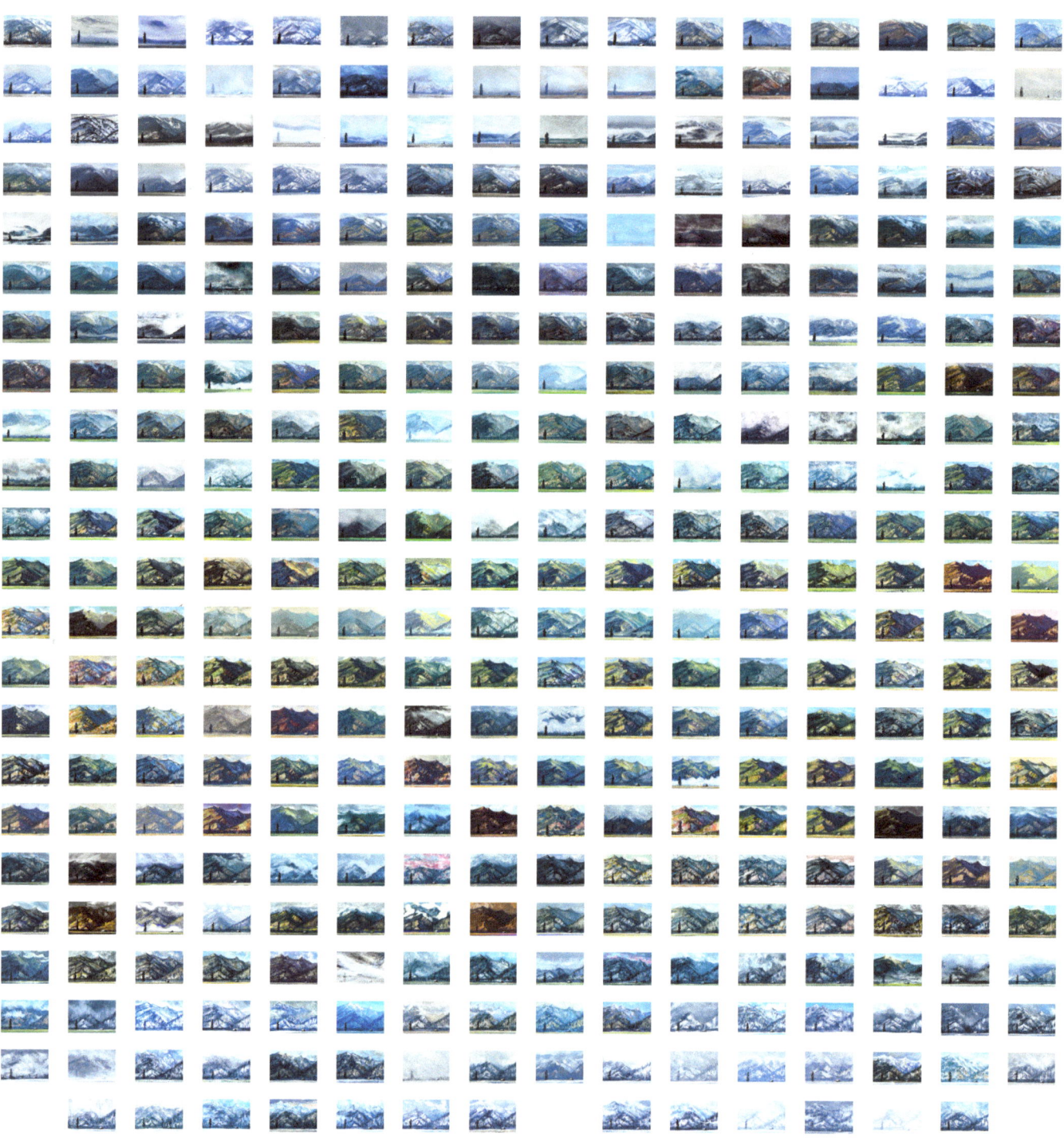

COUGAR PEAK-A-BOO

a year in the life of a mountain

dedication

This book is dedicated to my loving wife Jennifer, who though we were only dating at the time, put up with me and my wild obsession with the mountain.

contact info

For more information about me, and to view other artwork I have created please visit -

www.jaredshear.com

Layout: Jared Shear

Published by Shear Press   Printed in the United States
204 Gallatin Street
Thompson Falls, MT 59873   First Edition
E-mail: jashear@gmail.com

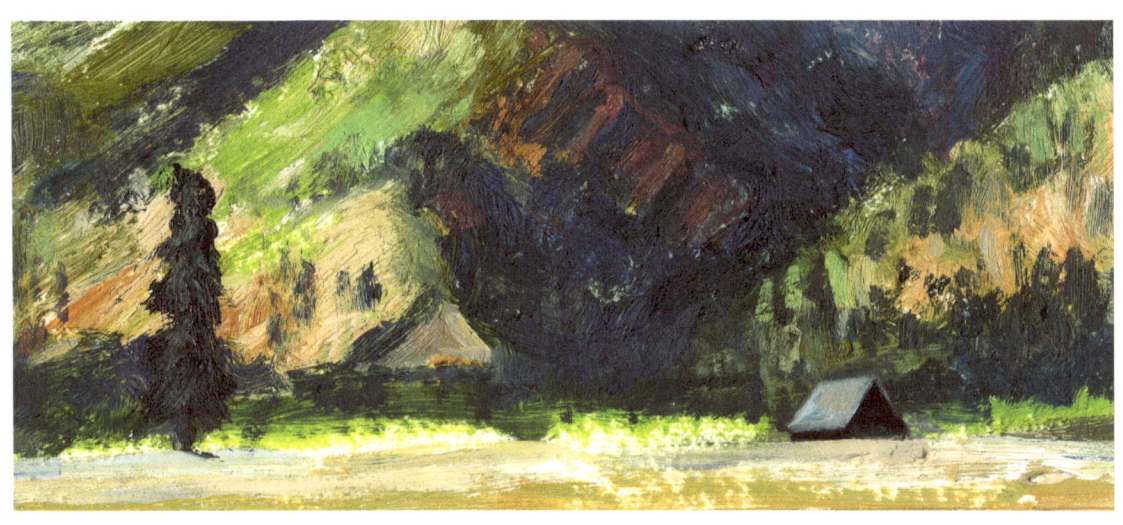

table of contents

introduction

The idea for the Cougar Peak series evolved late in the year of 2006. There were multiple factors that helped to shape the series into what it eventually became.

As long as I can remember I have always been fascinated with Cougar Peak. The mountain is nestled among the other peaks that surround my family's farm. It has always captured my attention, no matter the time of day, or season. Whenever I look upon it, I come away inspired, and am left with a sense of awe.

Perhaps though, it is not the mountain itself that I find so fascinating, but a much broader range of ideas and subjects that make up what I perceive as the "mountain". What I mean by this, is that the light, weather, temperature, seasons, etc... all help to form the mountain and how I observe it. Together as a whole they create this grand symphony, but individually they speak with a sort of music all their own. I am mesmerized by this ensemble, and the music, or rhythm of creation they play to. Yet, I am also in love with the individual musicians so to speak, and each their parts, as they contribute to the whole.

At that time I was interested in the daily painter movement that was taking off across the internet. A number of artists were painting images, and posting them online, nearly on a daily basis. I found the idea fascinating, and wanted to be part of that movement as well.

What also interested me about the daily painter movement was the idea of being accountable to myself as an artist. It is an important obstacle I think every artist must overcome, or deal with at some point if they are going to be serious about producing a body of work. As an artist, if you only paint when you feel like painting.....that is if you only paint when the sun shines, the planets are aligned, and you are feeling, "in the mood," then you will find yourself not painting very often.

One of my inspirations came from an artist named Nathan Fowkes. He produced a little series of sequential art out of his office window. All of the paintings, were of the same exact scene, but each one had a different look and feel, depending on the time of day and how he chose to capture the light. I realized in these paintings how much the mood, or emotional content of the image really depends on how you approach it in terms of lighting.

The last factor that went into helping shape this series was my desire, in the simplest sense, to just become a better painter. There were certain techniques, mediums, and ideas that I wanted to explore, and become more proficient at. This project gave me the perfect opportunity to explore those.

If you combine all of these factors together with a quickly approaching New Year, what you end up with is a recipe for a Cougar Peak-A-Boo.

My process for these paintings can be broken down into a couple of categories. These categories I will label as traditional, and digital.

The greater part of the series was painted in a traditional manner, that is with real paints outside of my studio in the true plein air style. All of the traditional pieces were painted on a pochade box manufactured by a company named Open Box M.

Choosing what surface to work on was always a fun part of keeping the project fresh for me. I painted on a variety of materials from illustration board, print making papers, tyvek, masonite, manila folders and even ice cream bar wrappers.

I would begin by drawing out a predefined border with a template I created to ensure each piece was the same size. After this I would mask off the outside of the border with tape, in order to assure the paint stayed within the boundaries. Once the taping was completed, I usually worked up a quick sketch of the mountain with either pastel, or pencil to give me a guideline to work by. Most of the time I would then seal this sketch down with an acrylic matte medium.

After my sketch was completed, I would then choose a medium to work in. Particular days would almost call out to me that the painting needed to be in a certain medium. Some paintings just screamed out to be painted in oils, or watercolor. Other days it was not so clear, and depending on my mood I would pick one.

The digital paintings for the series were painted in my studio that had a view of the mountain. I painted these on the computer with Adobe Photoshop. All of these images were started with a blank canvas, paint was applied in the same way you would a traditional painting, except that the digital paint is applied with a digital paintbrush, and digital paint.

Most of the paintings were completed from anywhere between 1 -1 1/2 hours. The time of day depended a great deal on when I was available to paint that day.

Once the painting was completed, I would scan in the image on a flatbed scanner, create an archived version, and then also a web friendly file to then post up on the internet. This process was then replicated each day, again, and again, and again.

It is my sincere hope that you enjoy this book, and will be able to share some of the fascination I have for Cougar Peak. Our world has become so busy, that we find it very difficult to devote our attention to a single subject longer than 5 minutes, much less a month or a year. You might not have a Cougar Peak in your back yard, but you might find you have something as equally fascinating.....if only you will take the time to sit and observe it.

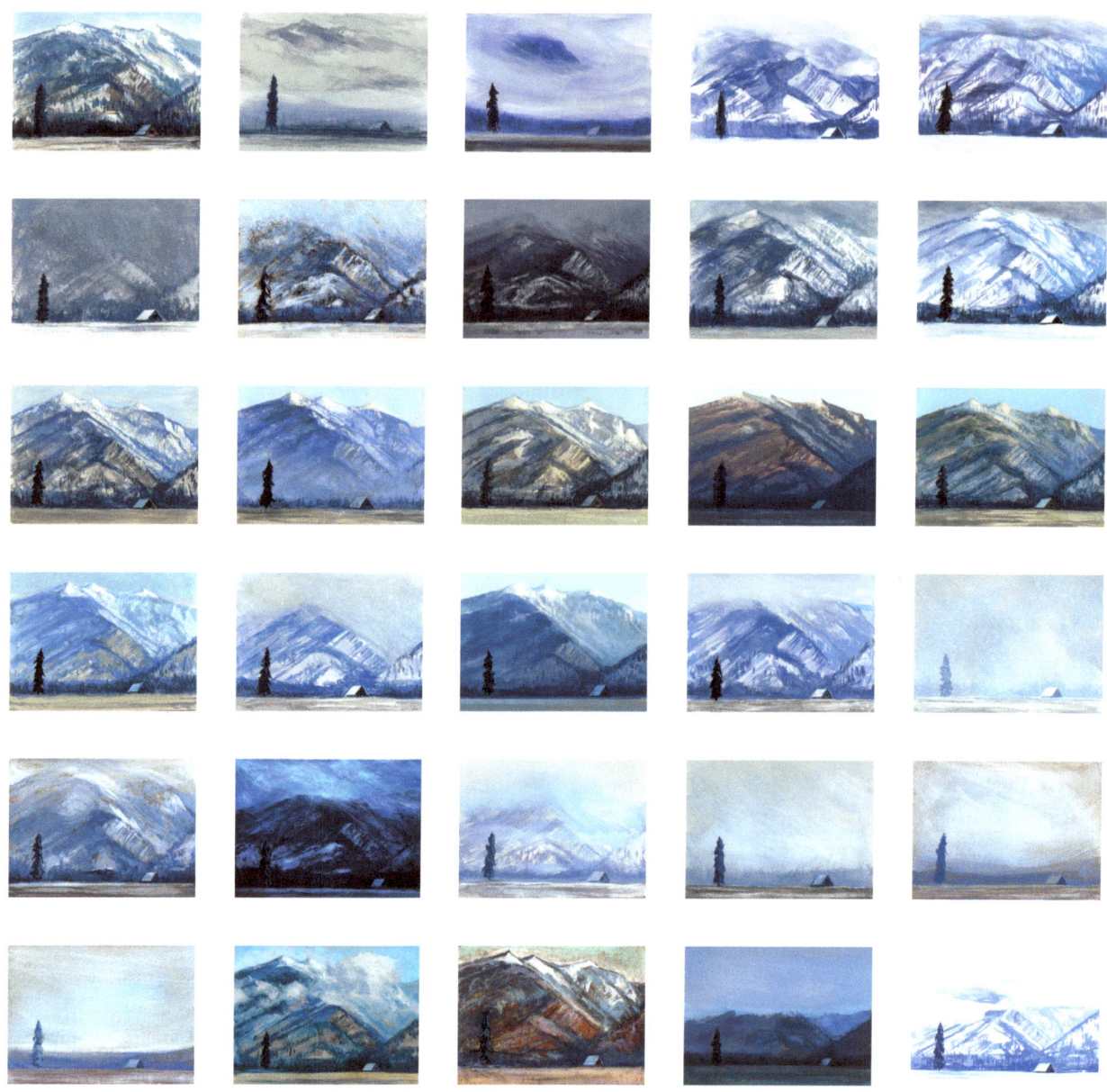

COUGAR PEAK·A·BOO
- The Art of Jared Shear -

JANUARY

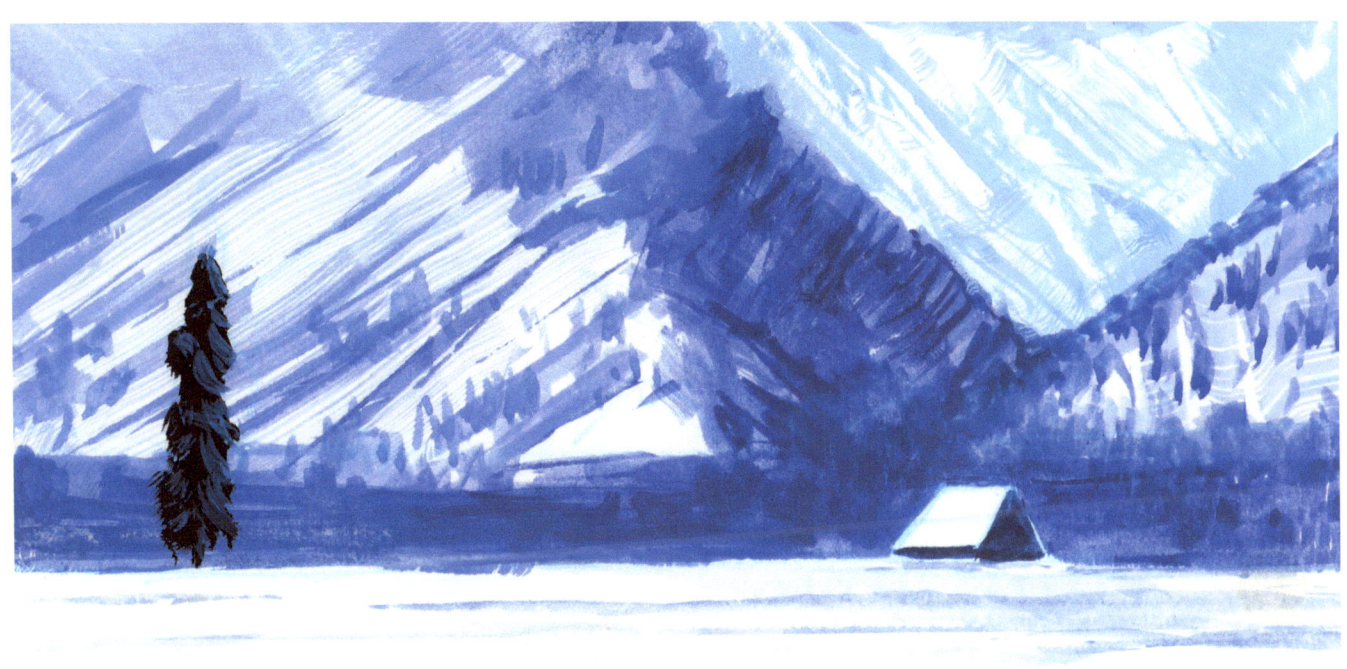

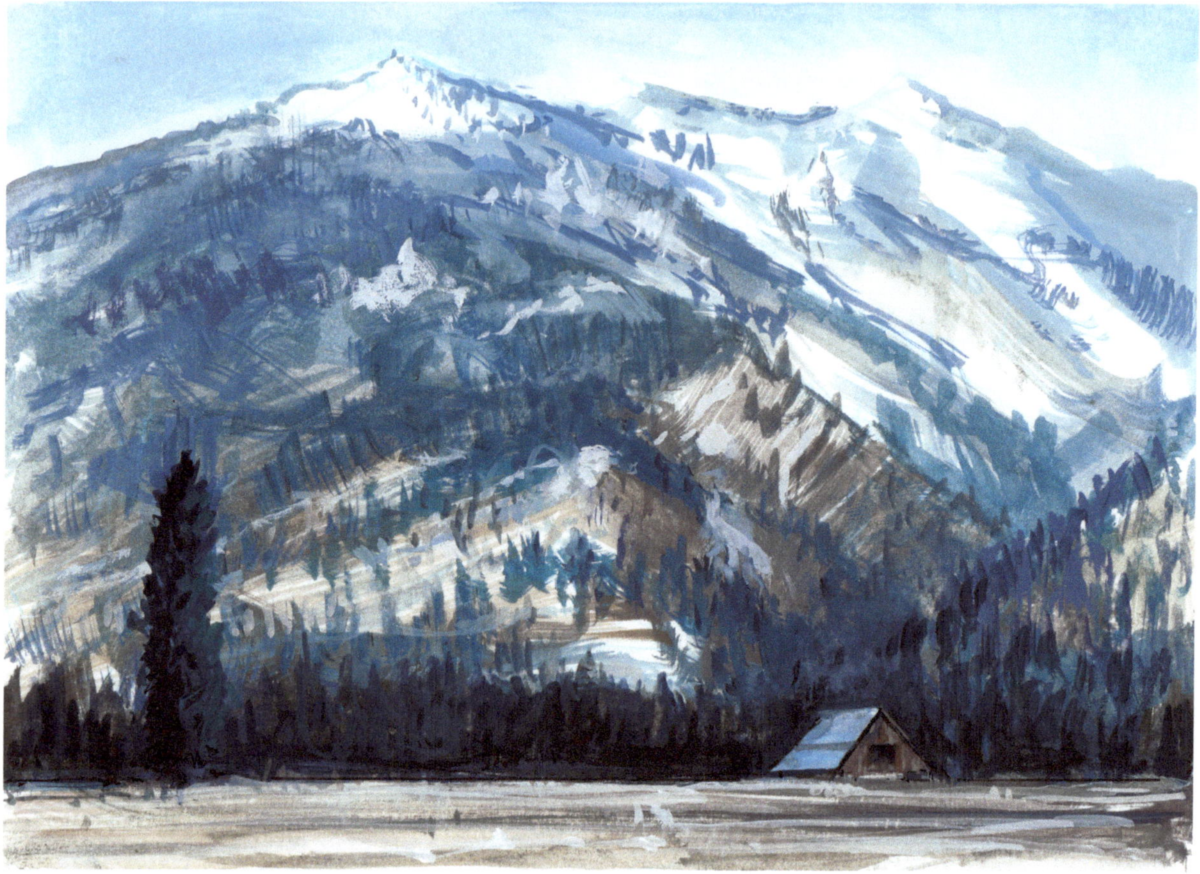

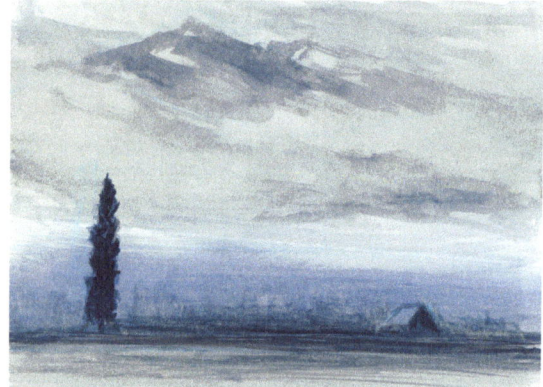

#1 Gouache on Paper   01/01/2007

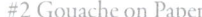

#2 Gouache on Paper   01/02/2007

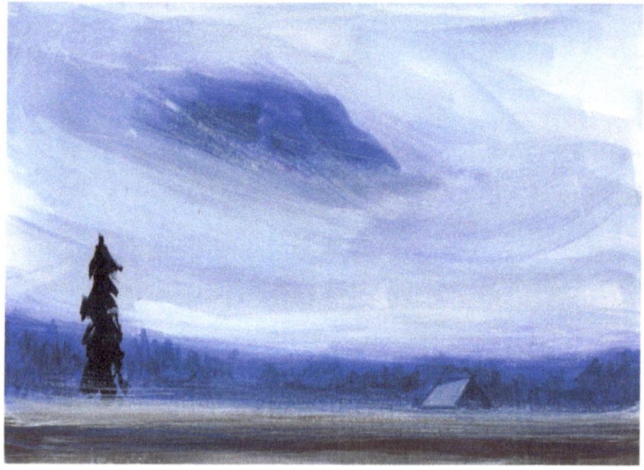

#3 Gouache on Paper   01/03/2007

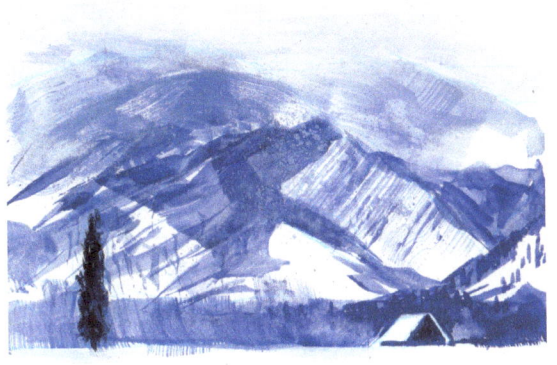

#4 Gouache on Paper   01/04/2007

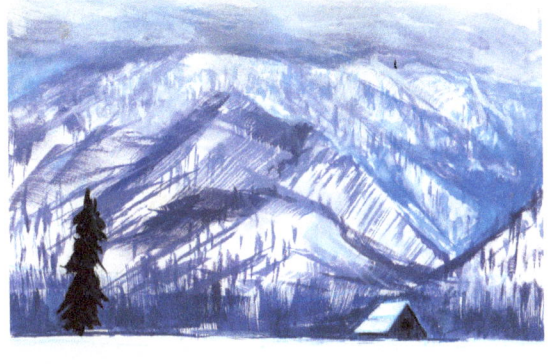

#5 Gouache on Paper   01/05/2007

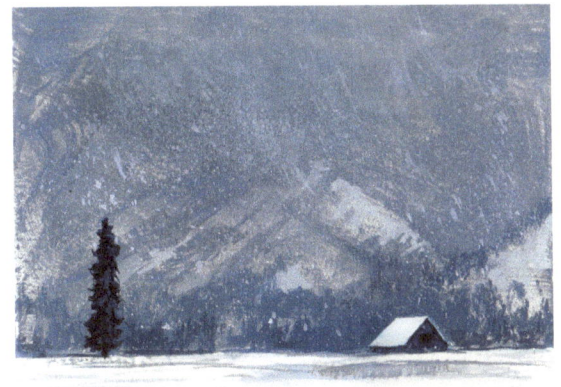

#6 Gouache on Paper   01/06/2007

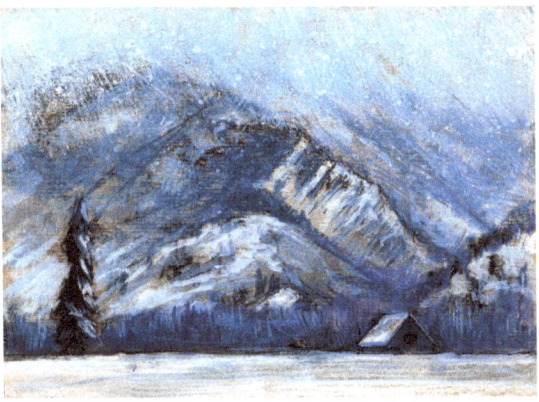

#7 Gouache on Paper   01/07/2007

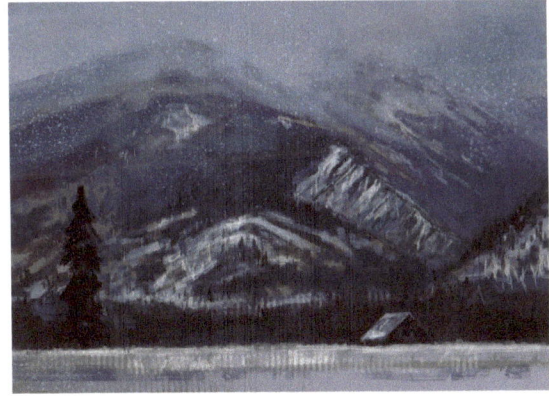

#8 Digital   01/08/2007

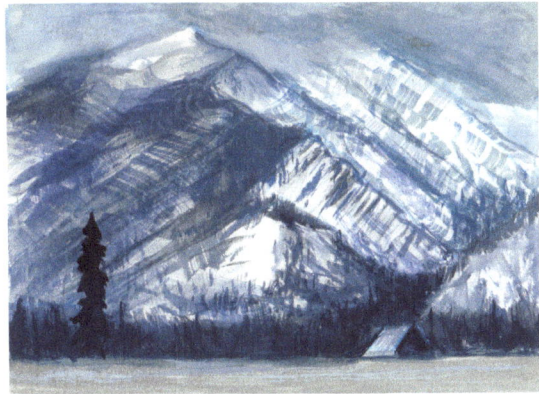

#9 Gouache on Paper   01/09/2007

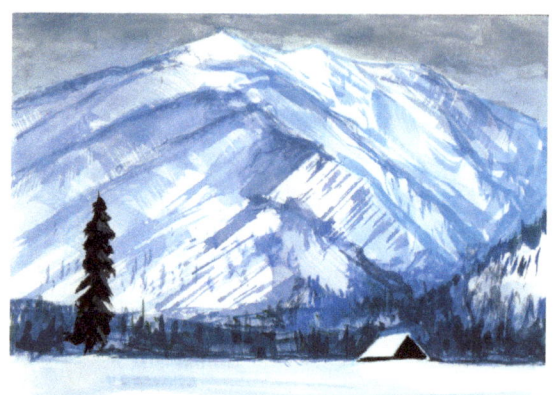

#10Gouache on Paper 01/10/2007

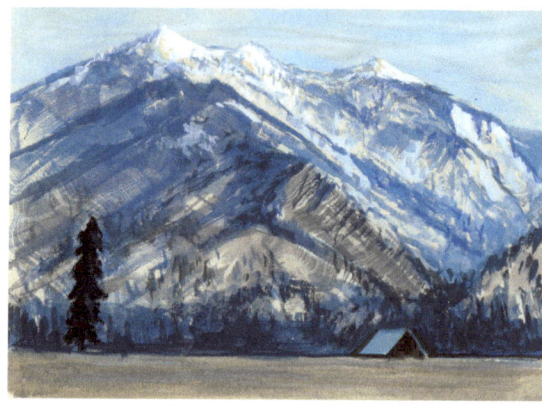

#11 Gouache on Paper 01/11/2007

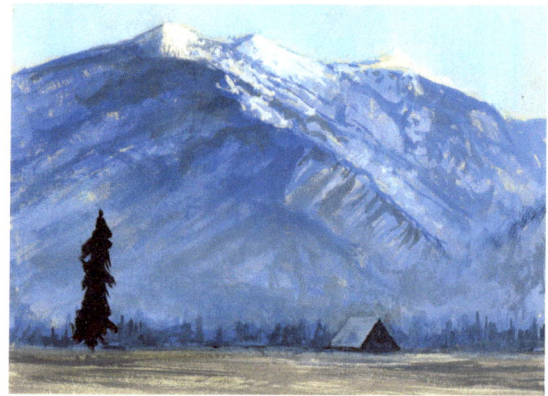

#12 Gouache on Paper 01/12/2007

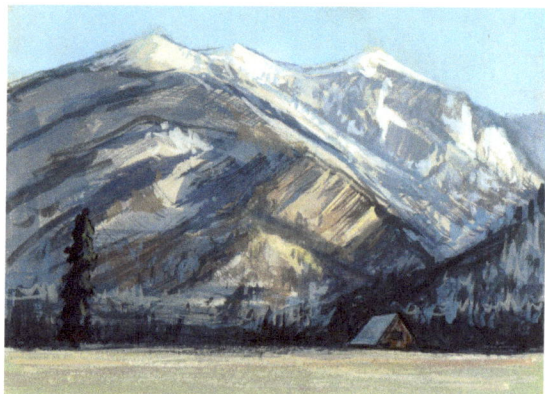

#13 Gouache on Paper 01/13/2007

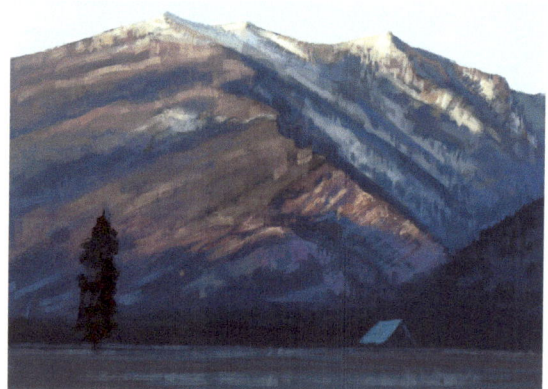

#14 Digital 01/14/2007

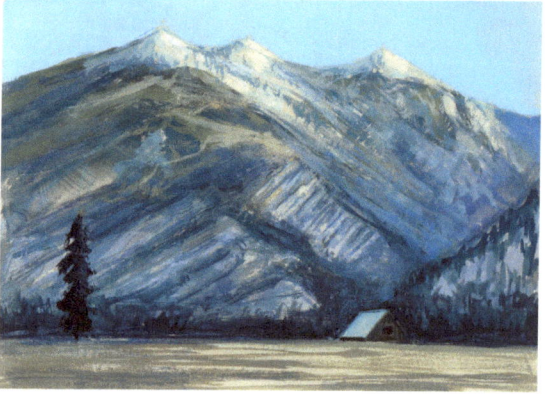

#15 Gouache on Paper 01/15/2007

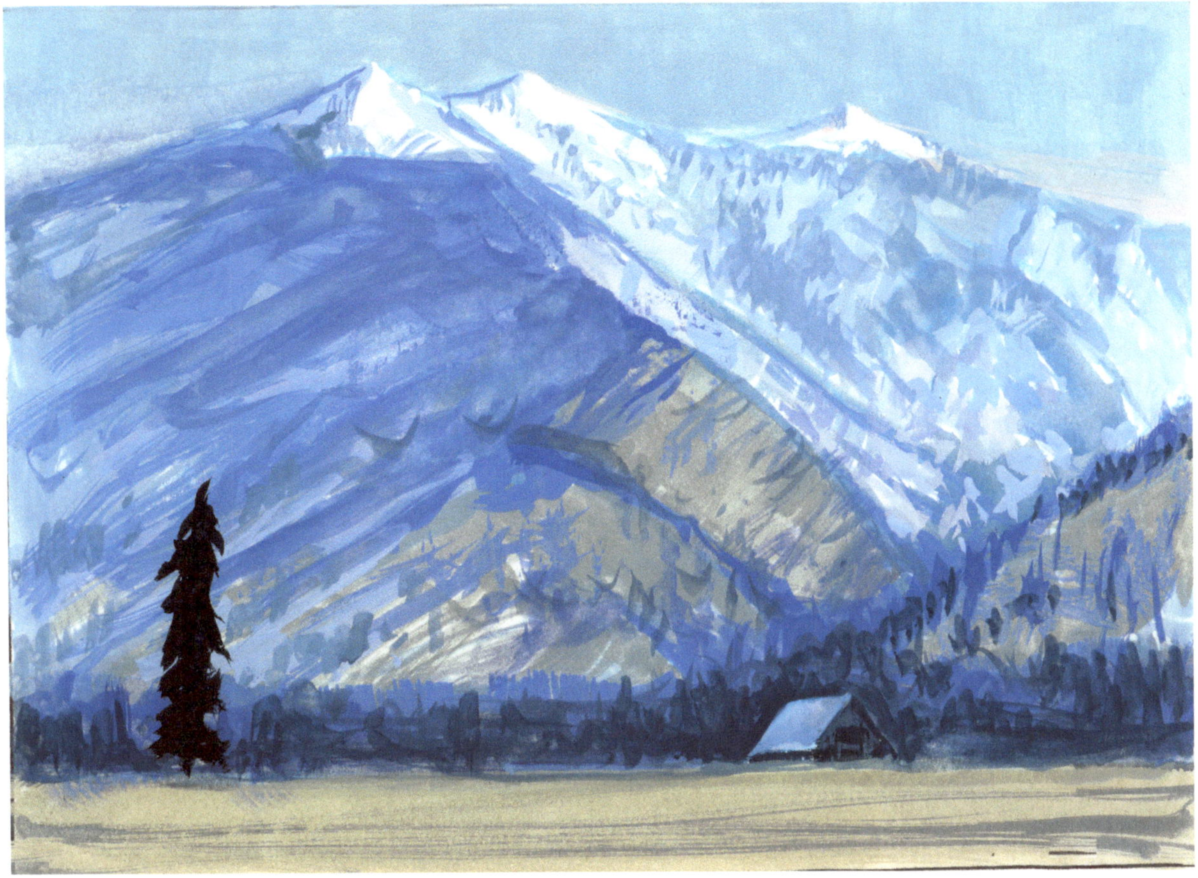

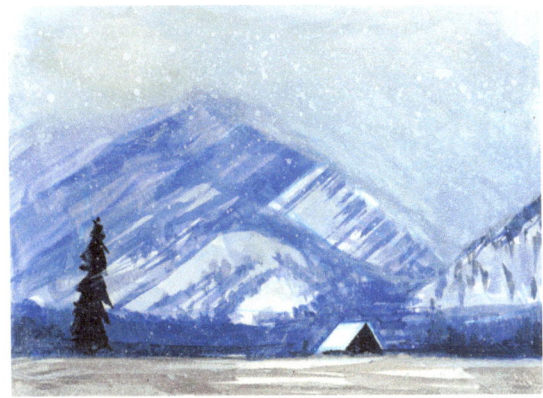

#16 Gouache on Paper   01/16/2007

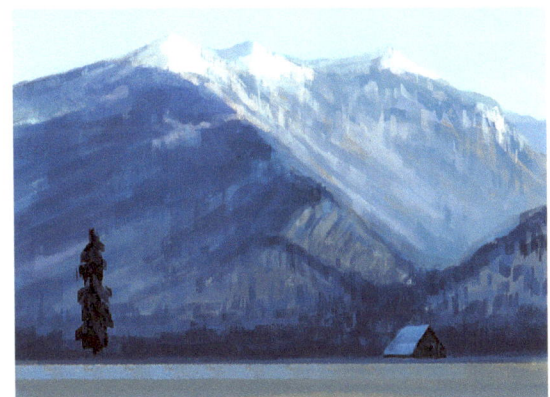

#17 Gouache on Paper   01/17/2007   #18 Digital   01/18/2007

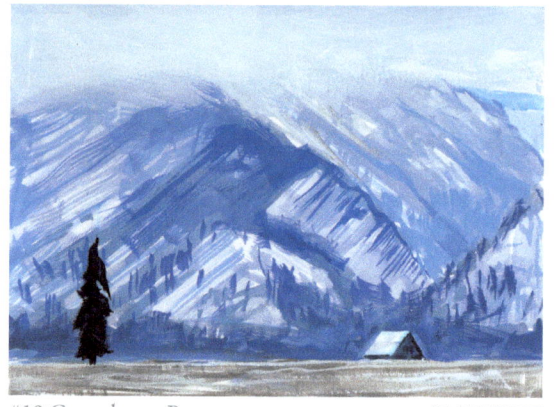

#19 Gouache on Paper   01/19/2007

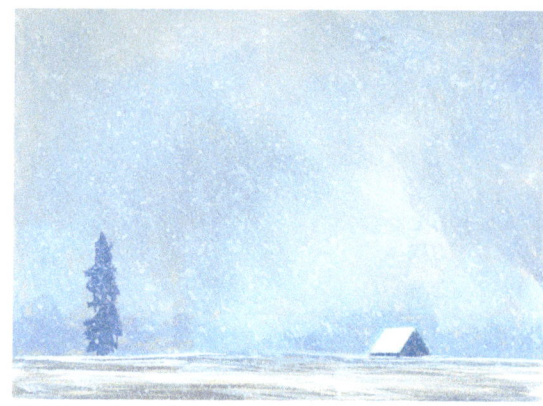

#20 Gouache on Paper   01/20/2007

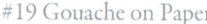

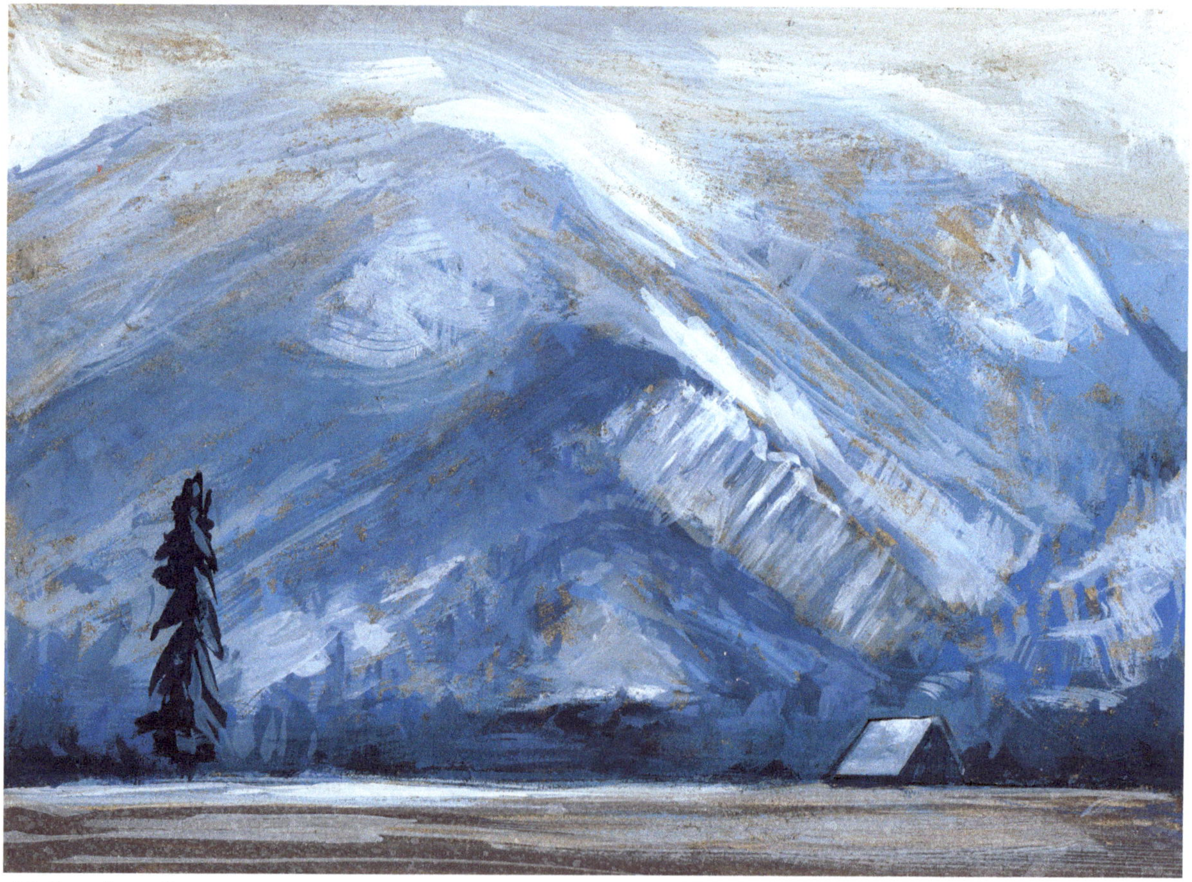

#21 Gouache on Paper   01/21/2007

COUGAR PEAK-A-BOO
- The Art of Jared Shear -

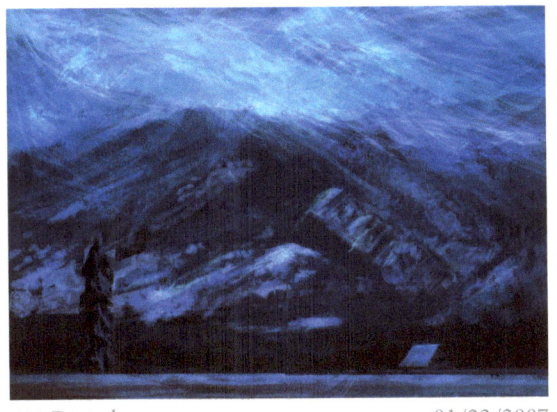

#22 Digital   01/22/2007

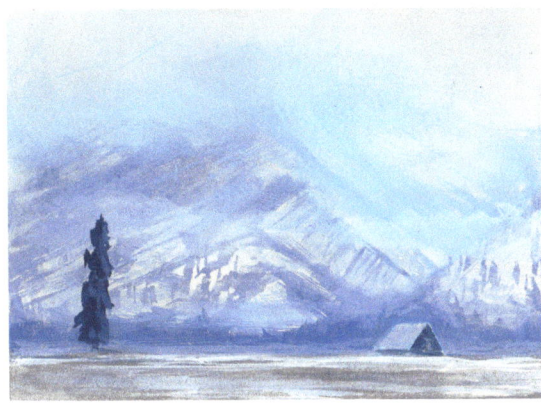

#23 Gouache on Paper   01/23/2007

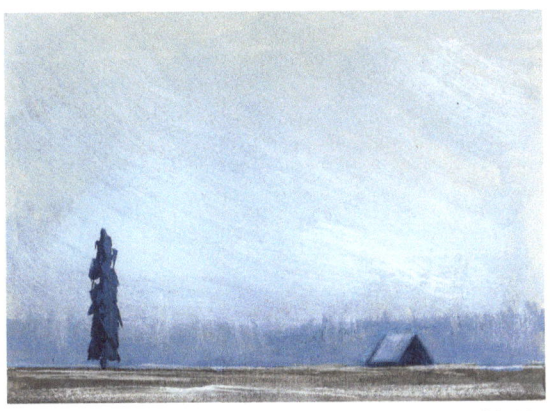

#24 Gouache on Paper   01/24/2007

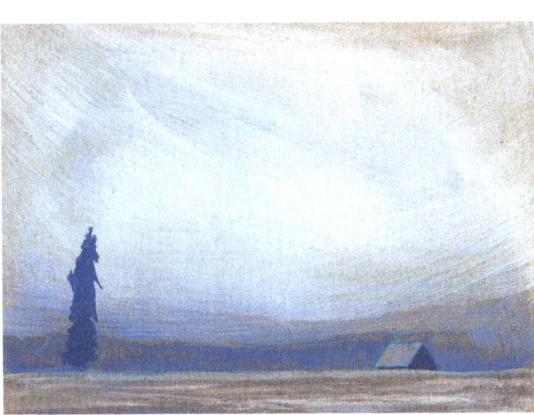

#25 Gouache on Paper   01/25/2007

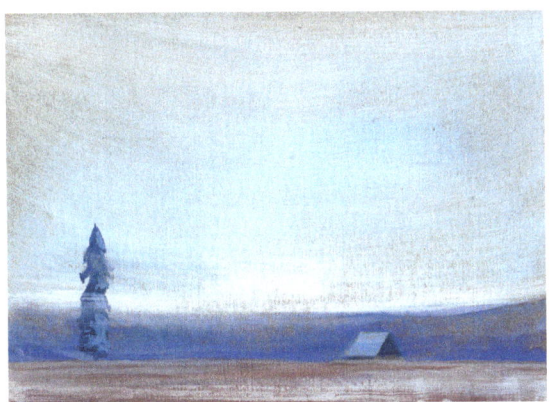

#26 Gouache on Paper   01/26/2007

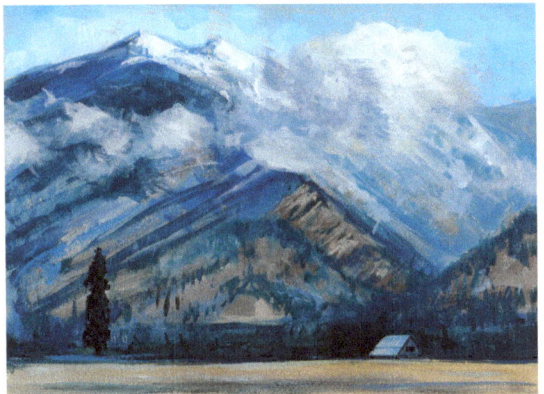

#27 Gouache on Paper   01/27/2007

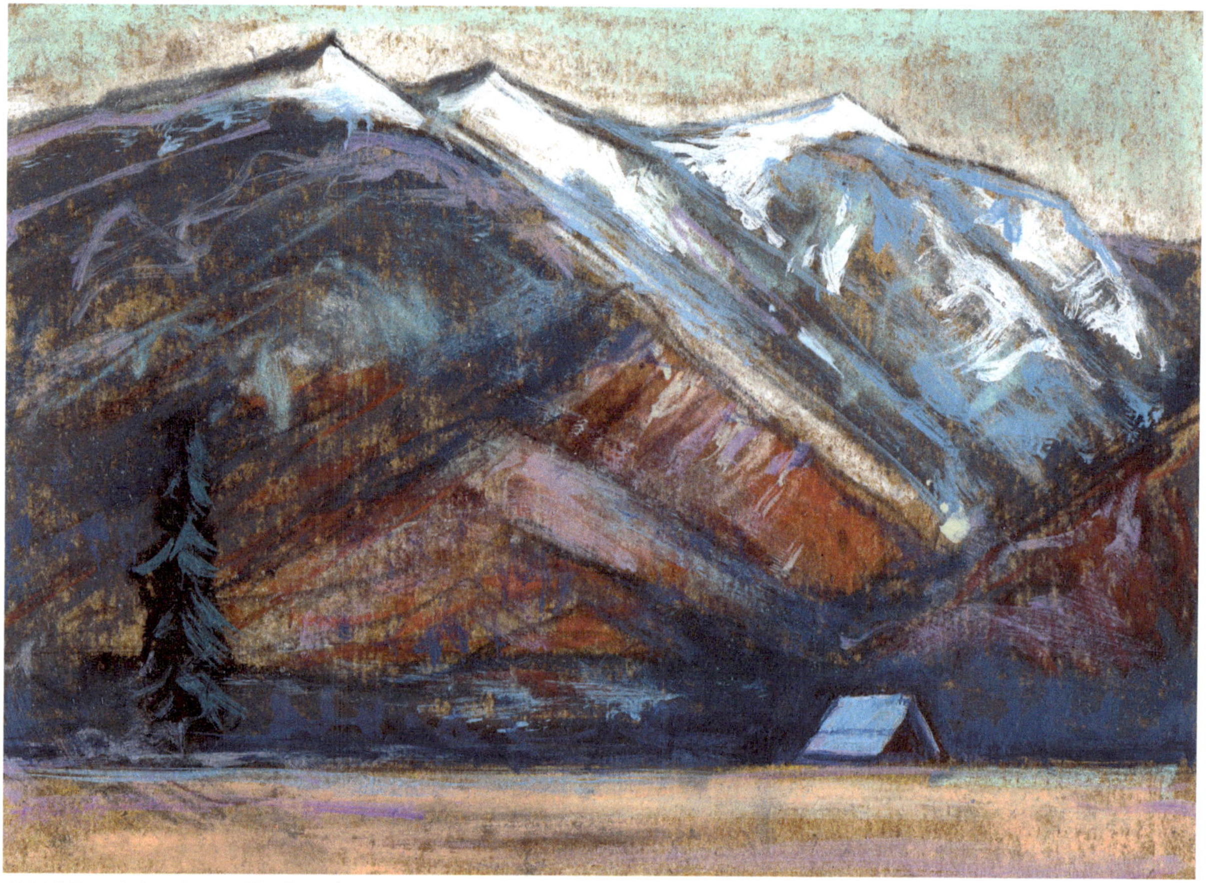

#28 NuPastel, Acrylic on Chipboard

01/28/2007

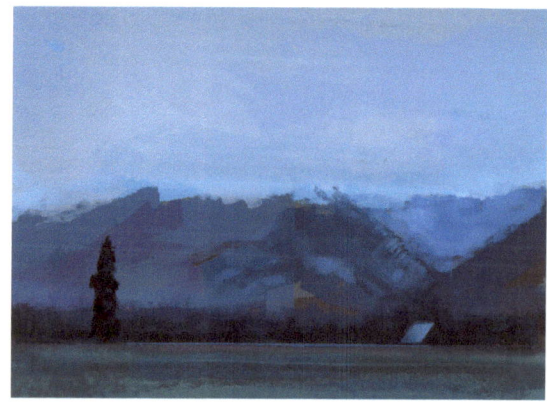

#29 Digital   01/29/2007

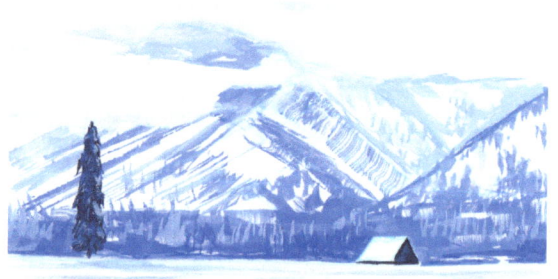

#30 Gouache on Paper   01/30/2007

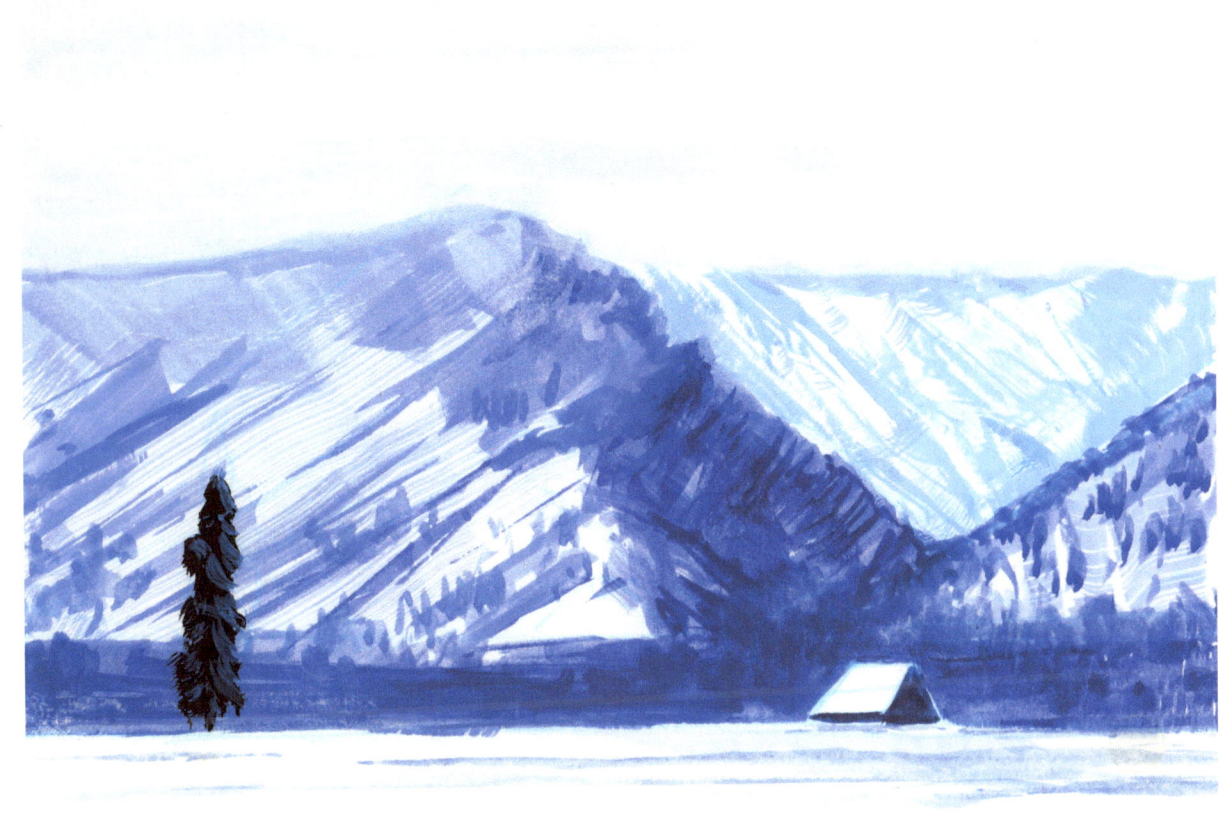

#31 Gouache on Paper

01/31/2007

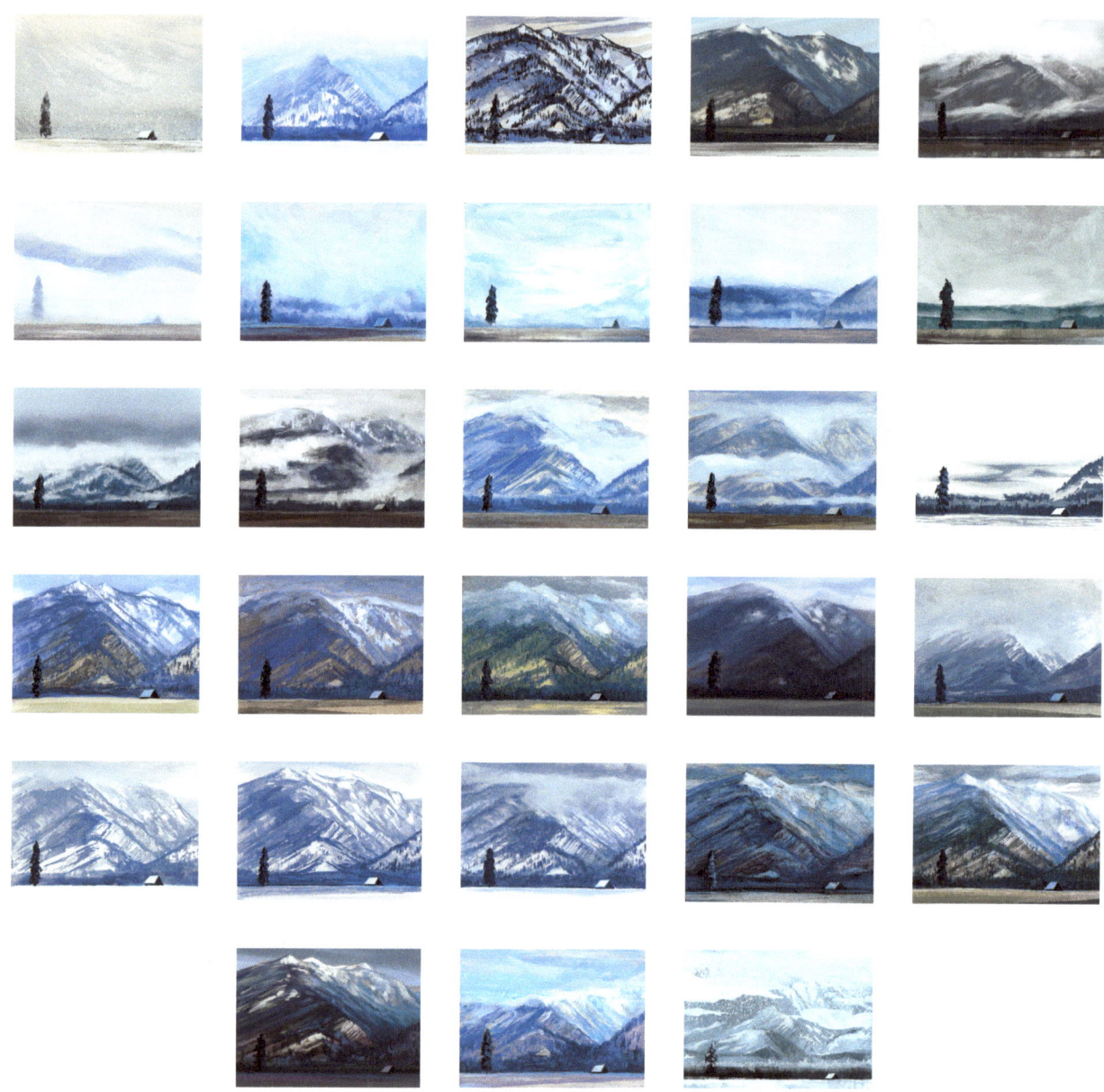

COUGAR PEAK-A-BOO
- The Art of Jared Shear -

FEBRUARY

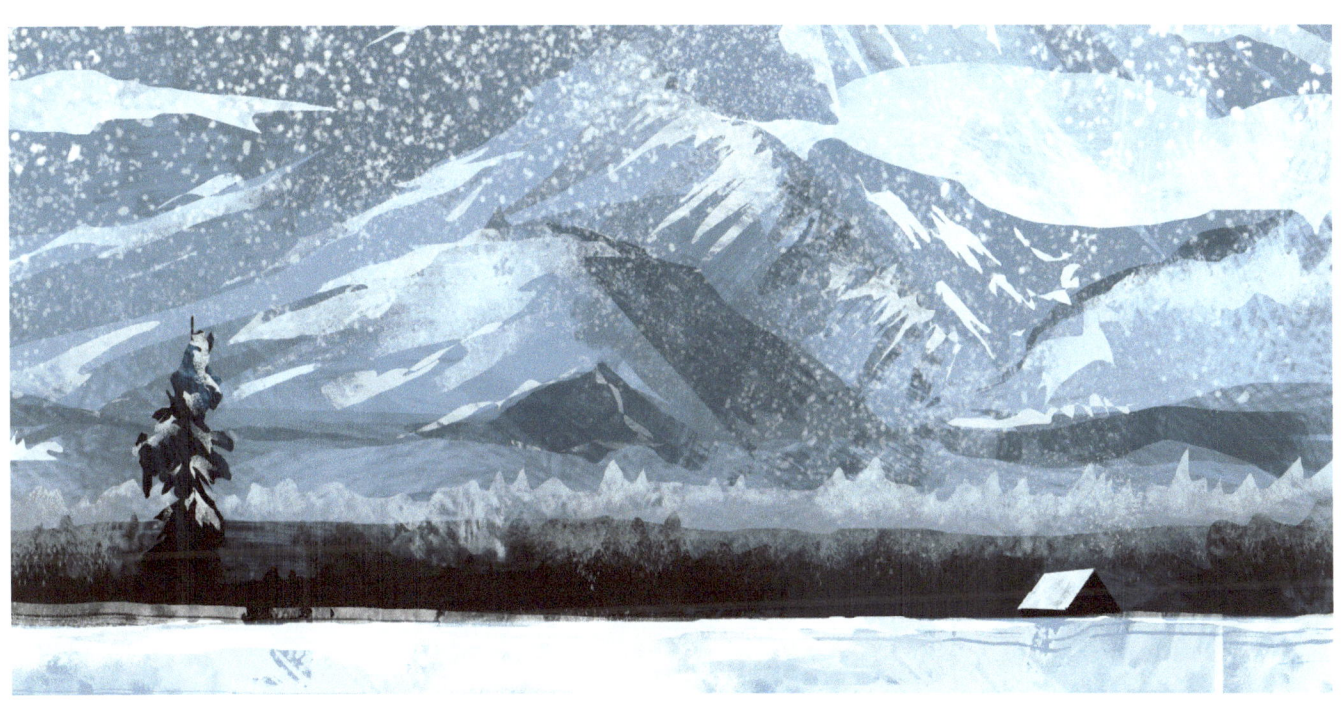

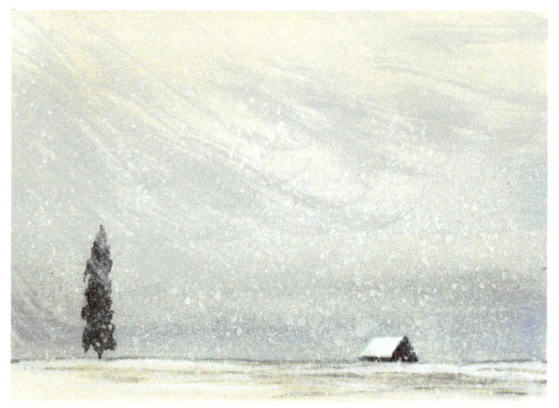

#32 Gouache/Digital on Paper   02/01/2007

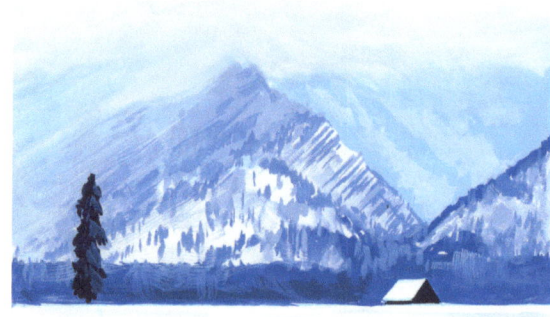

#33 Gouache/Digital on Paper   02/02/2007

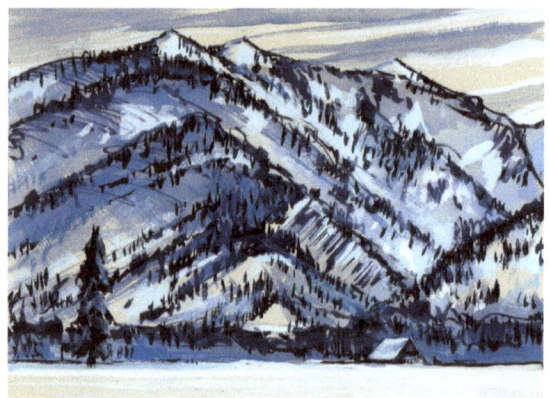

#34 Ink/Gouache on Paper   02/03/2007

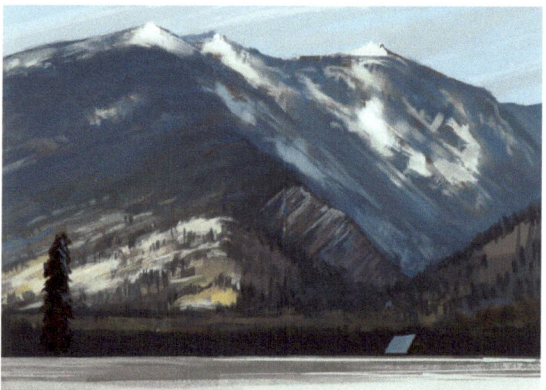

#35 Digital   02/04/2007

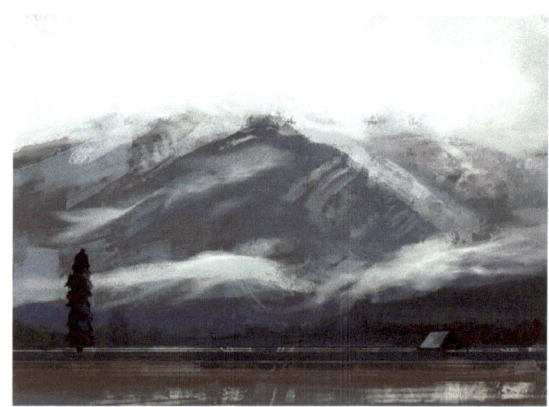

#36 Digital   02/05/2007

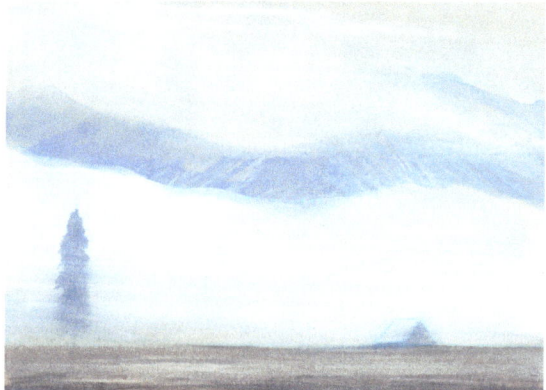

#37 Gouache on Paper   02/06/2007

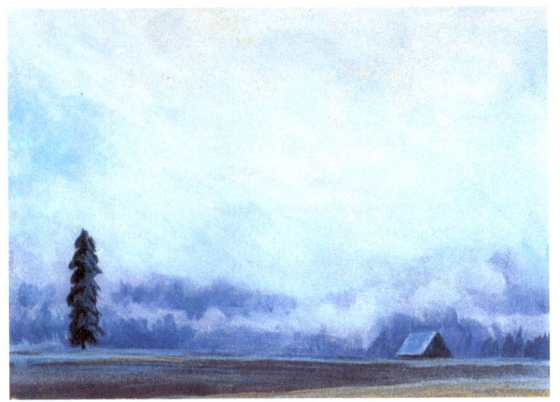

#38 Gouache on Paper   02/07/2007

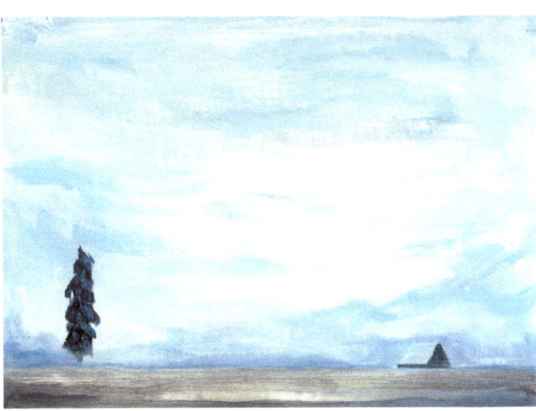

#39 Acrylic on Paper   02/08/2007

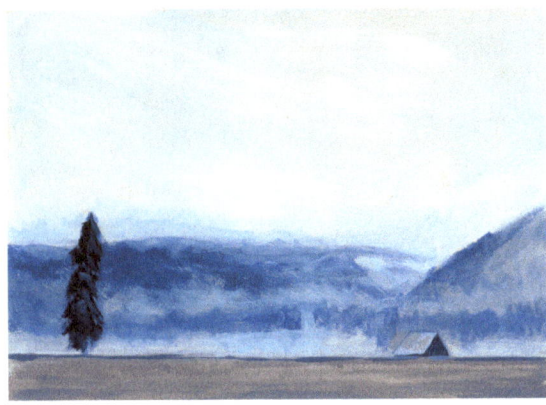

#40 Acrylic on Paper   02/09/2007

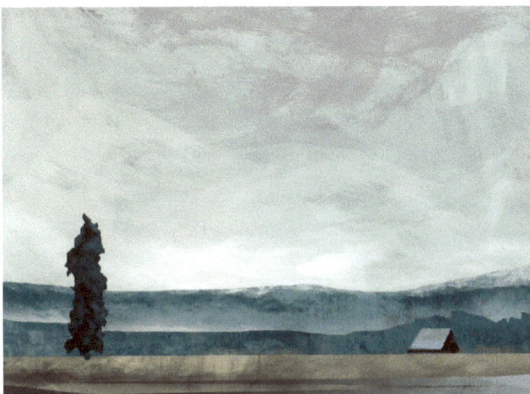

#41 Digital   02/10/2007

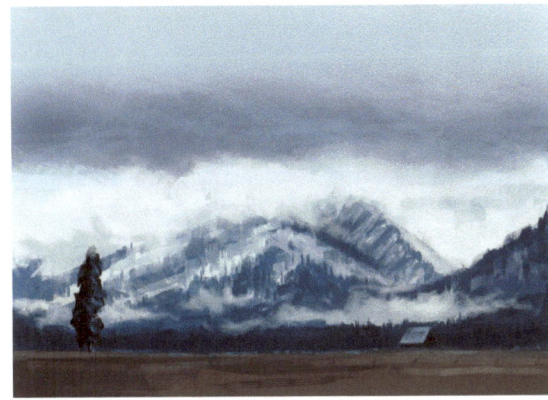

#42 Digital   02/11/2007

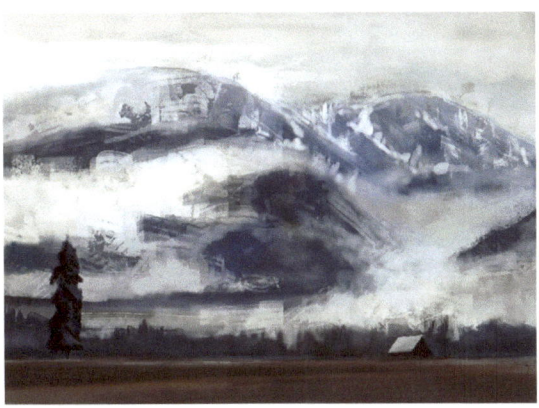

#43 Digital   02/12/2007

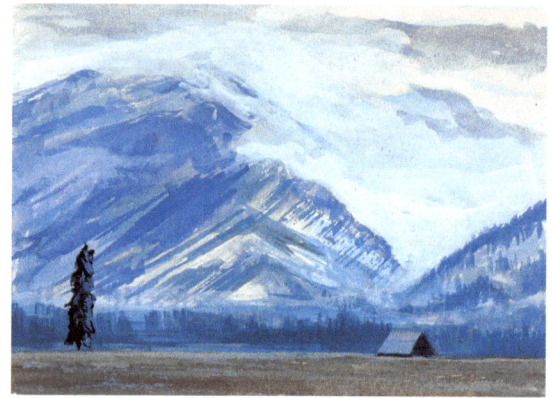

#44 Gouache on Paper   02/13/2007

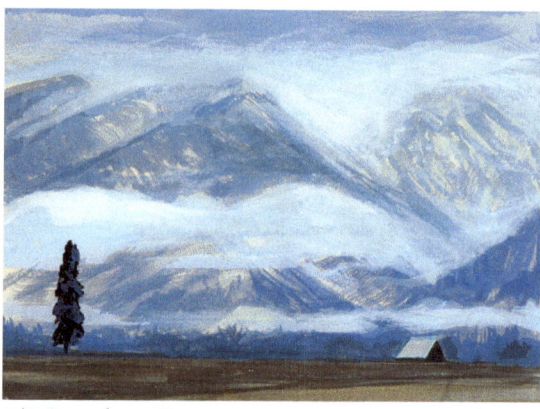

#45 Gouache on Paper   02/14/2007

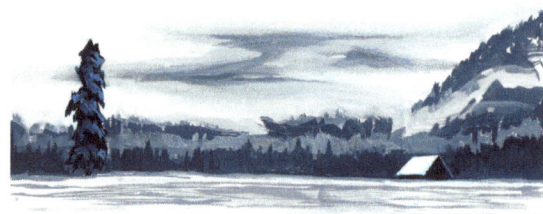

#46 Gouache on Paper   02/15/2007

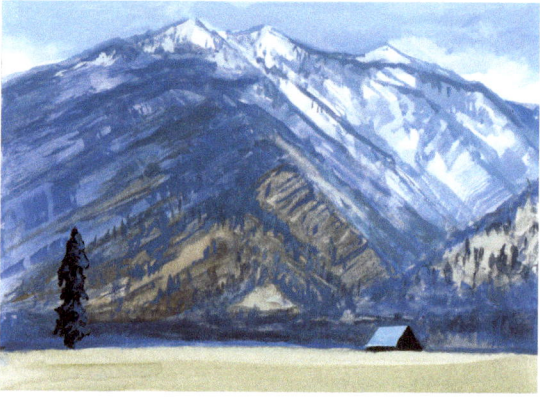

#47 Gouache on Paper   02/16/2007

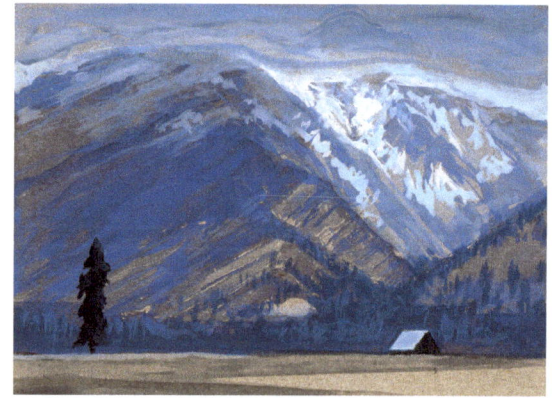

#48 Gouache on Chipboard   02/17/2007

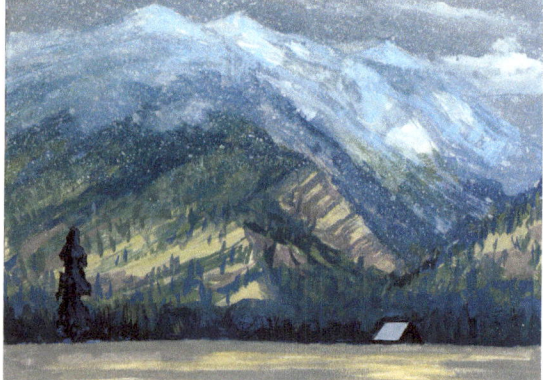

#49 Gouache on Paper   02/18/2007

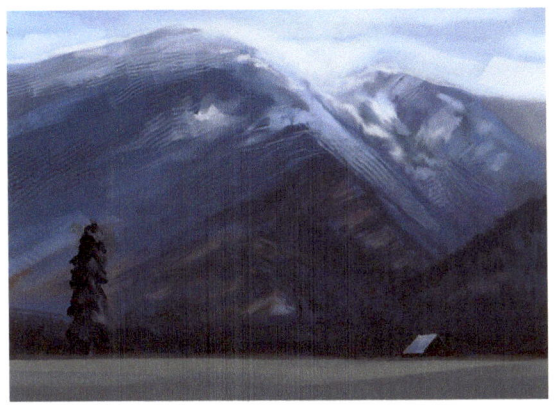

#50 Digital   02/19/2007

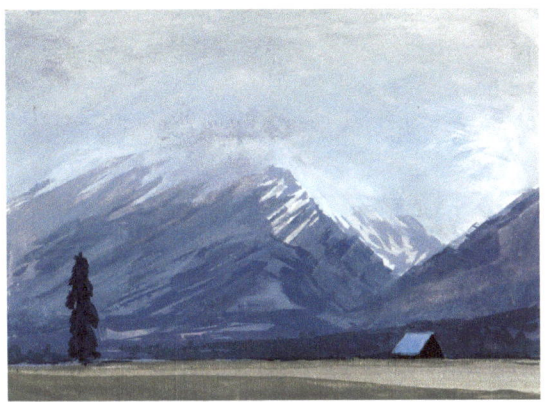

#51 Gouache on Paper   02/20/2007

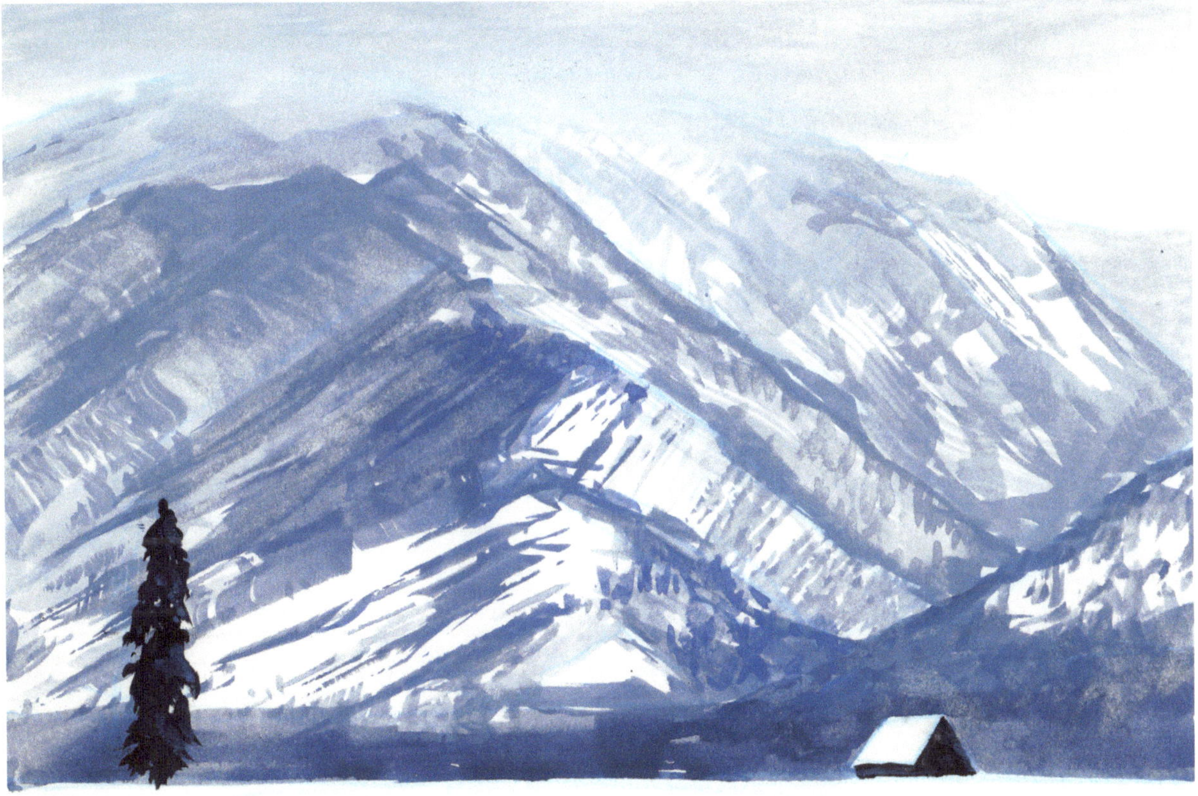

#52 Gouache on Paper   02/21/2007

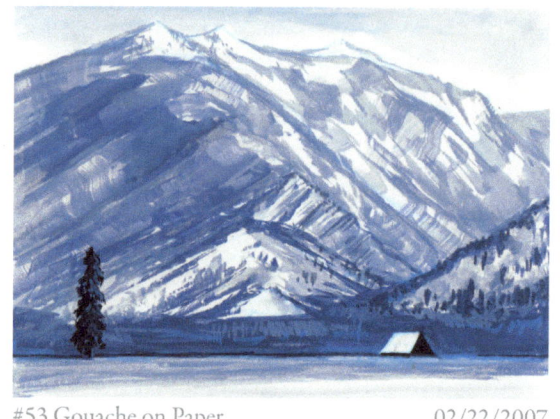

#53 Gouache on Paper   02/22/2007

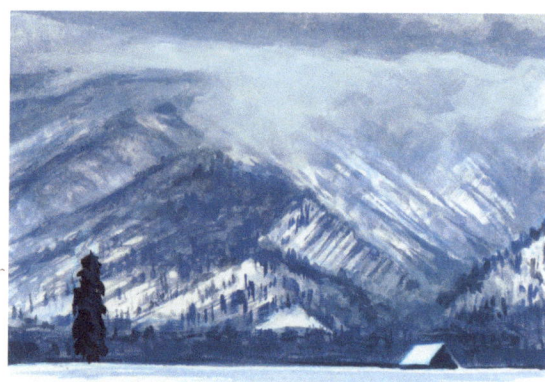

#54 Gouache on Paper   02/23/2007

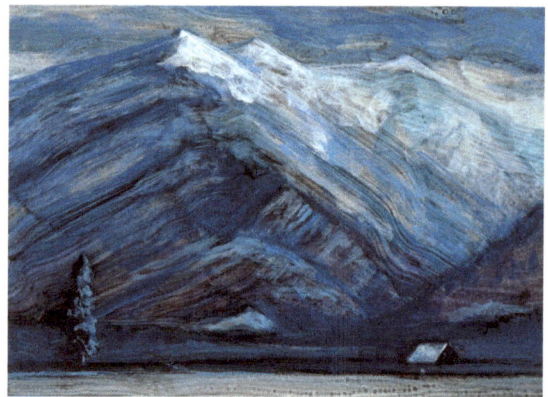

#55 Acrylic/Pastel on Paper   02/24/2007

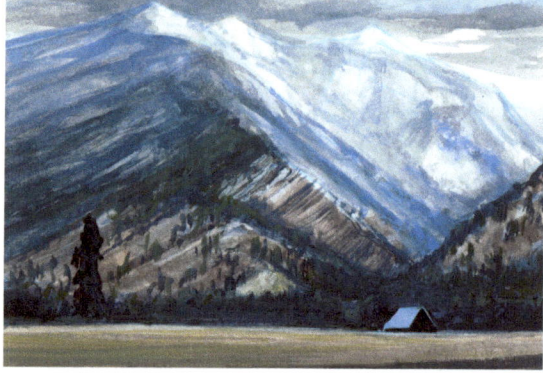

#56 Gouache on Paper   02/25/2007

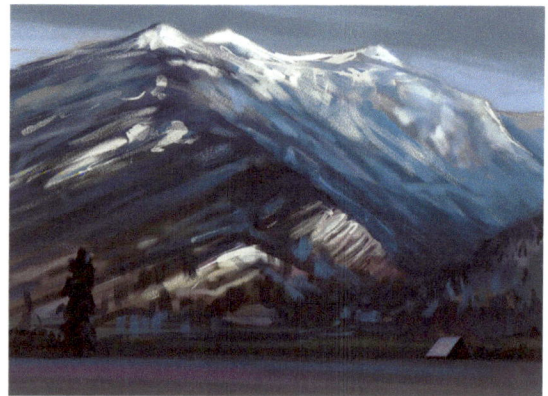

#57 Digital   02/26/2007

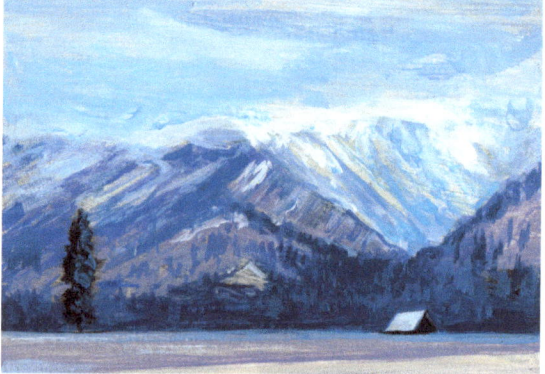

#58 Acrylic/Pastel on Paper   02/27/2007

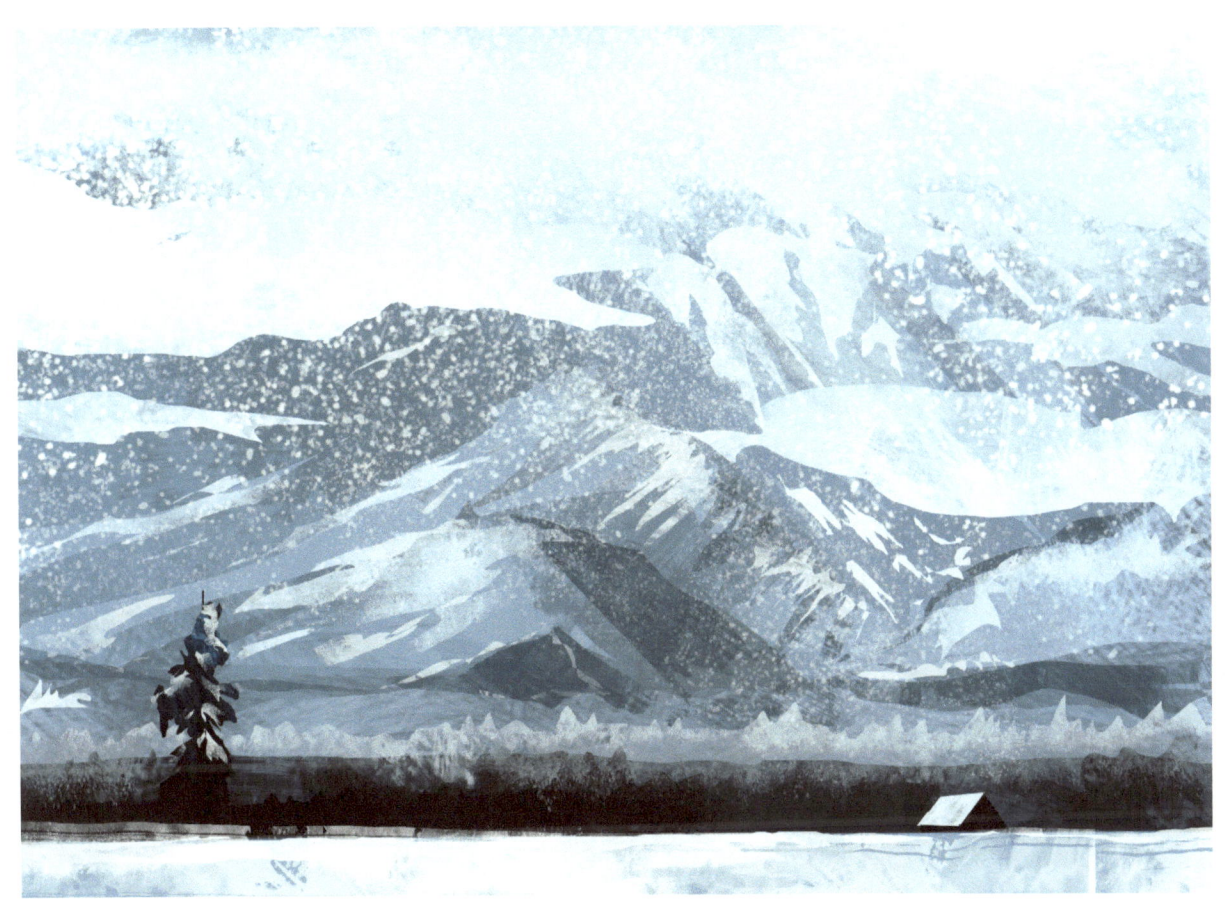

#59 Digital

02/28/2007

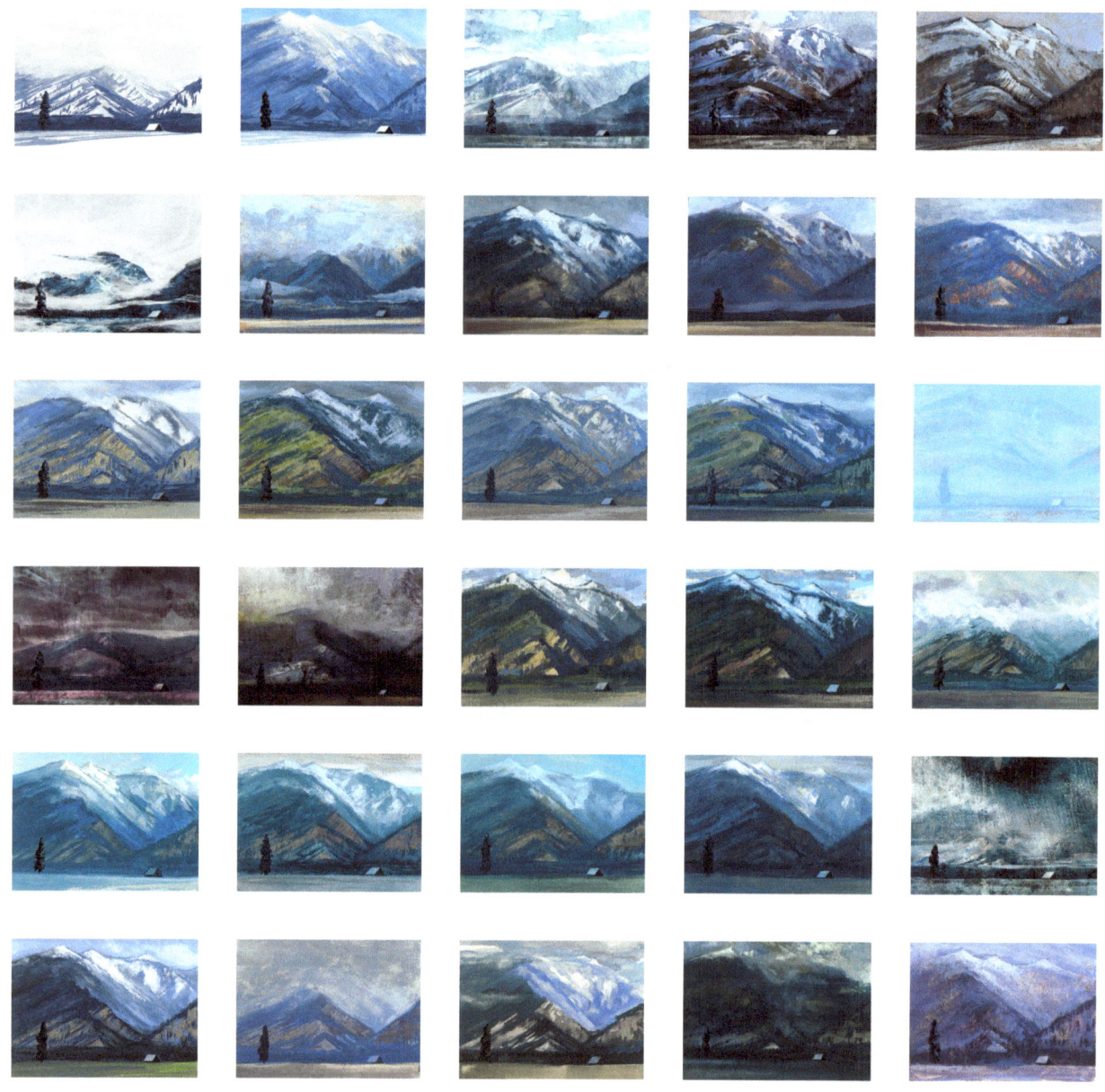

COUGAR PEAK-A-BOO
- The Art of Jared Shear -

MARCH

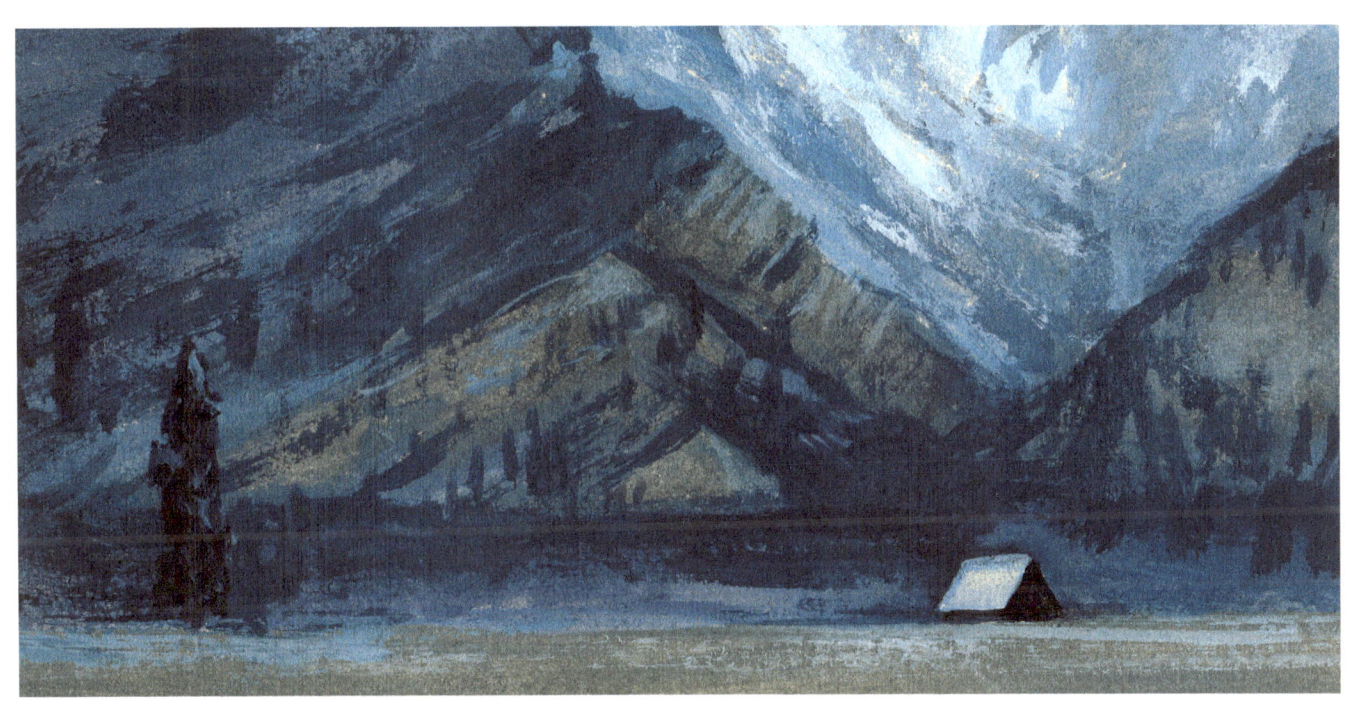

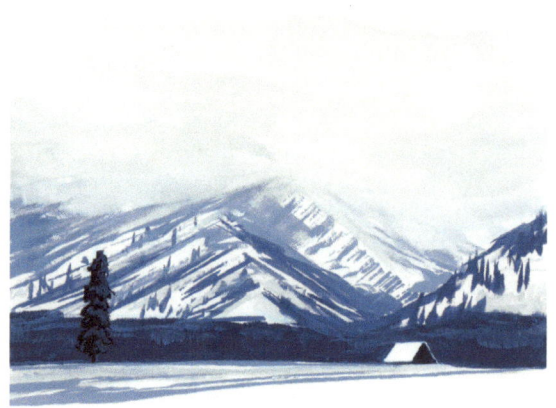

#60 Gouache on Paper   03/01/2007

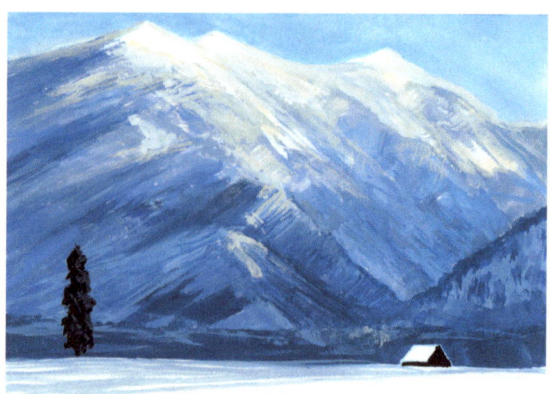

#61 Gouache on Paper   03/02/2007

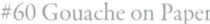

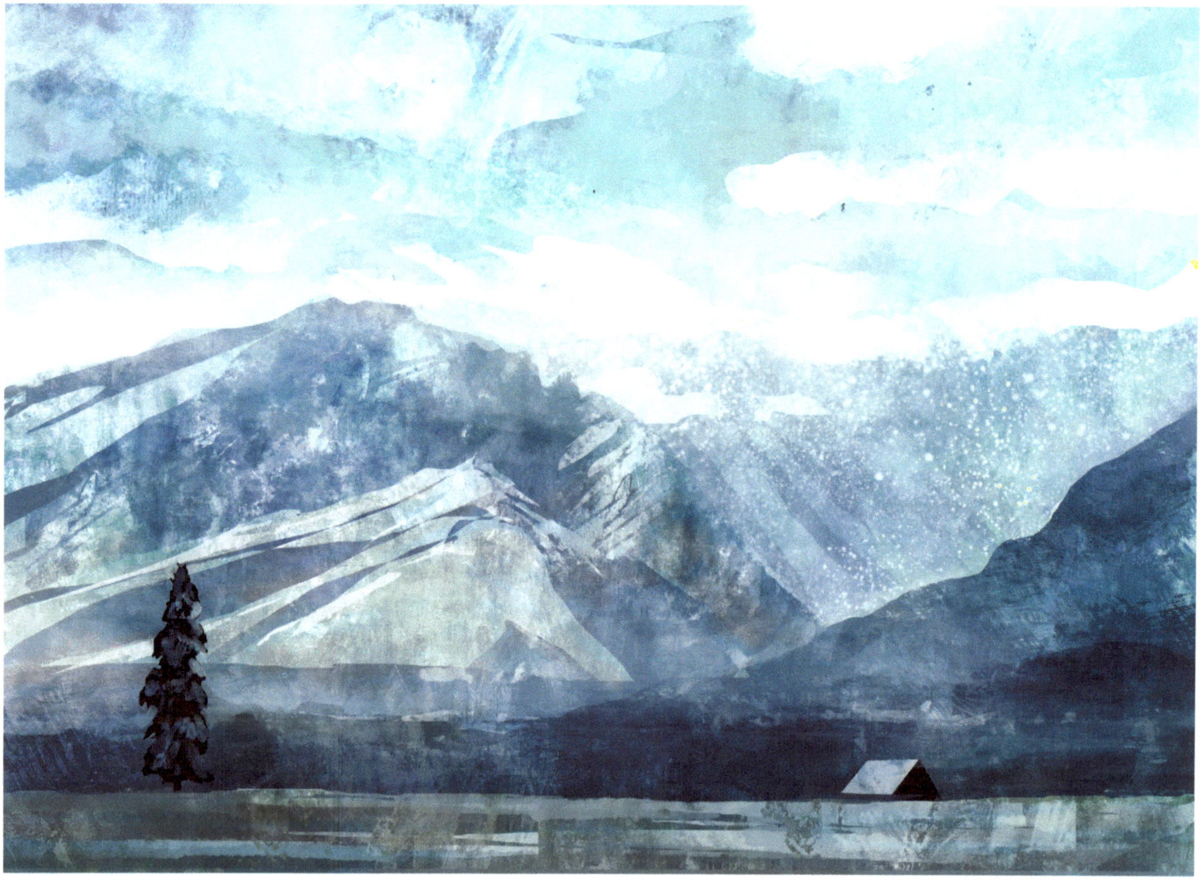

#62 Digital   03/03/2007

COUGAR PEAK-A-BOO
- The Art of Jared Shear -

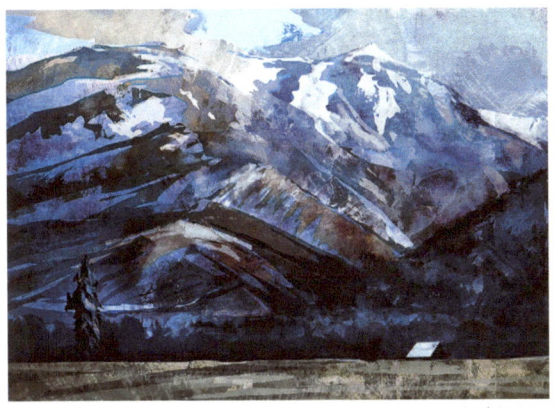

#63 Digital   03/04/2007

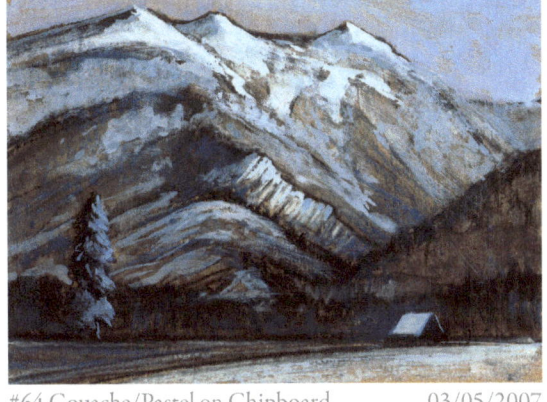

#64 Gouache/Pastel on Chipboard   03/05/2007

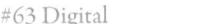

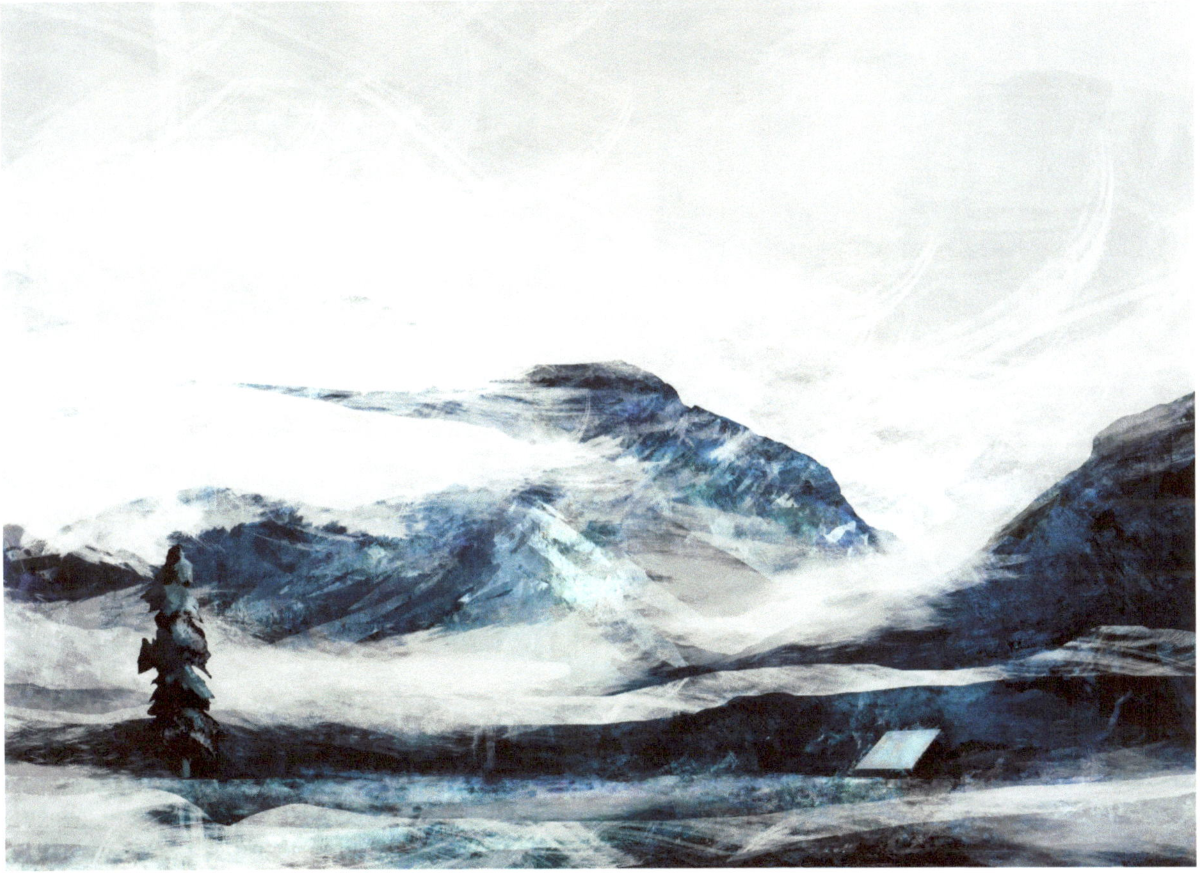

#65 Digital   03/06/2007

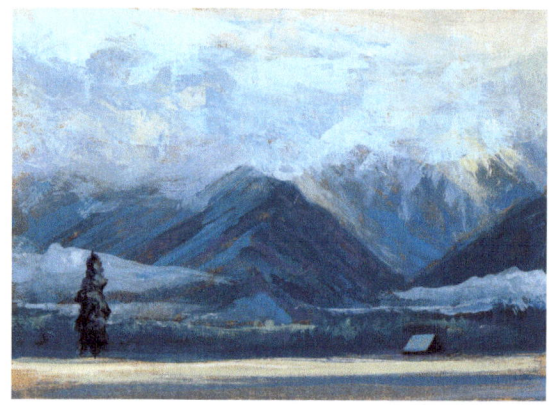

#66 Acrylic on Chipboard   03/07/2007

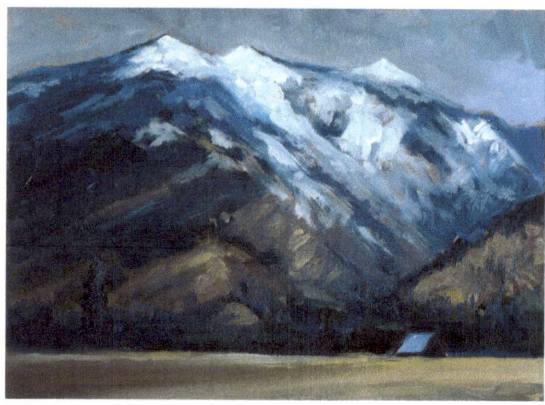

#67 Oil on Masonite   03/08/2007

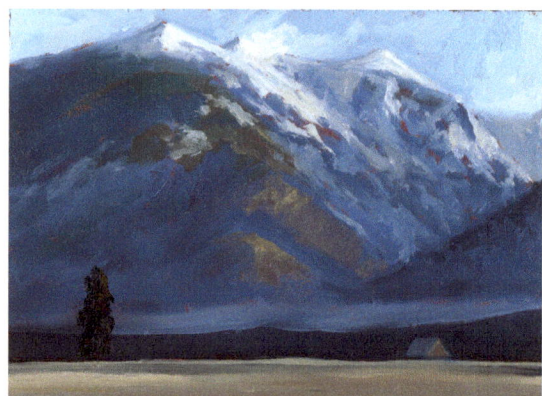

#68 Oil on Masonite   03/09/2007

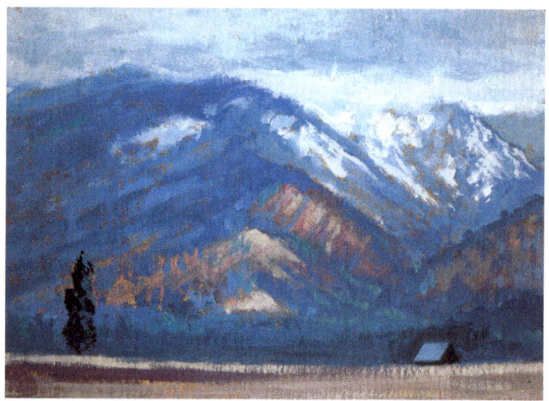

#69 Oil on Chipboard   03/10/2007

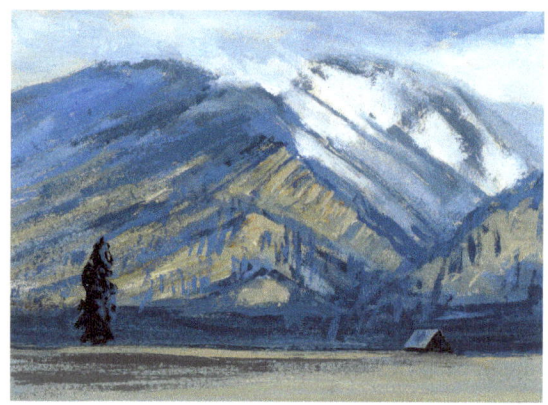

#70 Oil on Paper   03/11/2007

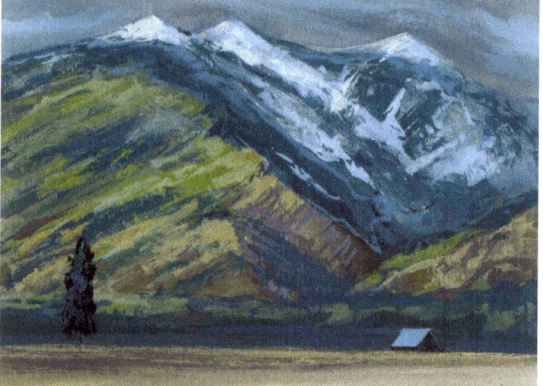

#71 Oil on Paper   03/12/2007

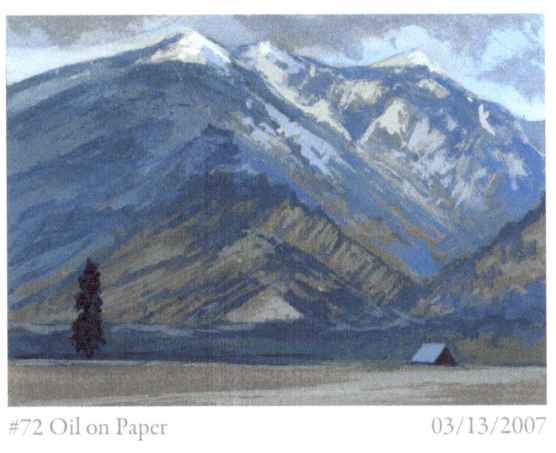

#72 Oil on Paper   03/13/2007

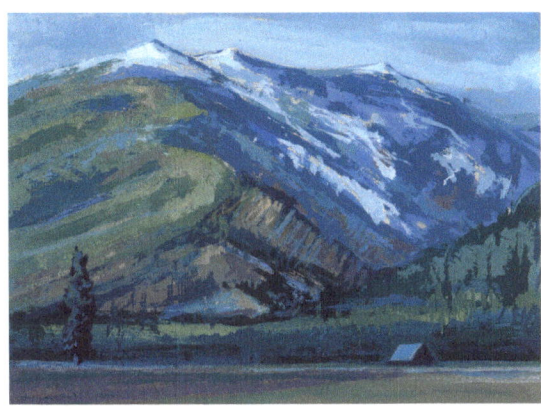

#73 Oil on Paper   03/14/2007

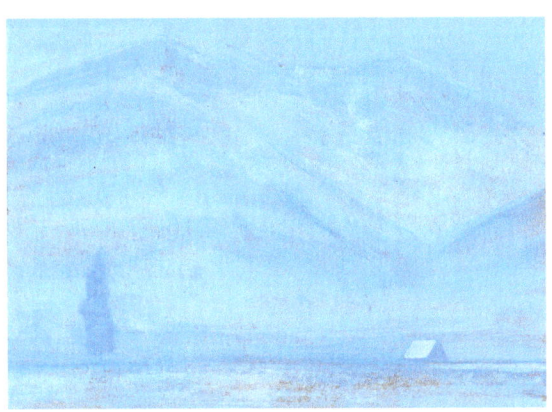

#74 Oil on Paper   03/15/2007

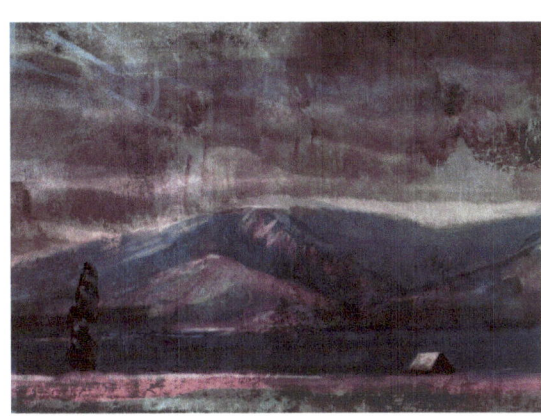

#75 Digital   03/16/2007

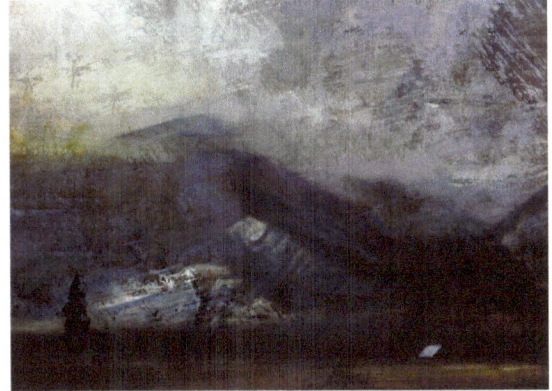

#76 Digital   03/17/2007

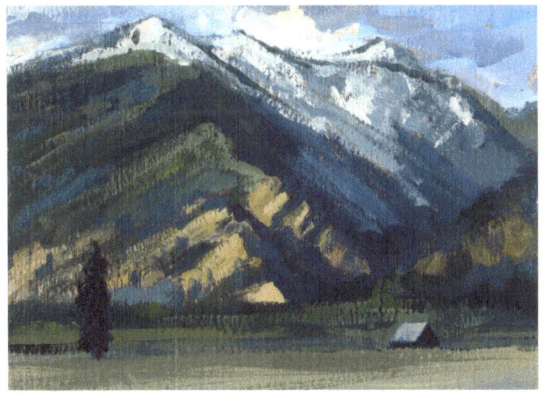

#77 Oil on Chipboard   03/18/2007

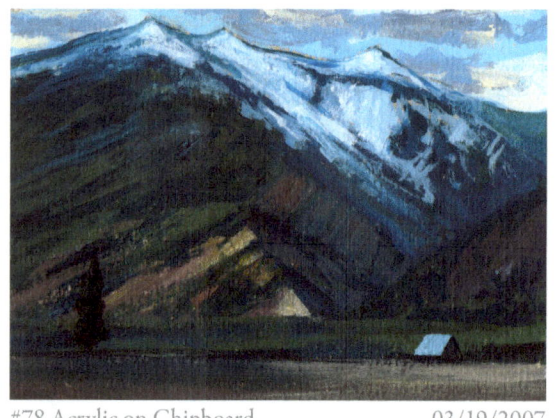

#78 Acrylic on Chipboard   03/19/2007

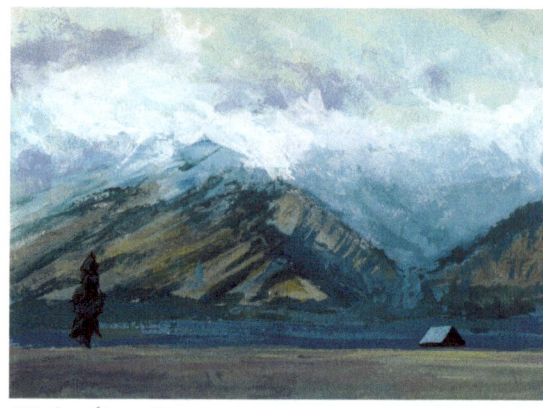

#79 Acrylic on Paper   03/20/2007

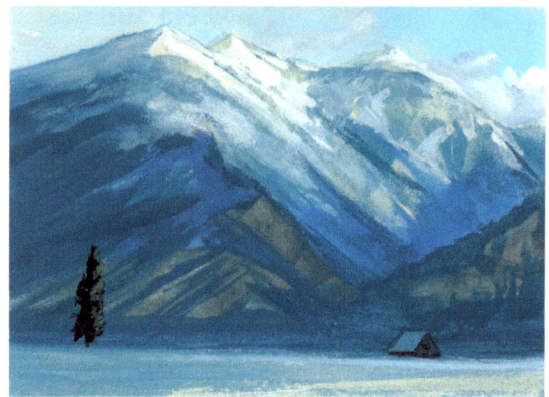

#80 Acrylic on Paper   03/21/2007

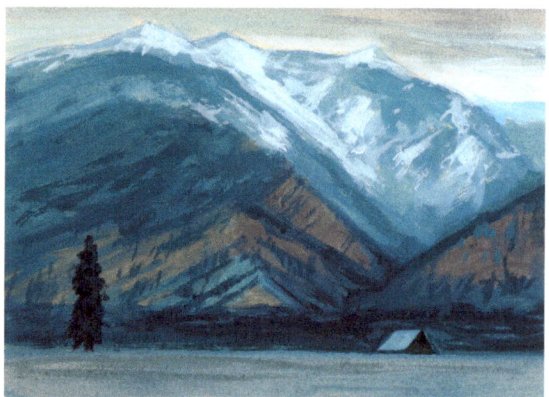

#81 Acrylic on Paper   03/22/2007

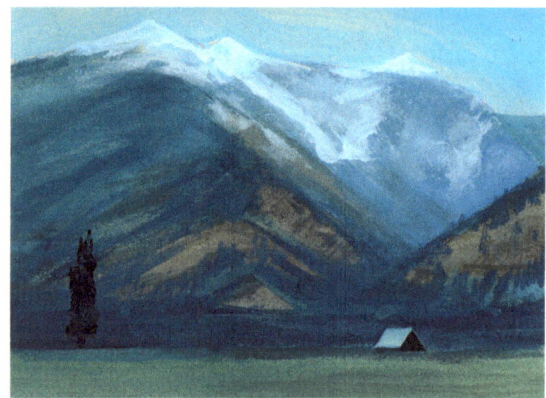

#82 Acrylic on Paper   03/23/2007

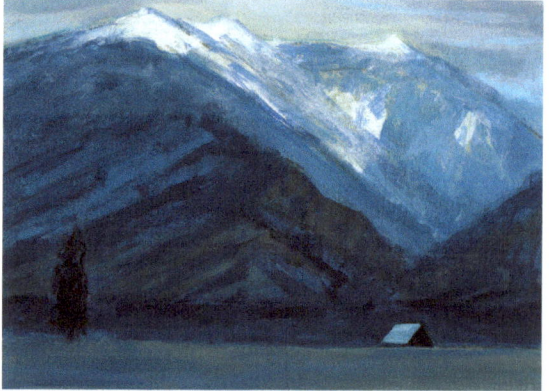

#83 Acrylic on Paper   03/24/2007

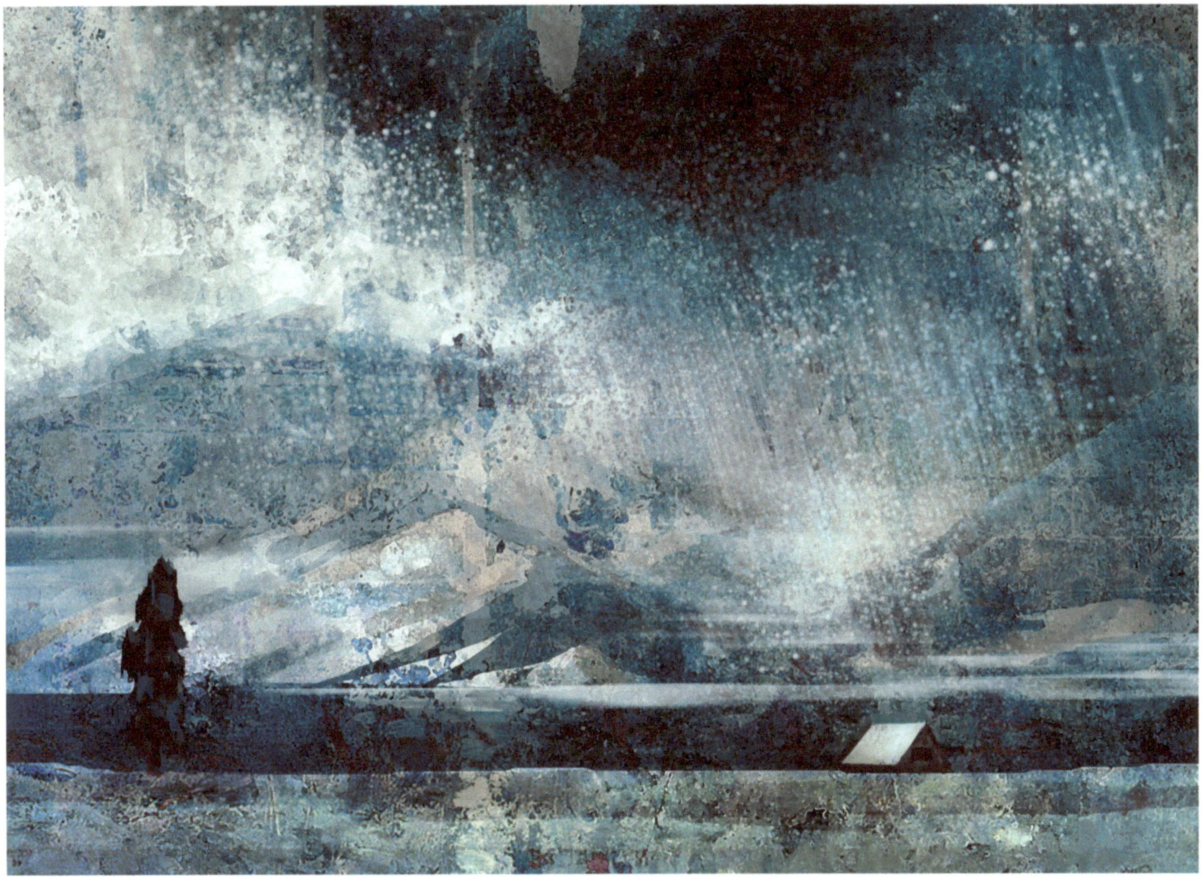

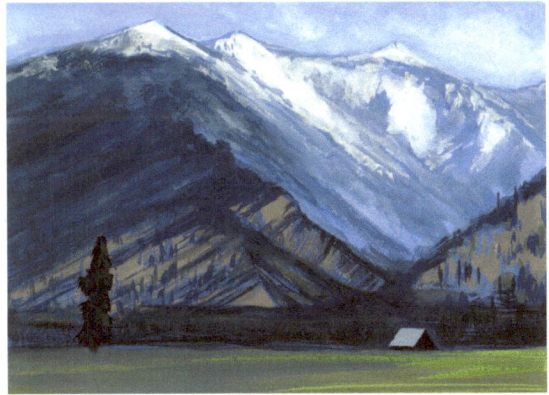

#84 Digital   03/25/2007

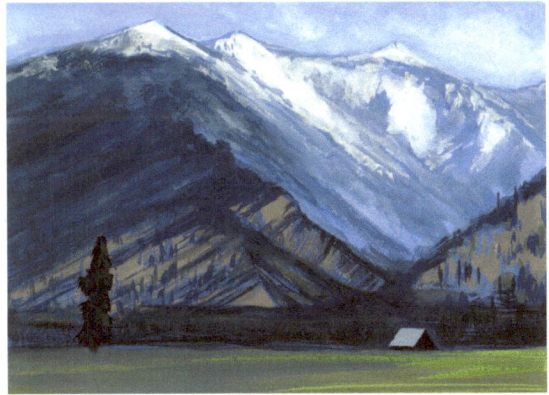

#85 Gouache on Paper   03/26/2007

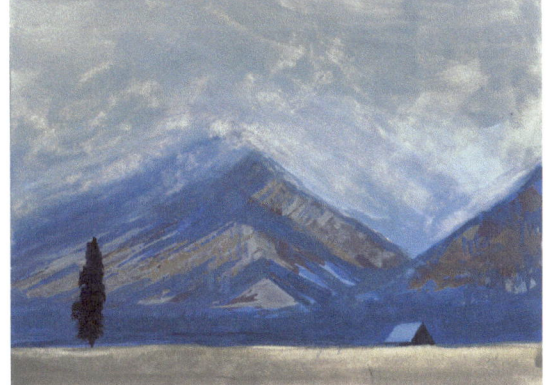

#86 Gouache on Paper   03/27/2007

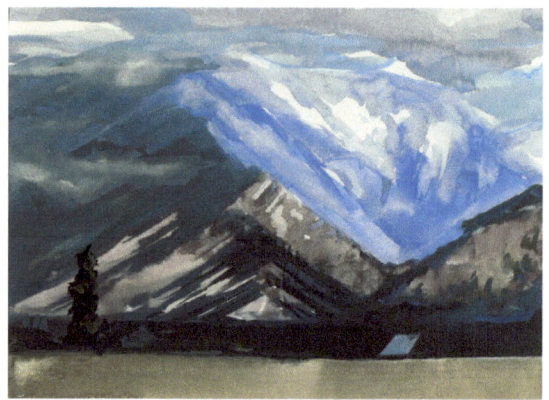

#87 Gouache on Paper   03/28/2007

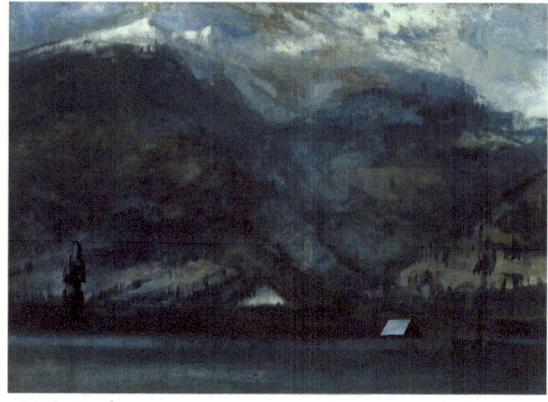

#88 Digital   03/29/2007

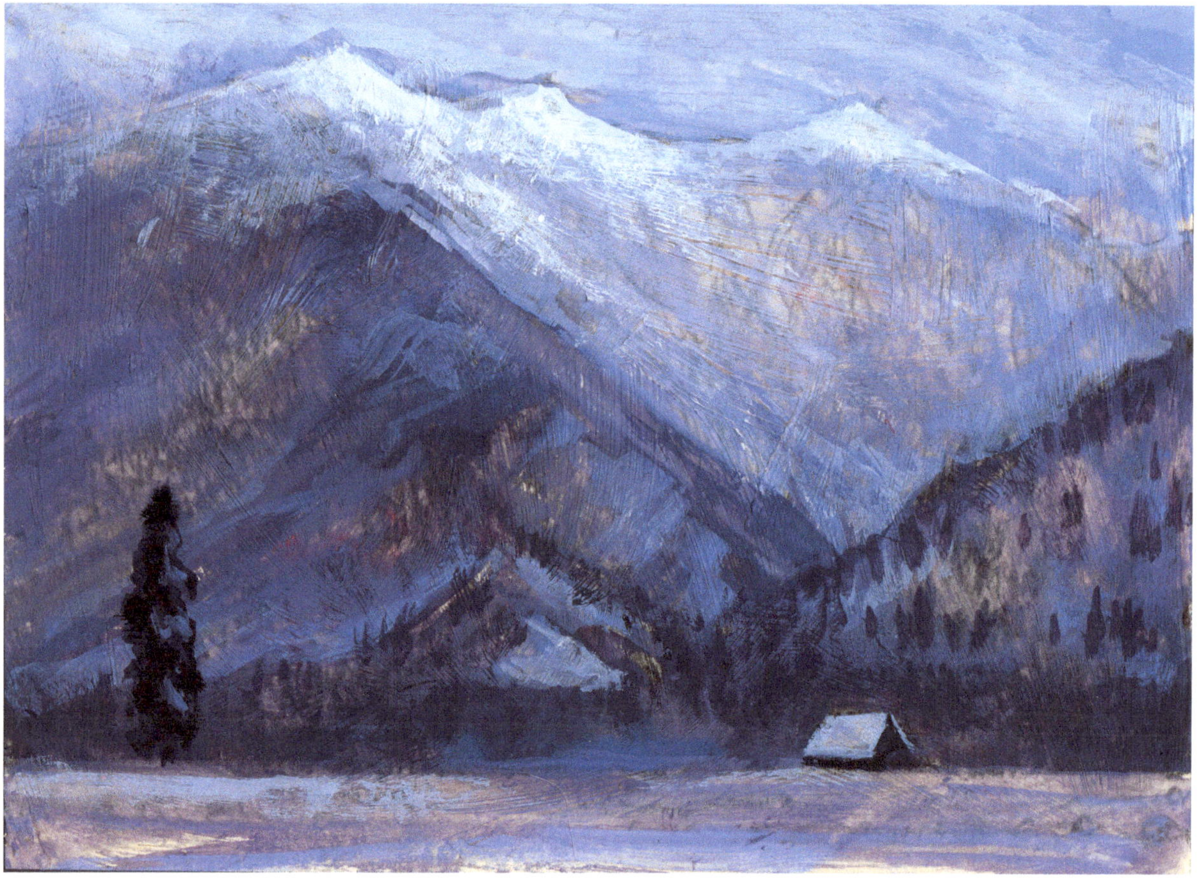

#89 Gouache on Manilla Folder   03/30/2007

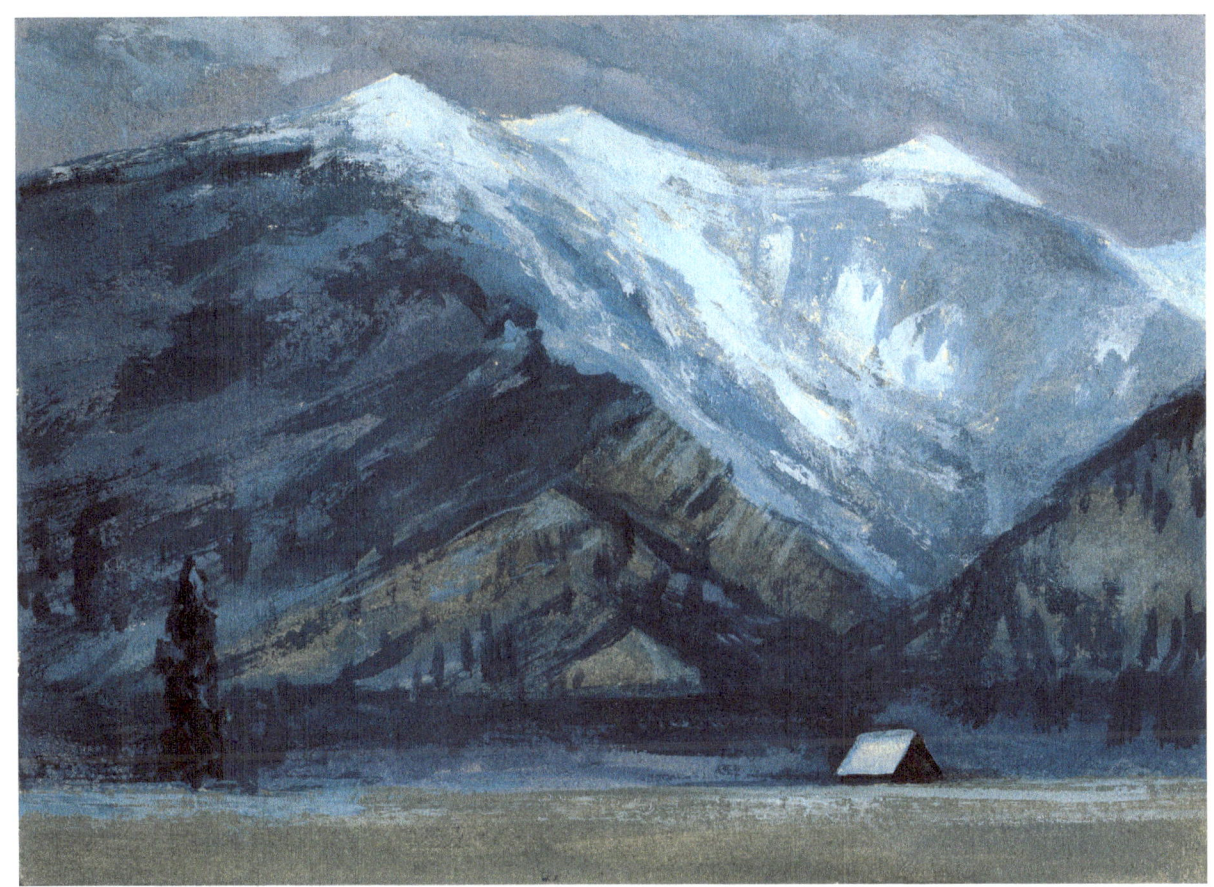

#90 Acrylic on Paper   03/31/2007

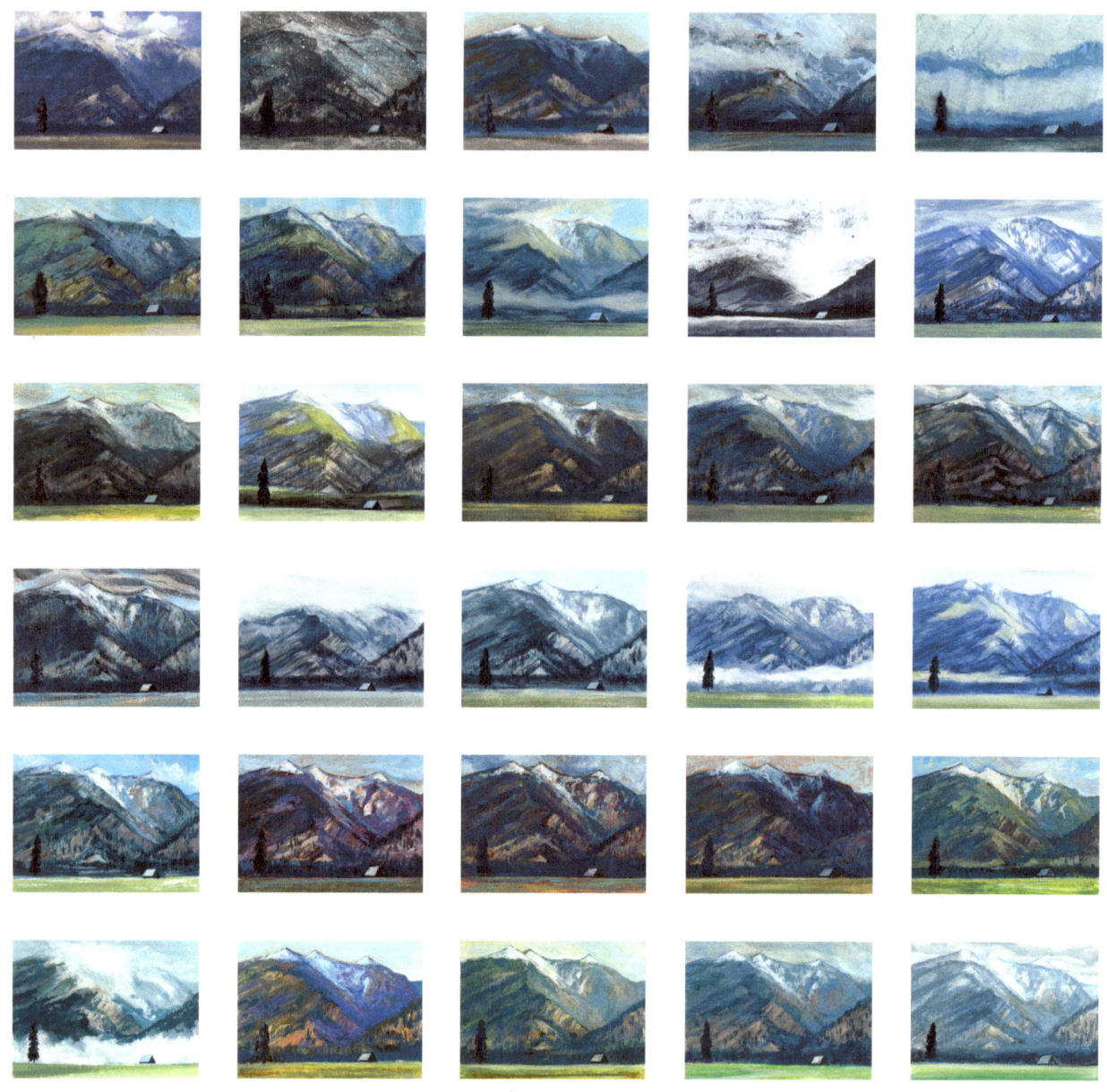

COUGAR PEAK-A-BOO
- The Art of Jared Shear -

APRIL

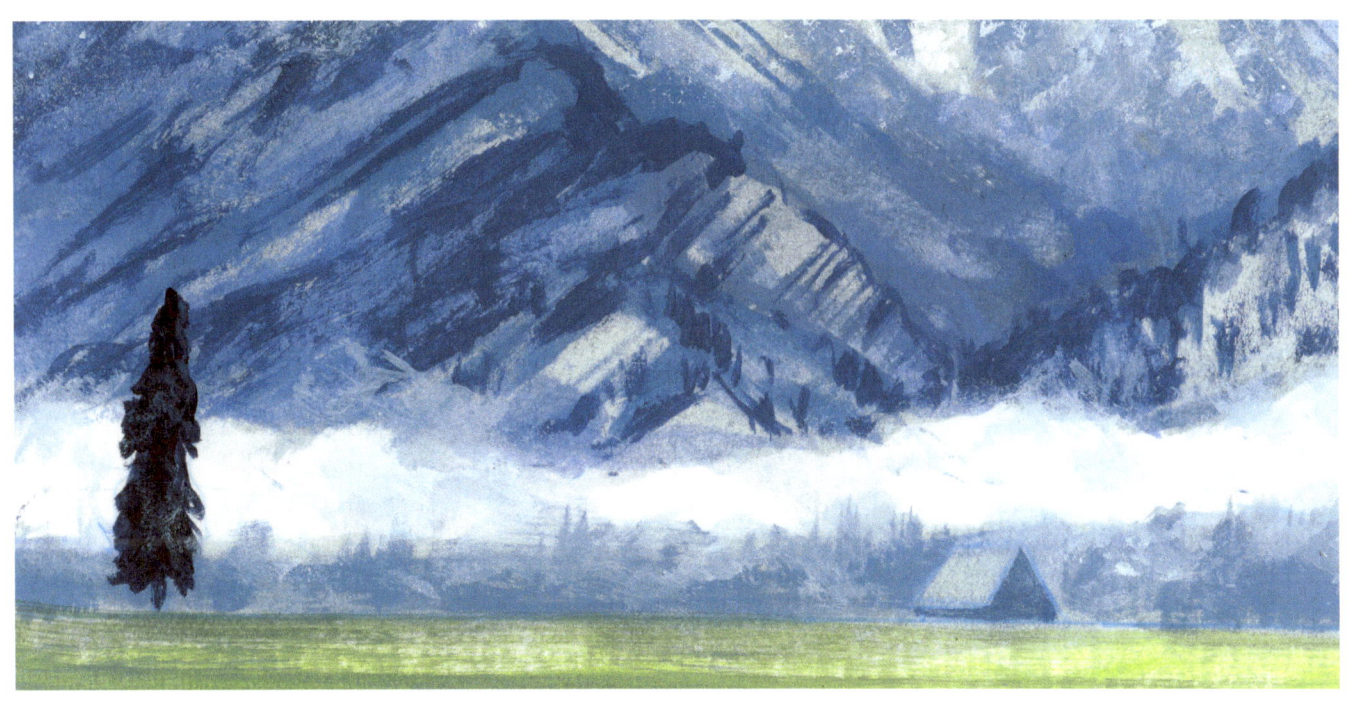

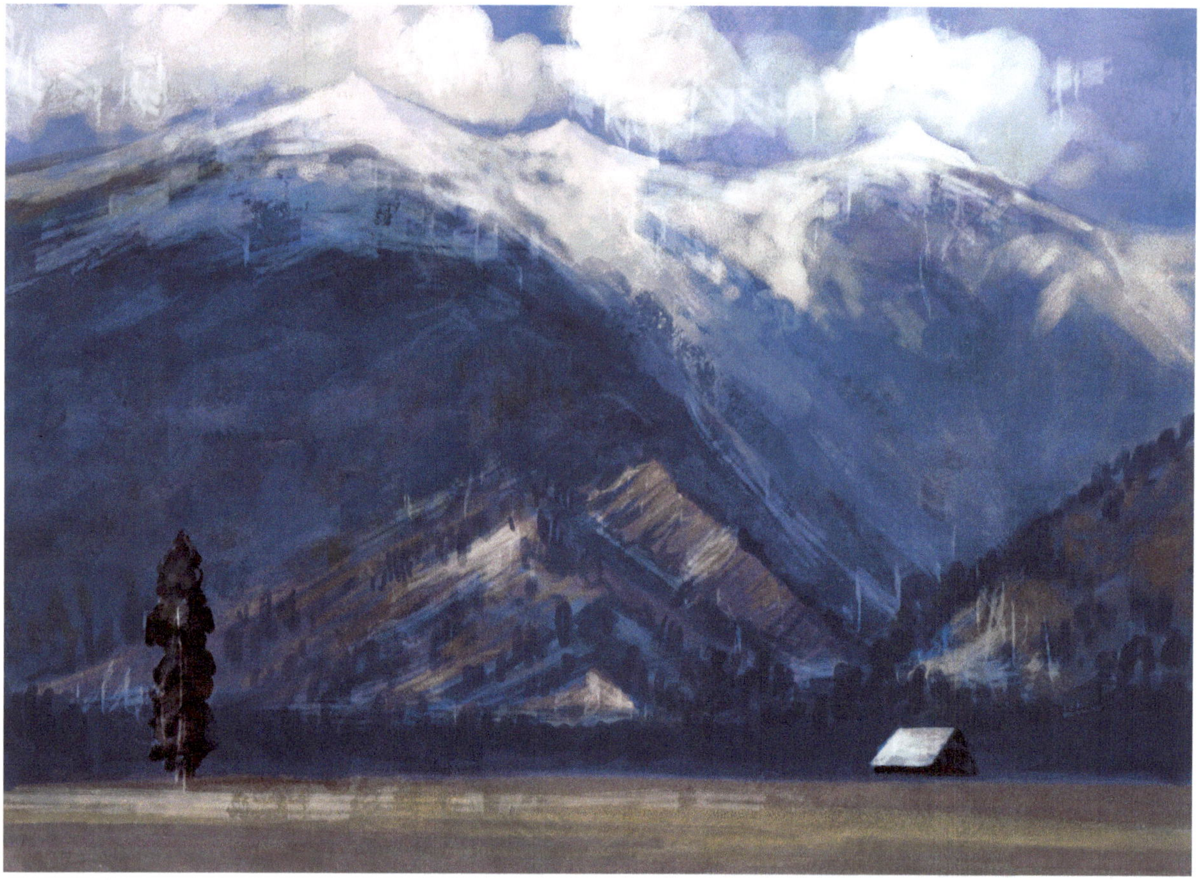

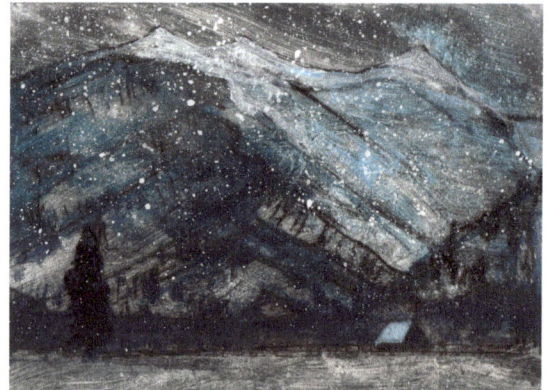

#91 Digital   04/01/2007

#92 Acrylic on Paper   04/02/2007   #93 Acrylic on Paper   04/03/2007

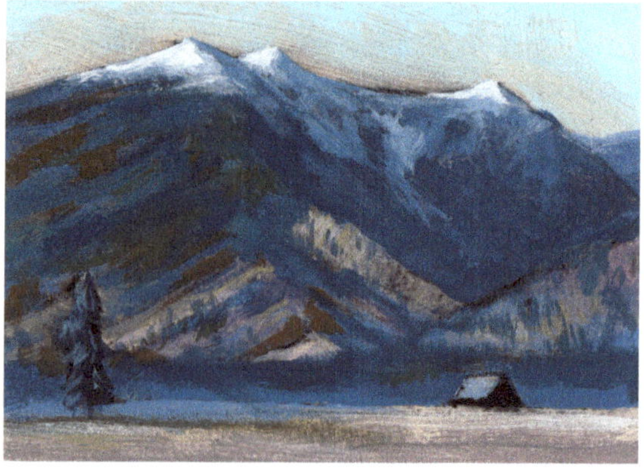

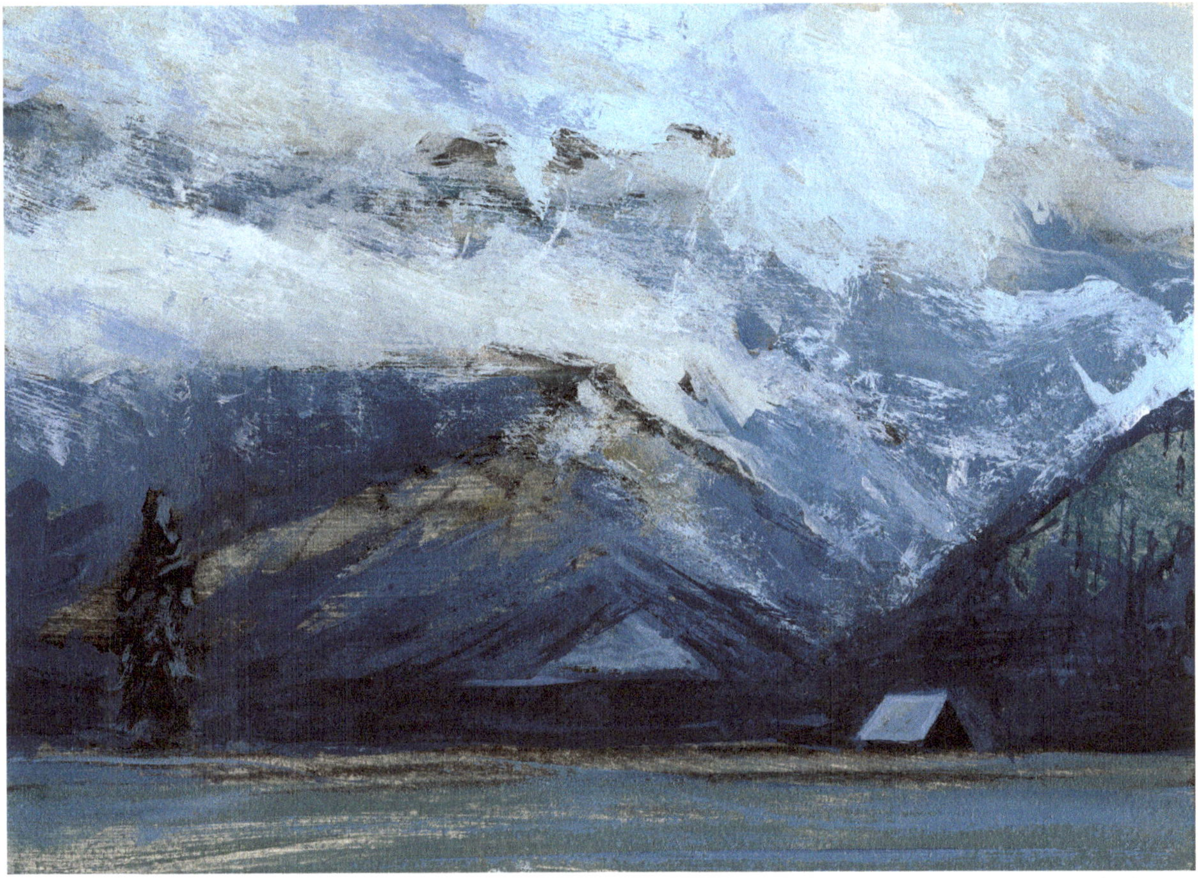

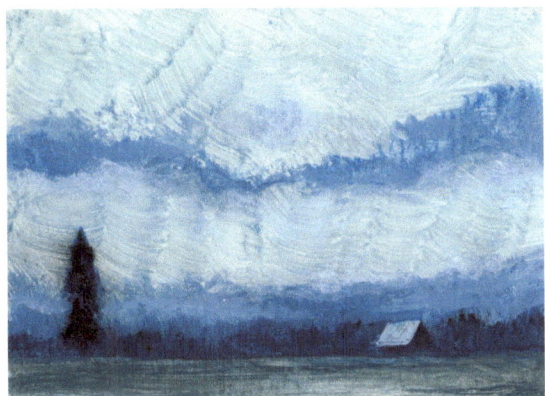

#94 Acrylic on Paper   04/04/2007

#95 Acrylic on Paper   04/05/2007

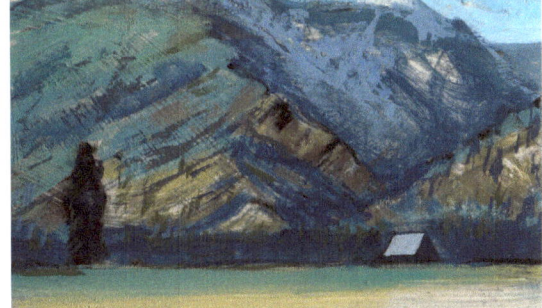

#96 Acrylic on Paper   04/06/2007

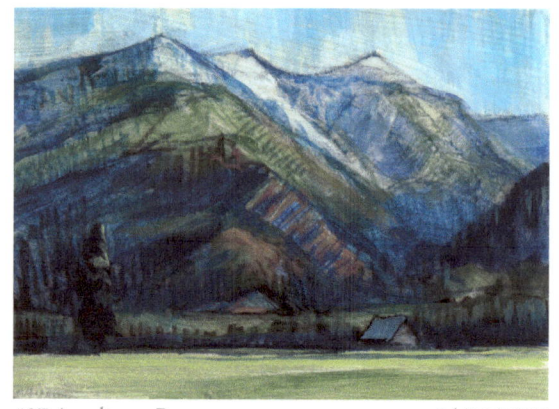

#97 Acrylic on Paper   04/07/2007

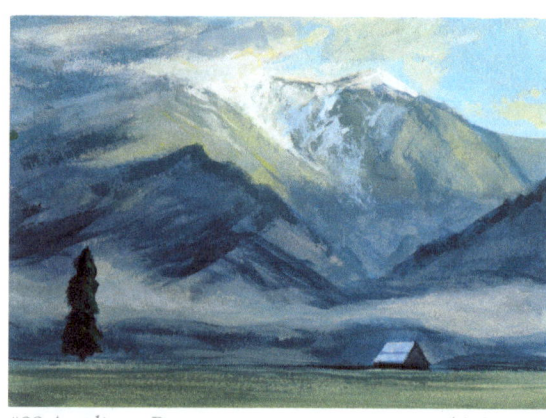

#98 Acrylic on Paper   04/08/2007

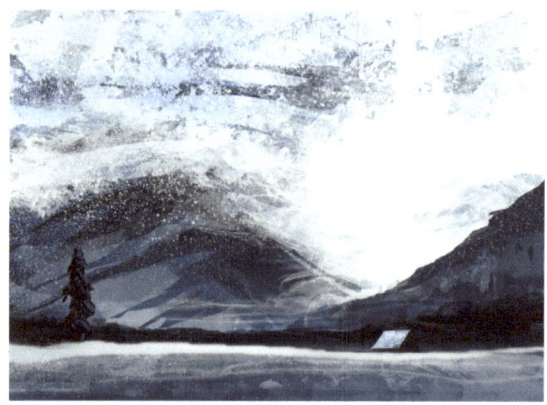

#99 Digital   04/09/2007

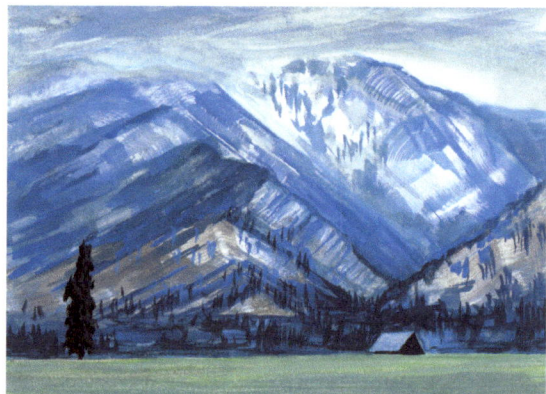

#100 Goauche on Paper   04/10/2007

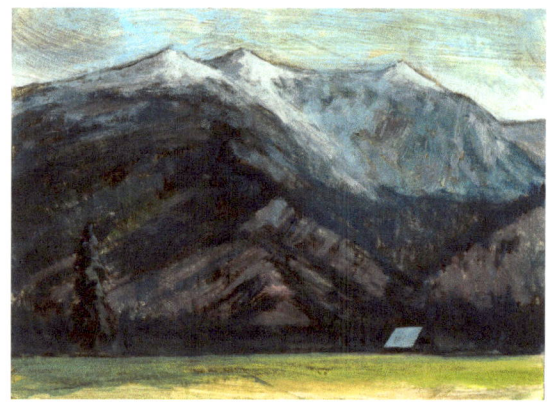

#101 Acrylic on Paper   04/11/2007

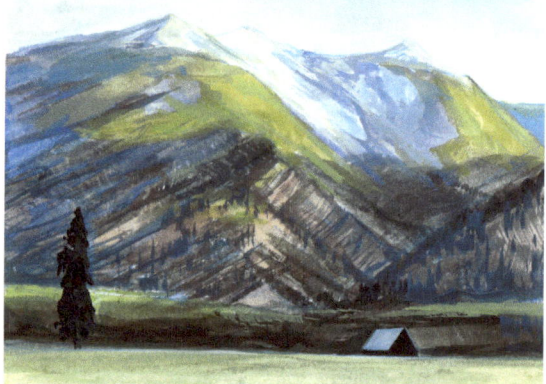

#102 Gouache on Paper   04/12/2007

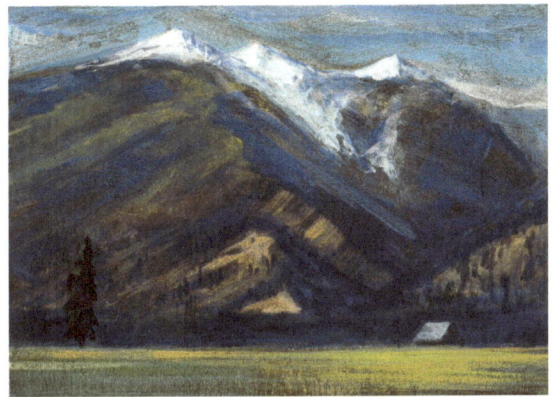

#103 Acrylic on Paper   04/13/2007

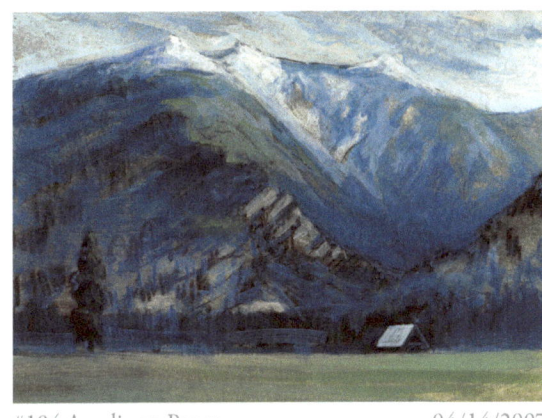

#104 Acrylic on Paper   04/14/2007

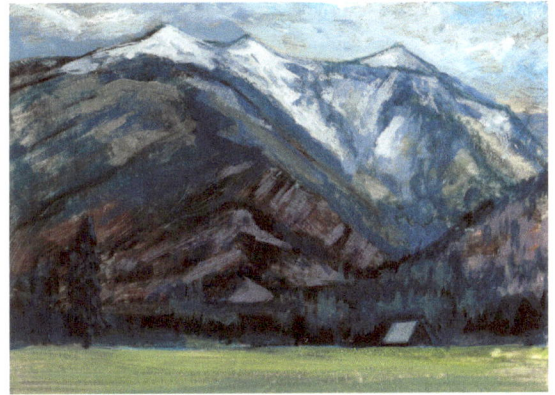

#105 Acrylic on Paper   04/15/2007

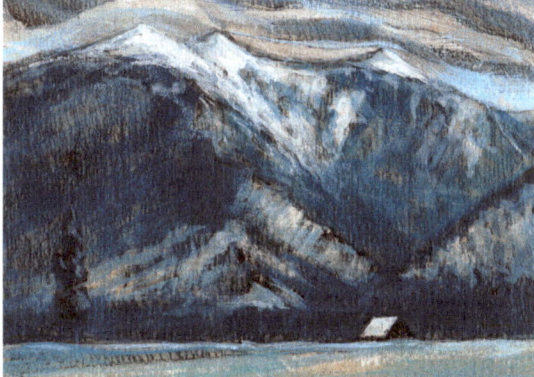

#106 Acrylic on Chipboard   04/16/2007

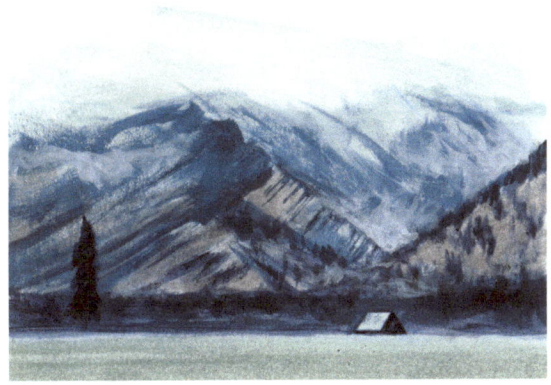

#107 Acrylic on Paper   04/17/2007

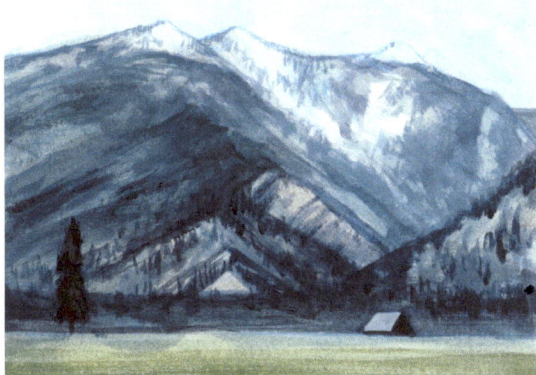

#108 Acrylic on Paper   04/18/2007

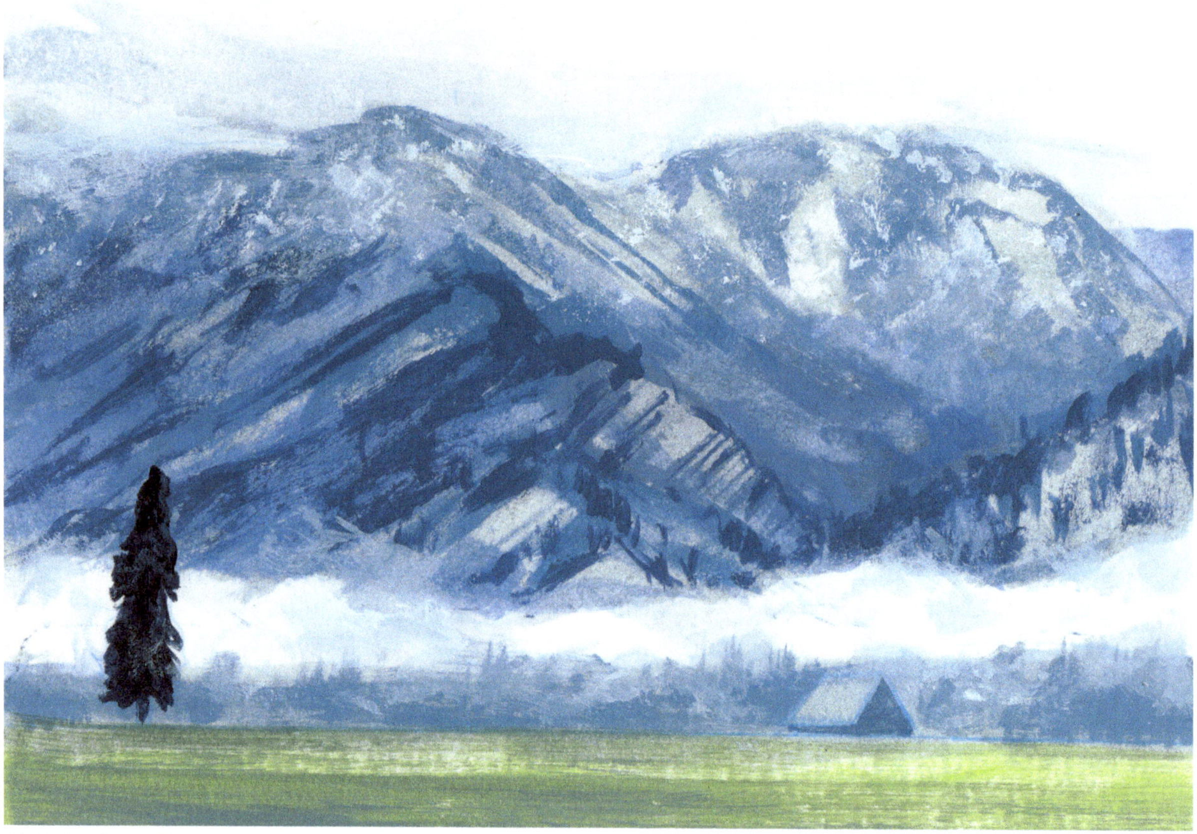

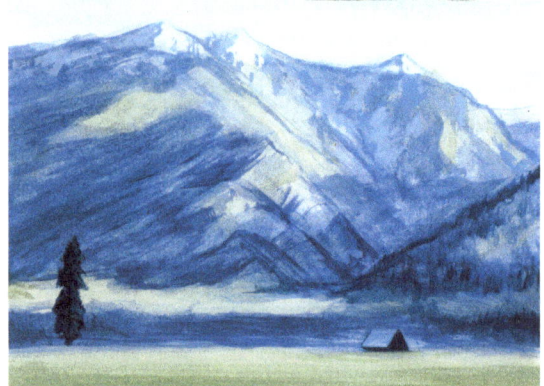

#109 Acrylic on Paper   04/19/2007

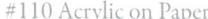

#110 Acrylic on Paper   04/20/2007

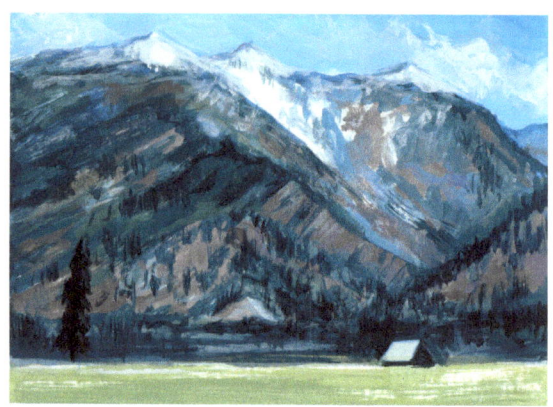

#111 Acrylic on Paper   04/21/2007

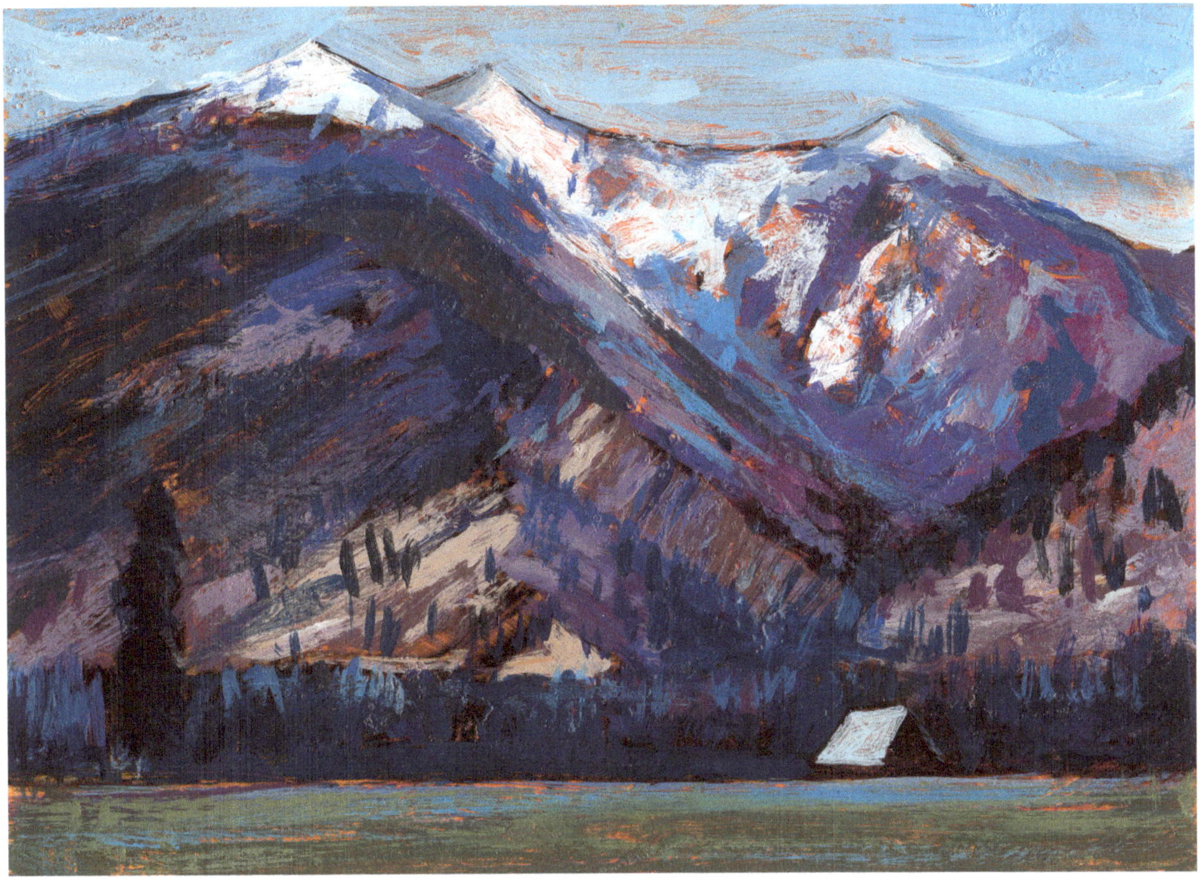

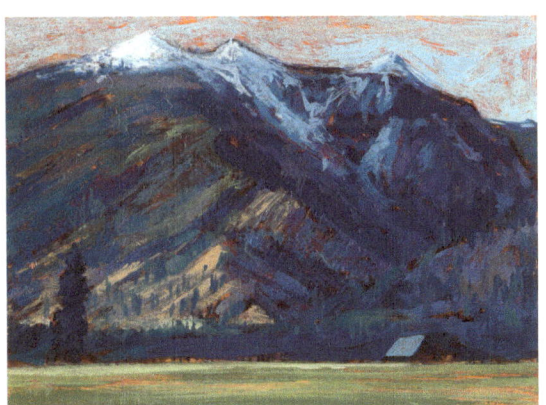

#112 Acrylic on Paper   04/22/2007

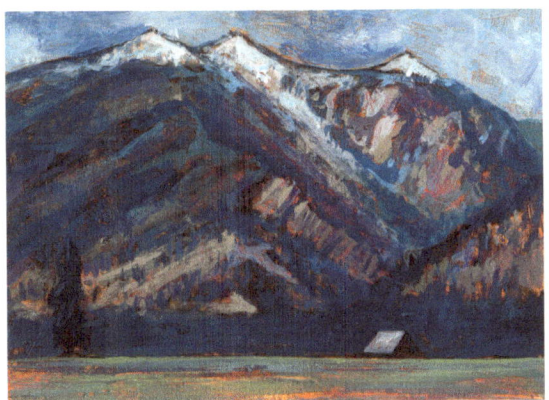

#113 Acrylic on Paper   04/23/2007

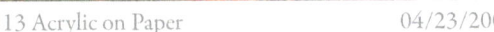

#114 Acrylic on Paper   04/24/2007

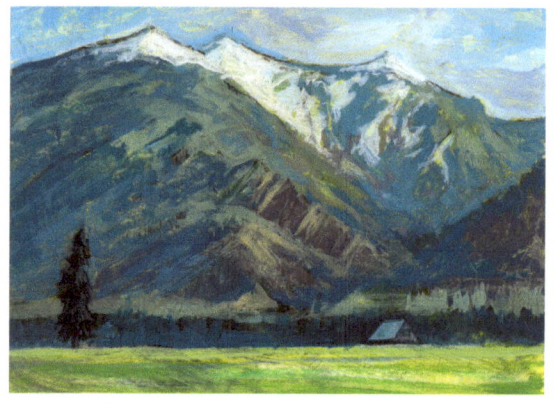

#115 Acrylic on Paper   04/25/2007

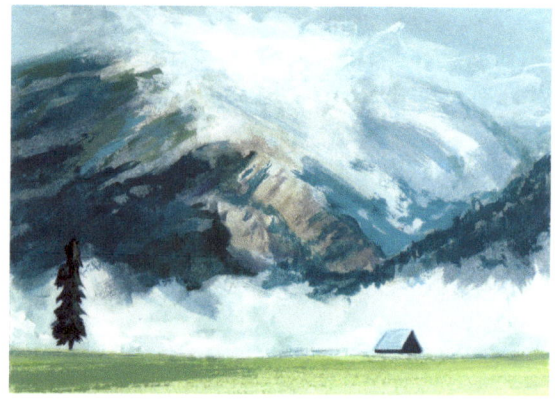

#116 Acrylic on Paper   04/26/2007

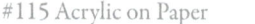

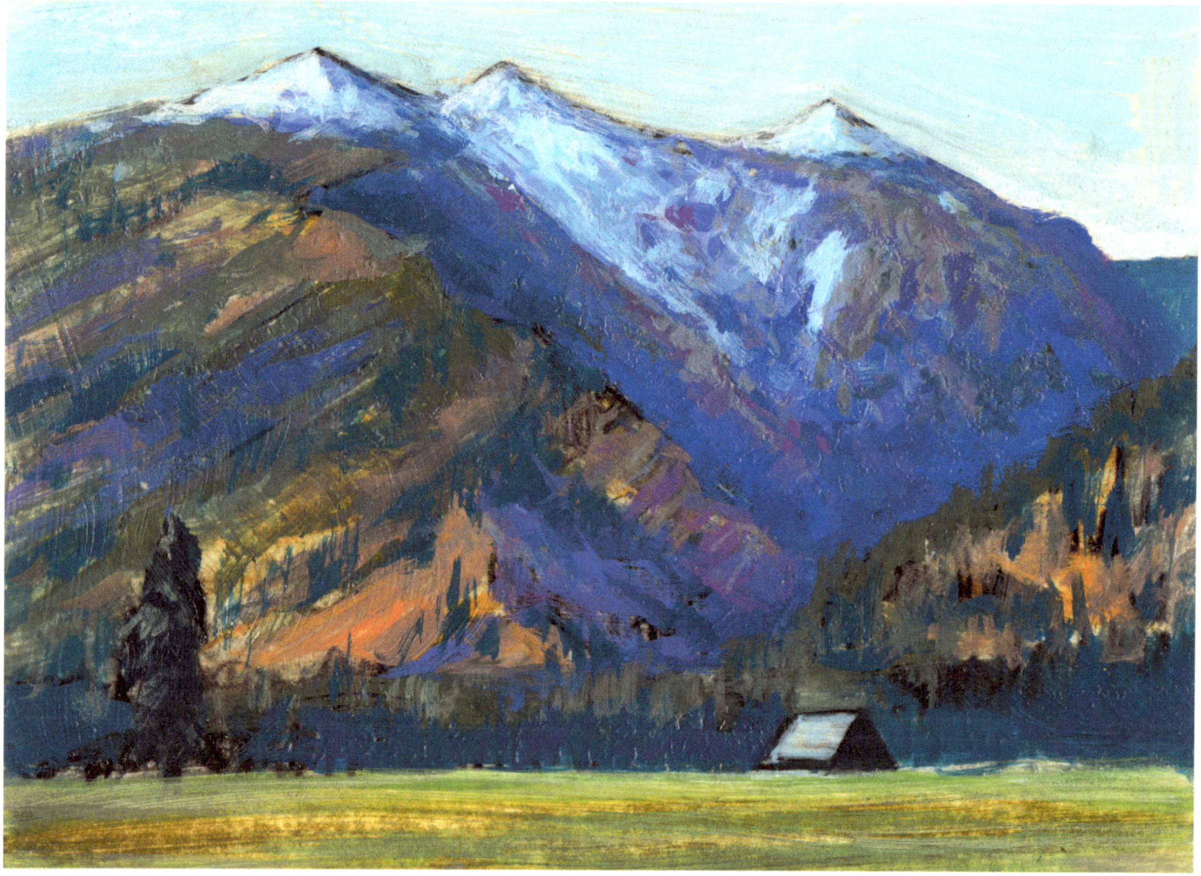

#117 Acrylic on Paper   04/27/2007

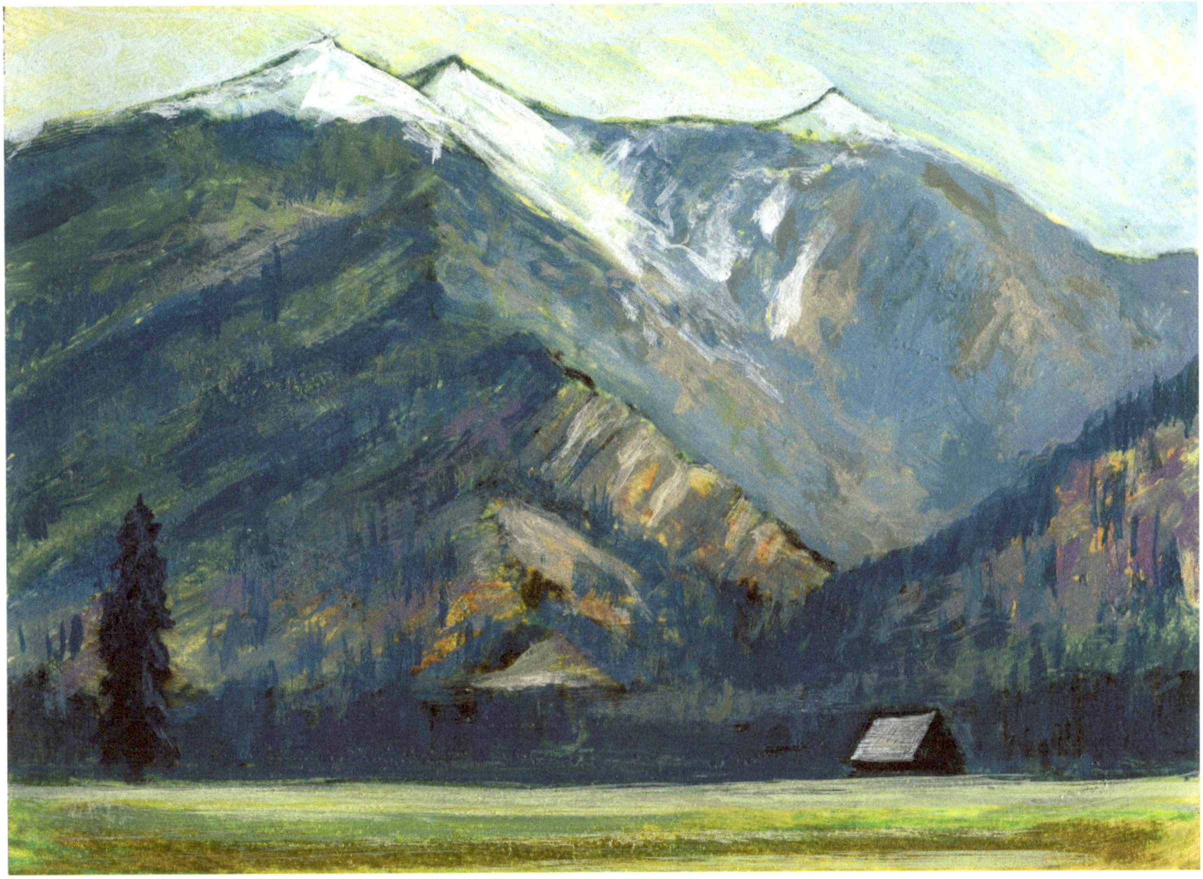

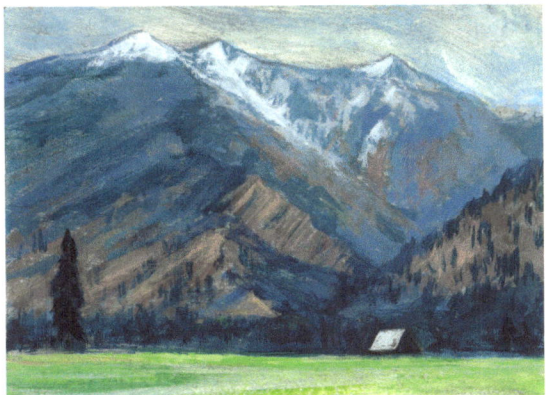

#118 Acrylic on Paper   04/28/2007

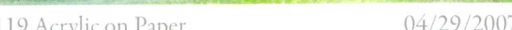

#119 Acrylic on Paper   04/29/2007

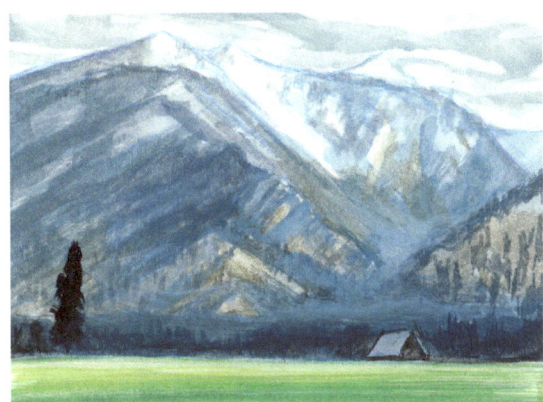

#120 Gouache on Paper   04/30/2007

COUGAR PEAK-A-BOO
- The Art of Jared Shear -

45

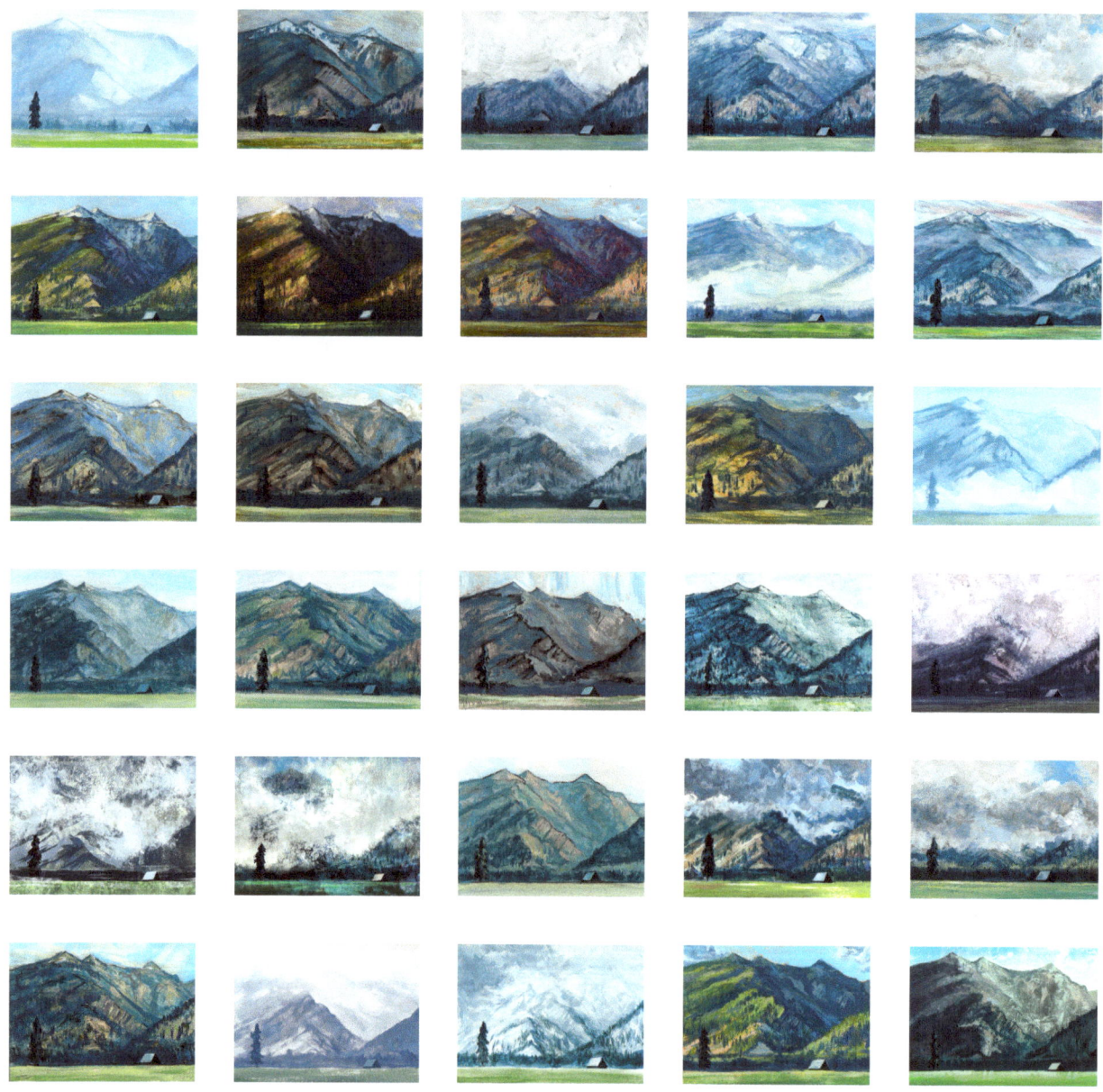

COUGAR PEAK-A-BOO
- The Art of Jared Shear -

MAY

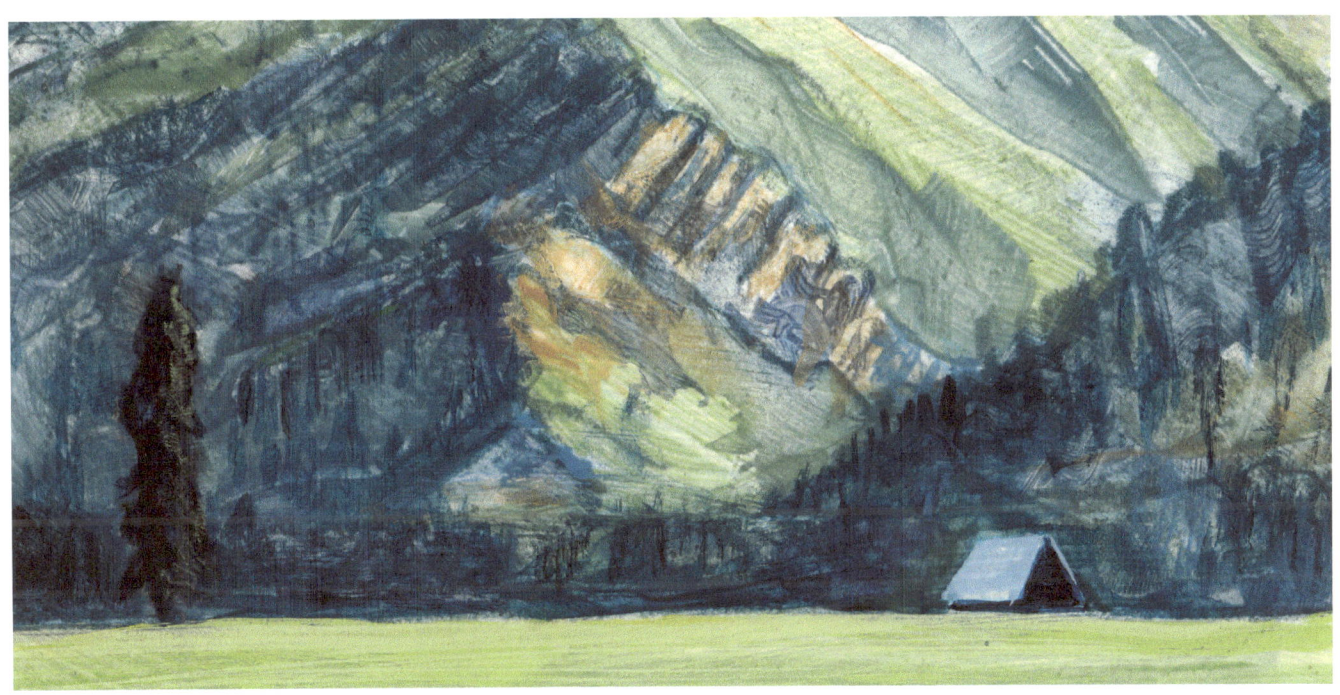

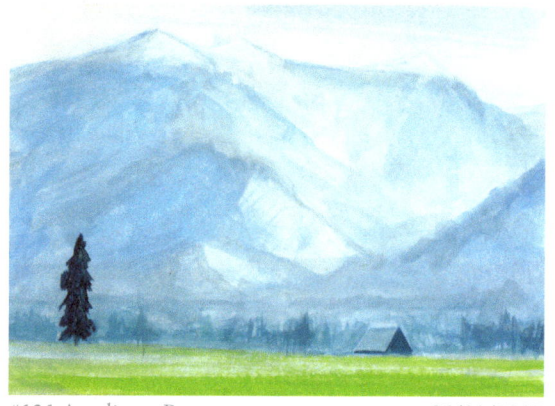

#121 Acrylic on Paper   05/01/2007

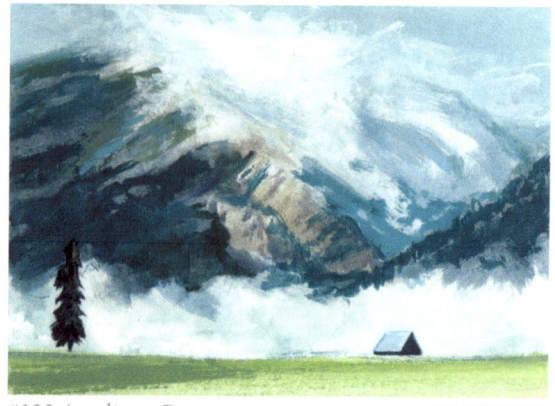

#122 Acrylic on Paper   05/02/2007

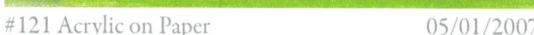

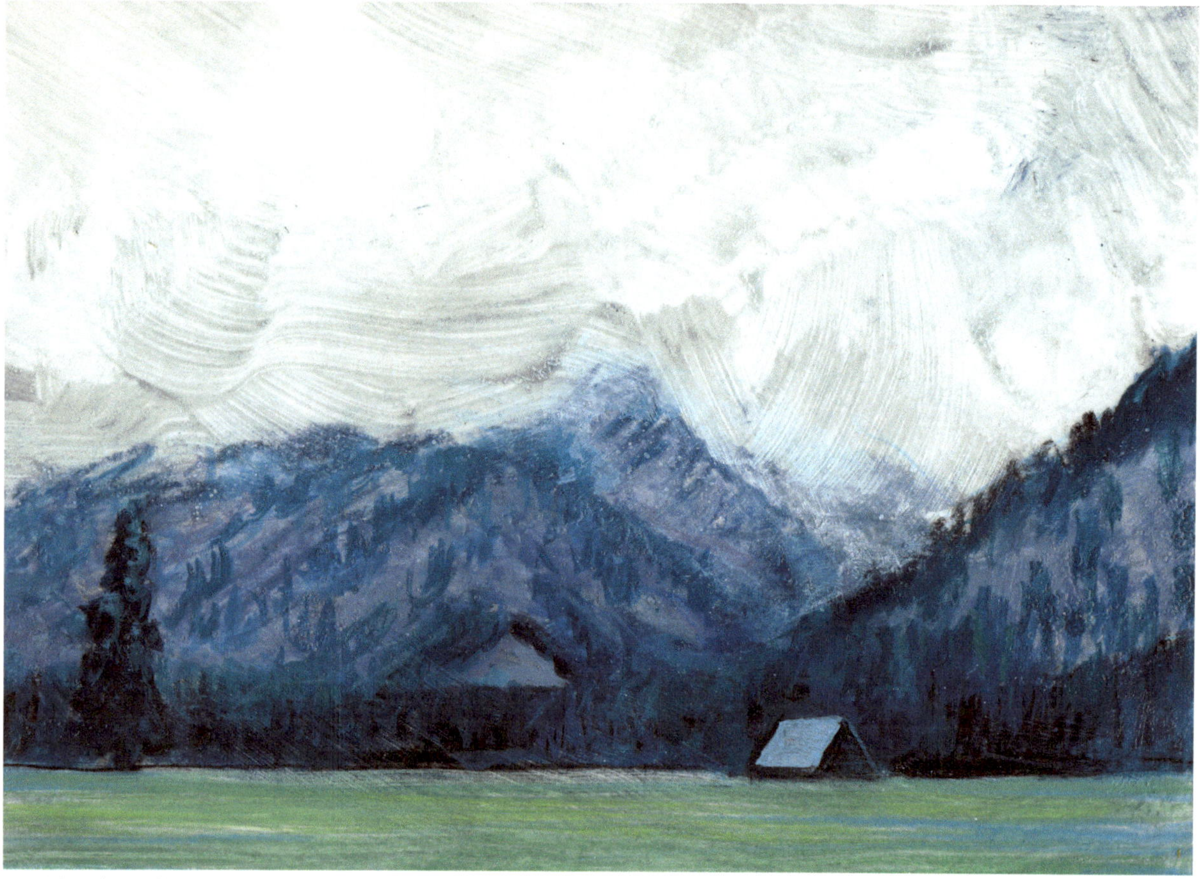

#123 Acrylic on Paper   05/03/2007

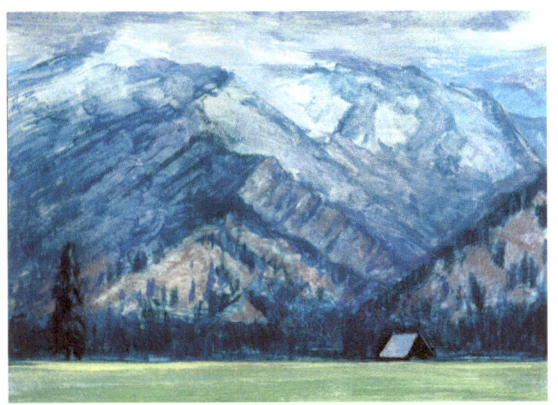

#124 Acrylic on Paper   05/04/2007

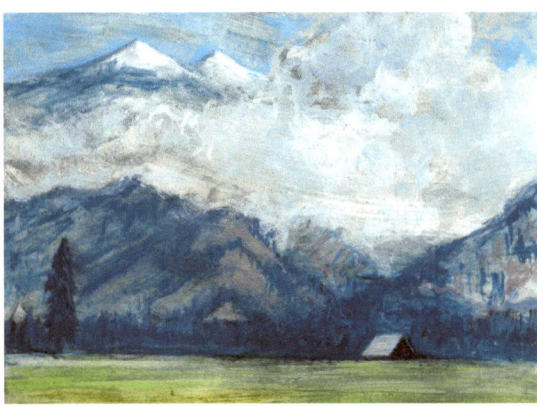

#125 Acrylic on Paper   05/05/2007

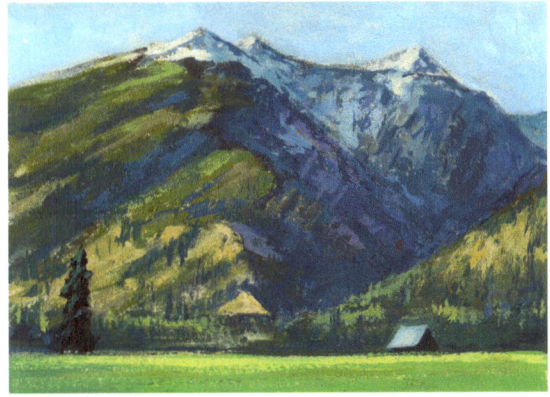

#126 Oil on Paper   05/06/2007

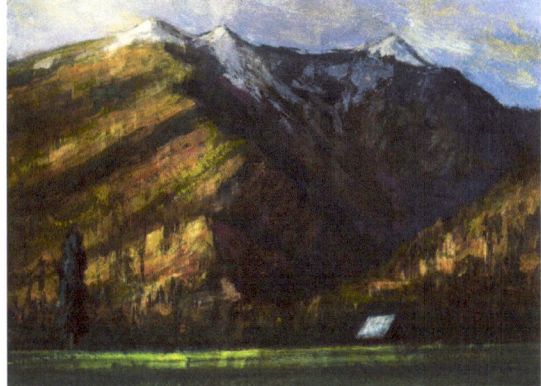

#127 Digital   05/07/2007

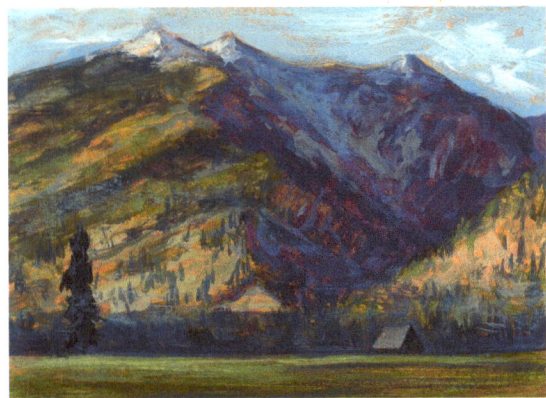

#128 Acrylic on Paper   05/08/2007

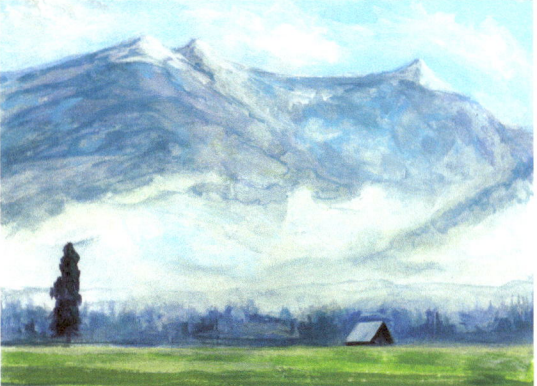

#129 Acrylic on Paper   05/09/2007

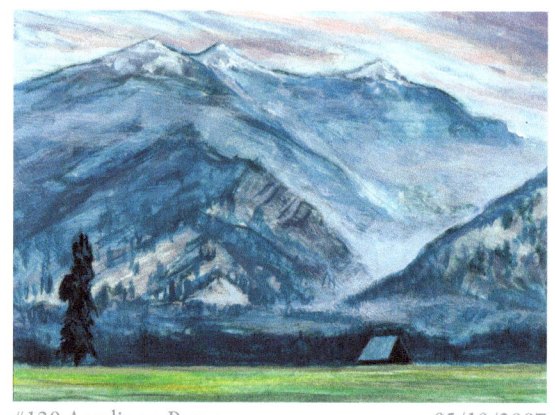

#130 Acrylic on Paper   05/10/2007

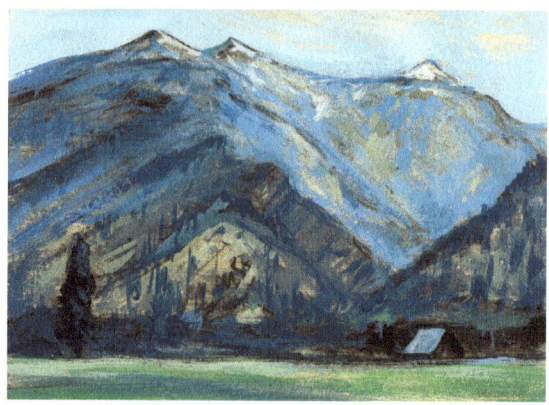

#131 Acrylic on Paper   05/11/2007

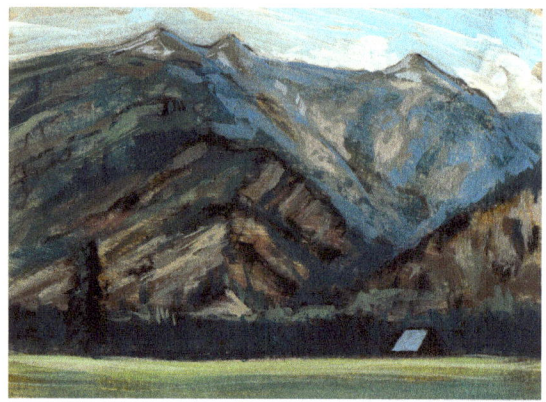

#132 Acrylic on Paper   05/12/2007

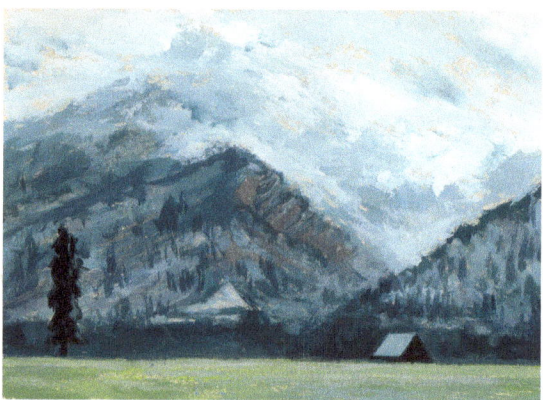

#133 Acrylic on Paper   05/13/2007

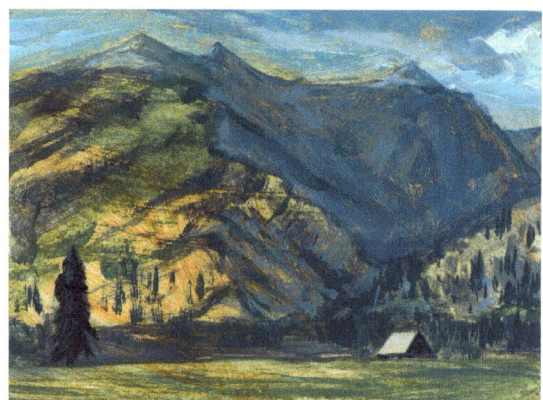

#134 Acrylic on Paper   05/14/2007

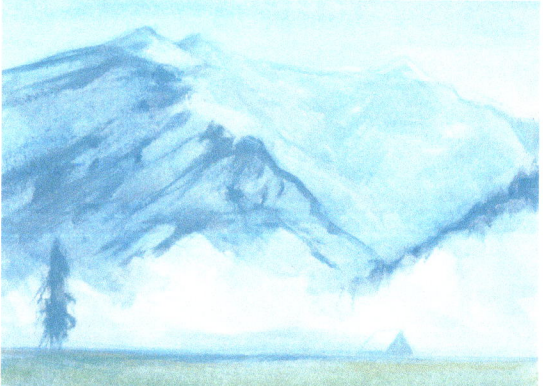

#135 Acrylic on Paper   05/15/2007

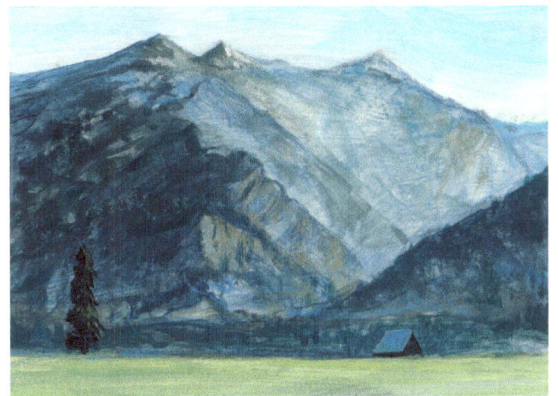

#136 Acrylic on Paper   05/16/2007

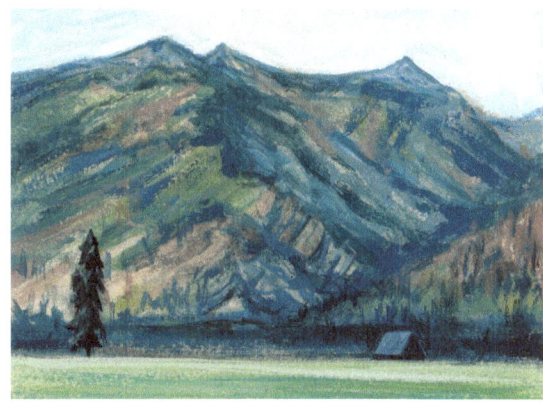

#137 Acrylic on Paper   05/17/2007

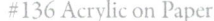

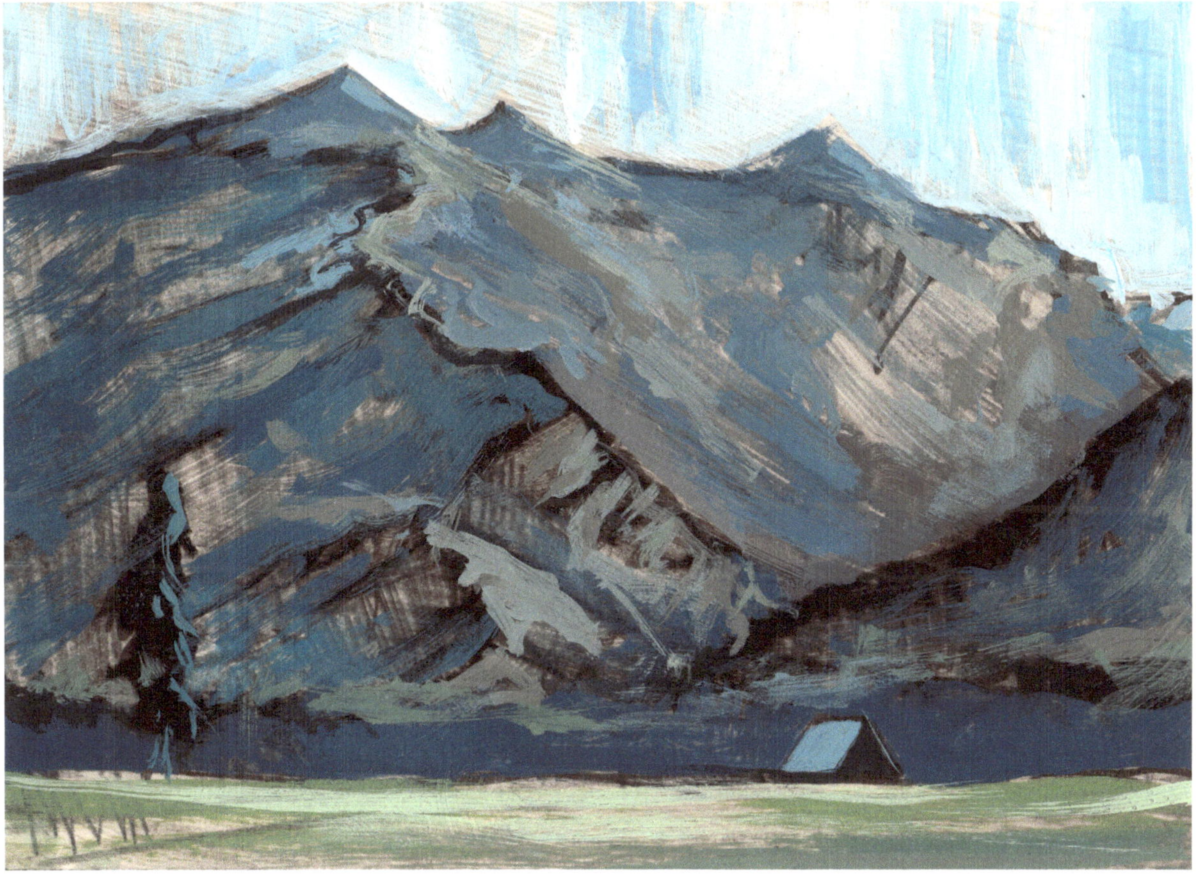

#138 Acrylic/India Ink on Paper   05/18/2007

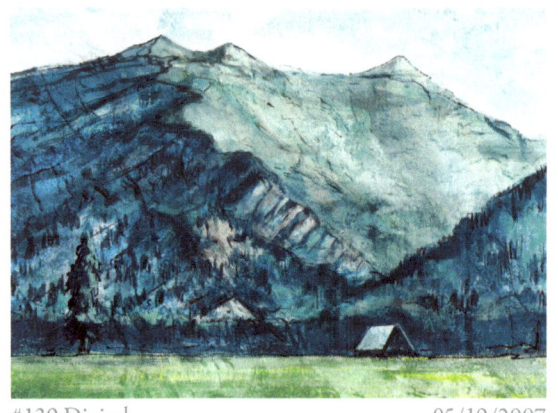

#139 Digital   05/19/2007

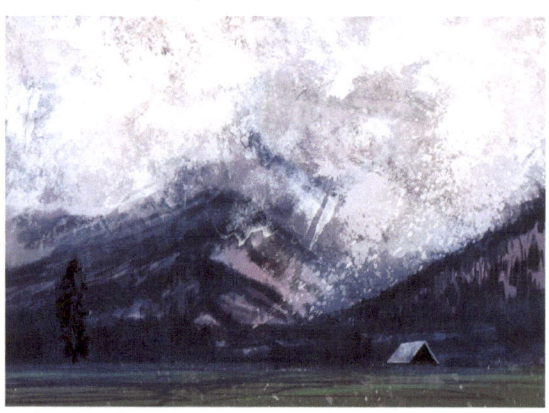

#140 Digital   05/20/2007

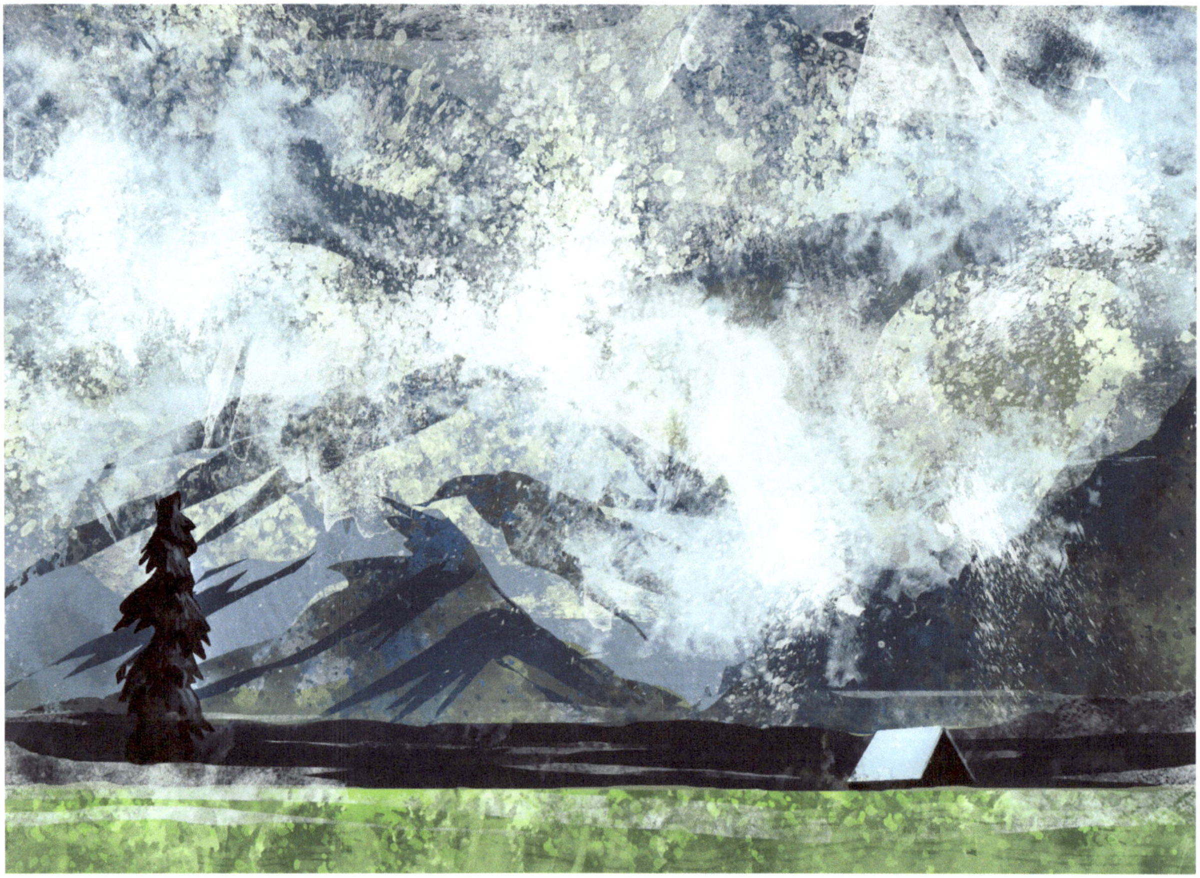

#141 Digital   05/21/2007

COUGAR PEAK-A-BOO
- The Art of Jared Shear -

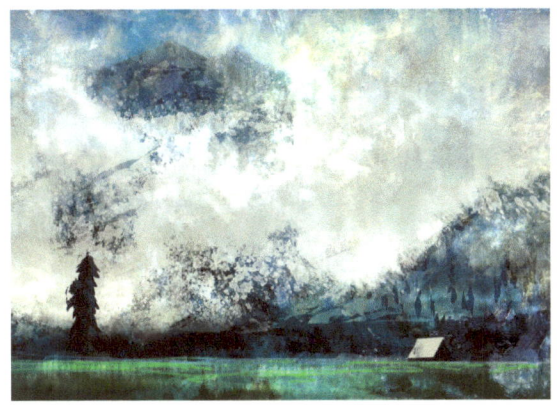

#142 Digital   05/22/2007

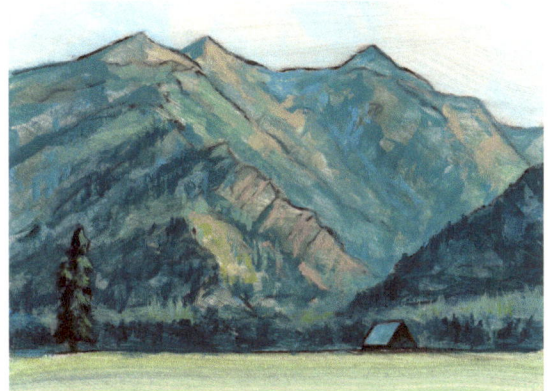

#143 Acrylic on Paper   05/23/2007

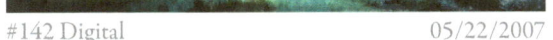

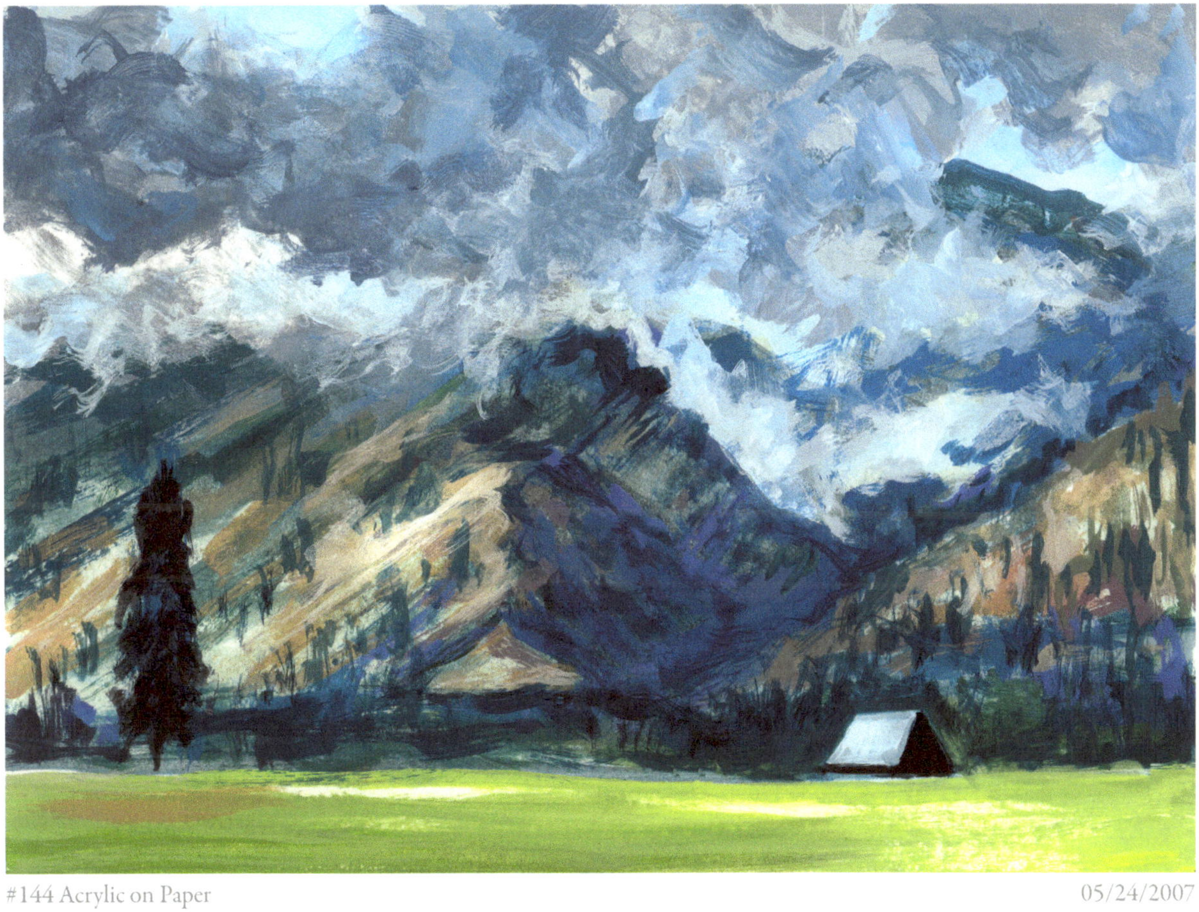

#144 Acrylic on Paper   05/24/2007

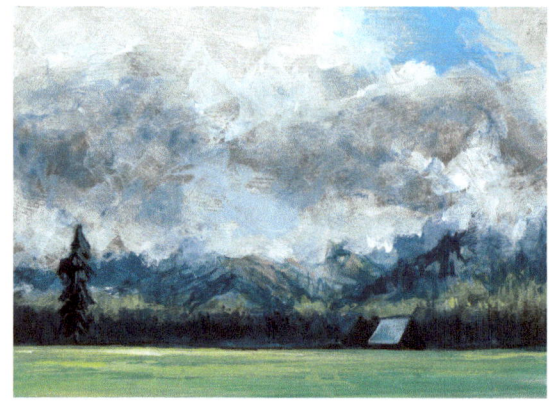

#145 Acrylic on Paper   05/25/2007

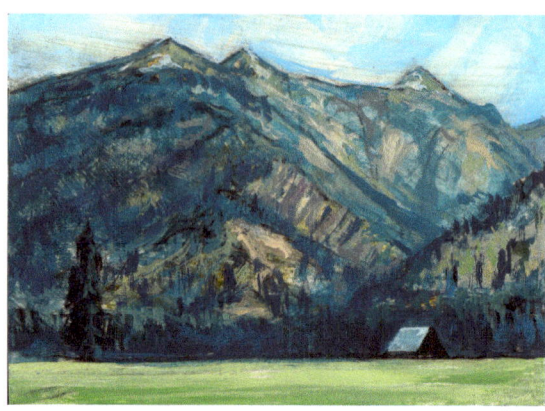

#146 Acrylic on Paper   05/26/2007

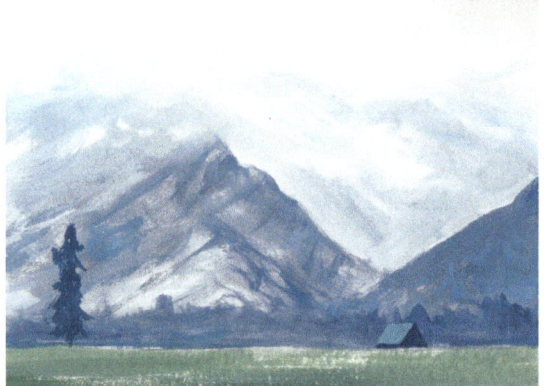

#147 Acrylic on Paper   05/27/2007

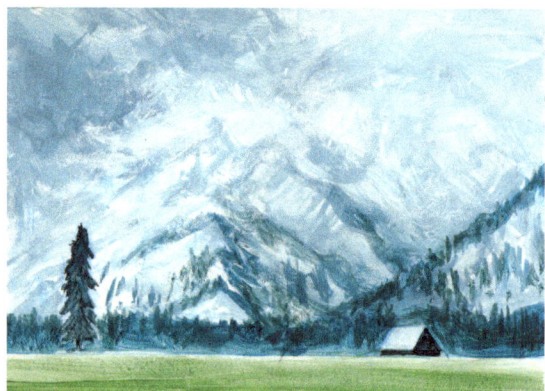

#148 Acrylic on Paper   05/28/2007

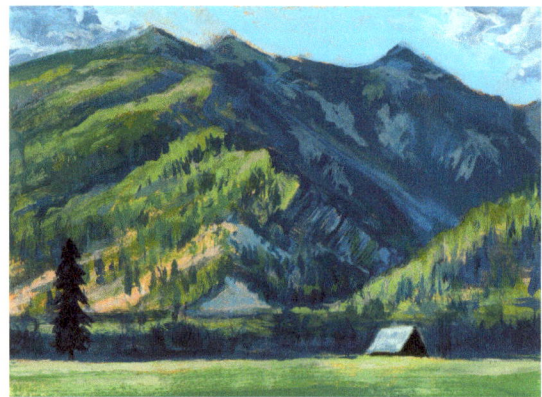

#149 Acrylic on Paper   05/29/2007

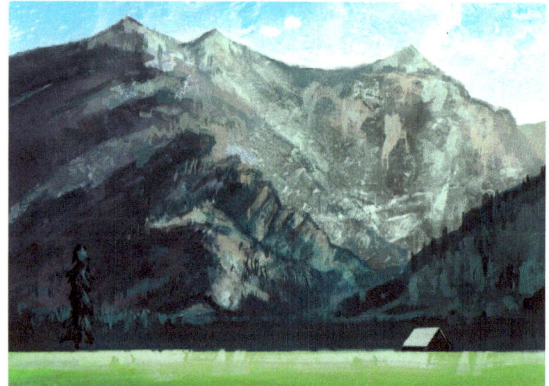

#150 Digital   05/30/2007

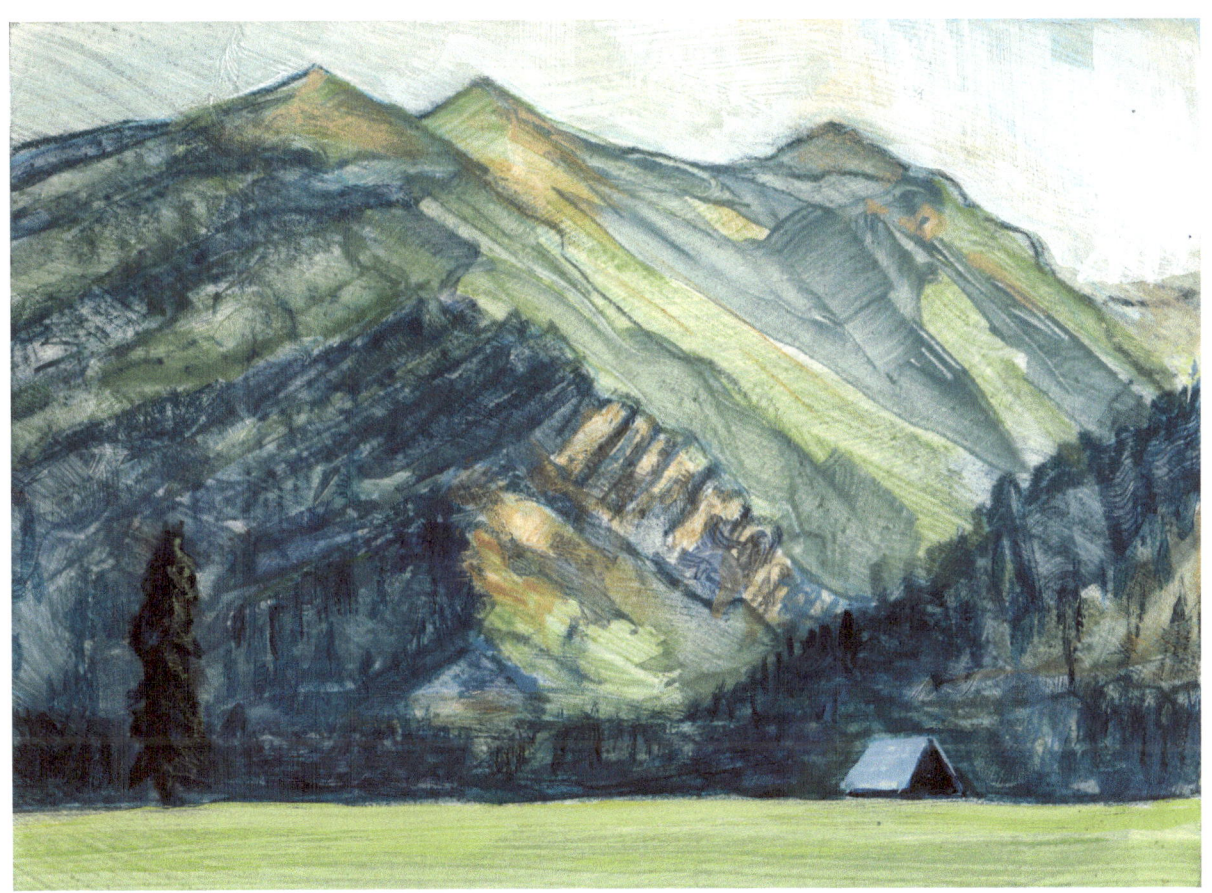

#151 Acrylic on Paper

05/31/2007

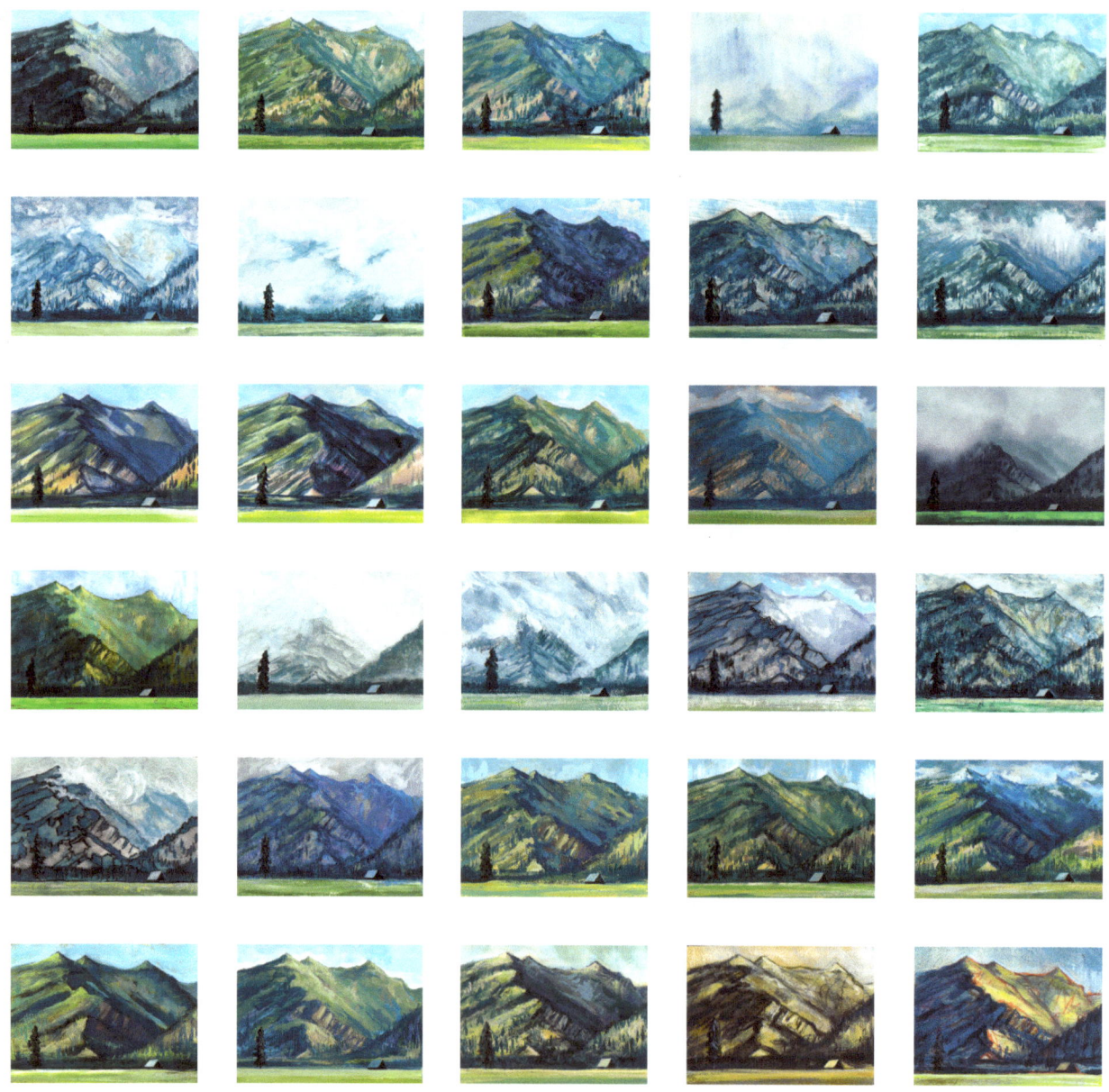

COUGAR PEAK-A-BOO
- The Art of Jared Shear -

JUNE

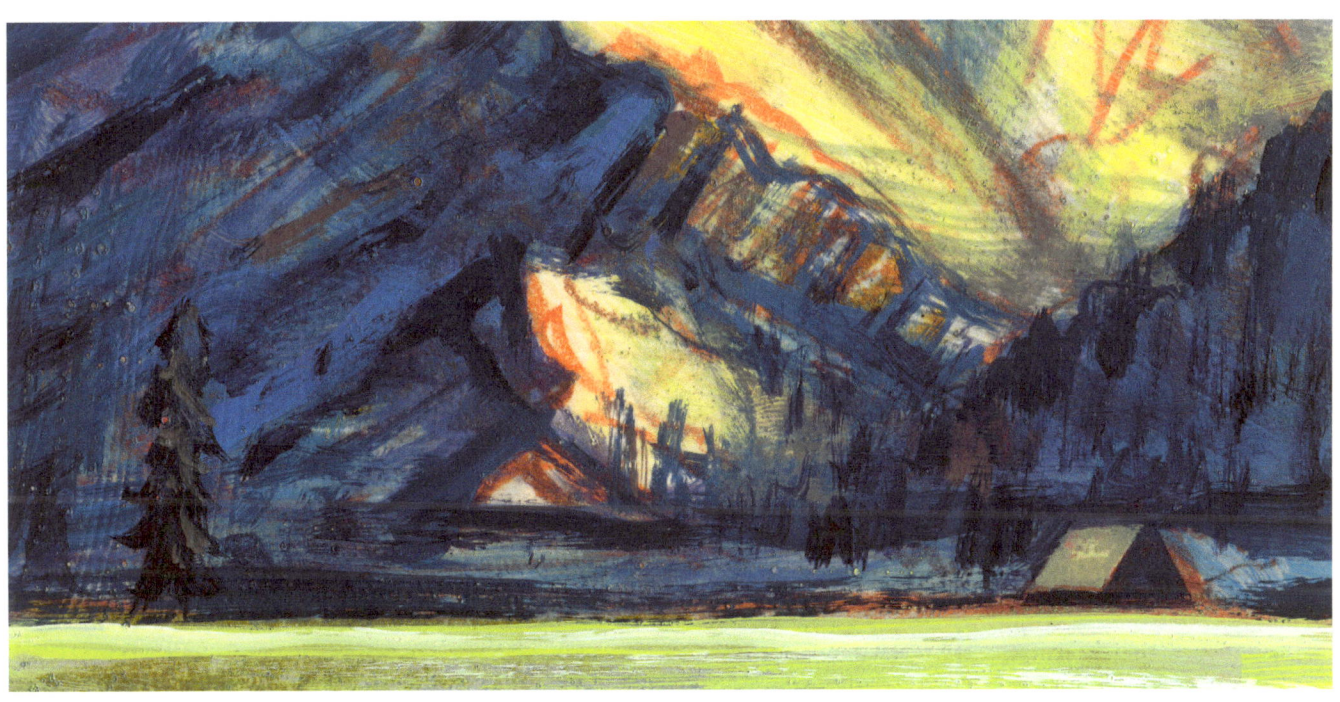

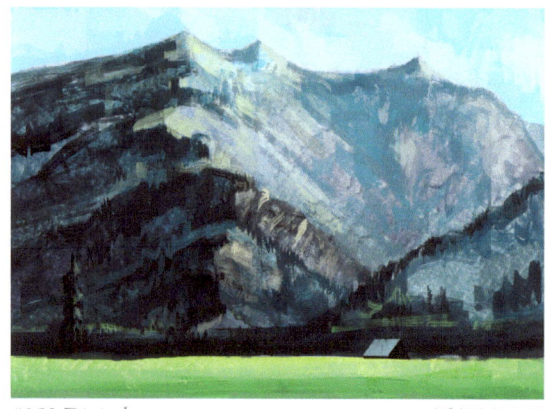

#152 Digital   06/01/2007

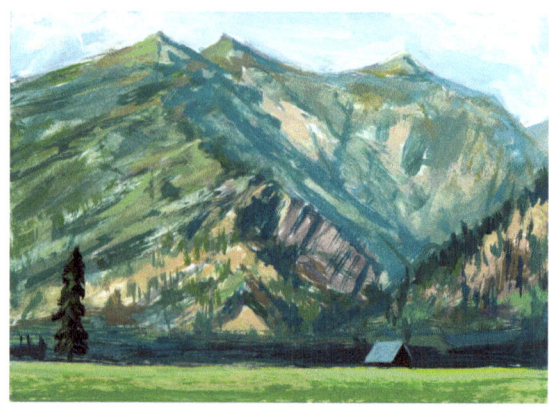

#153 Acrylic on Paper   06/02/2007

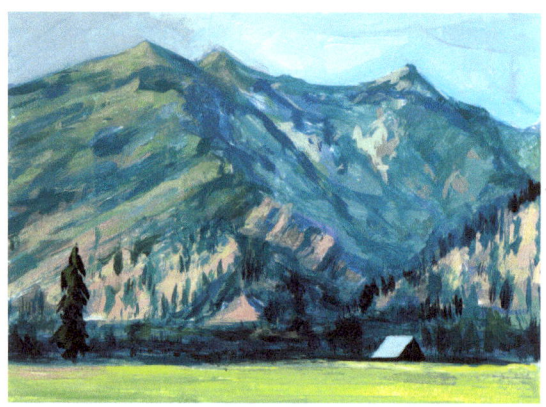

#154 Acrylic on Paper   06/03/2007

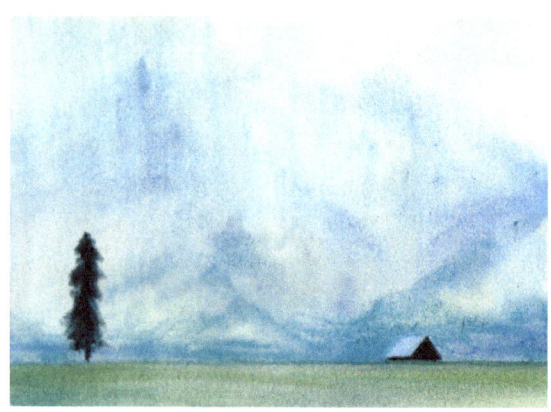

#155 Acrylic on Paper   06/04/2007

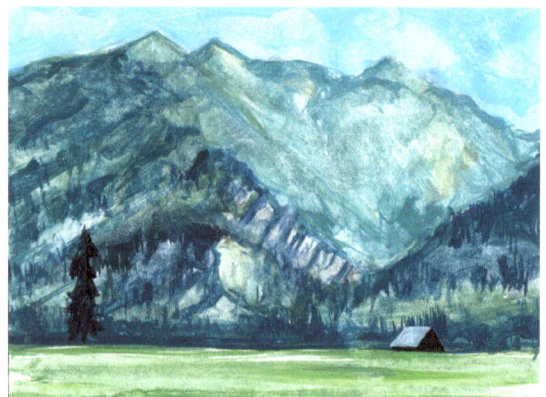

#156 Acrylic on Tyvek   06/05/2007

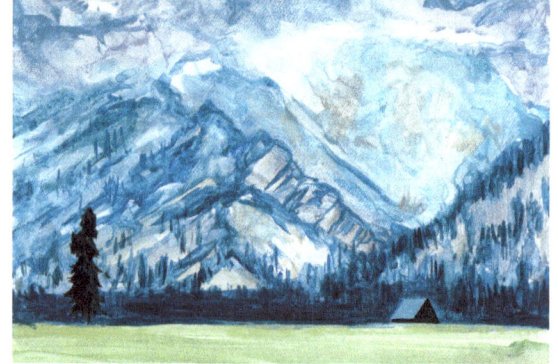

#157 Acrylic on Tyvek   06/06/2007

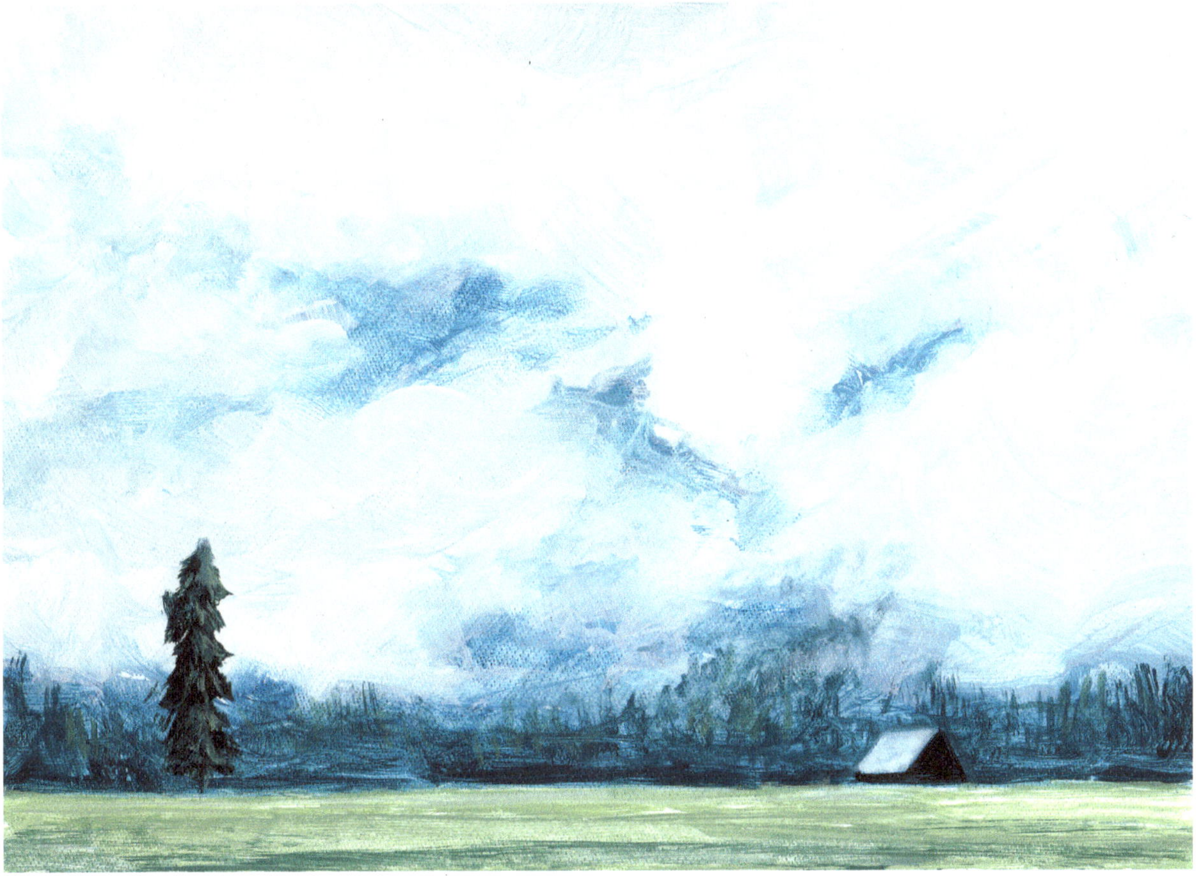

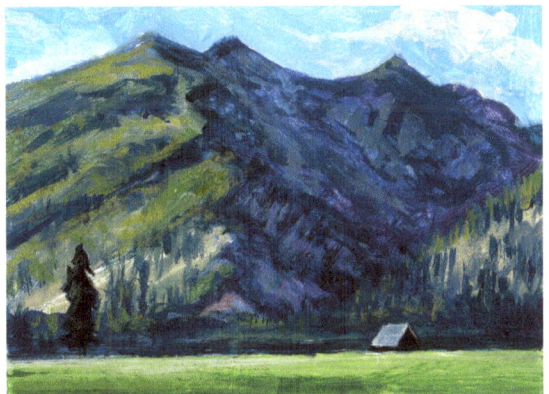

#158 Acrylic on Tyvek   06/07/2007

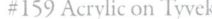

#159 Acrylic on Tyvek   06/08/2007

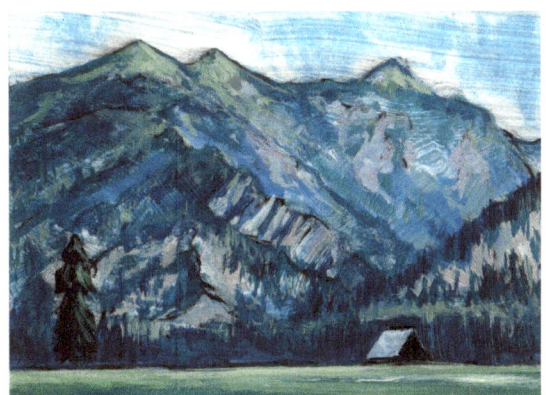

#160 Acrylic on Paper   06/09/2007

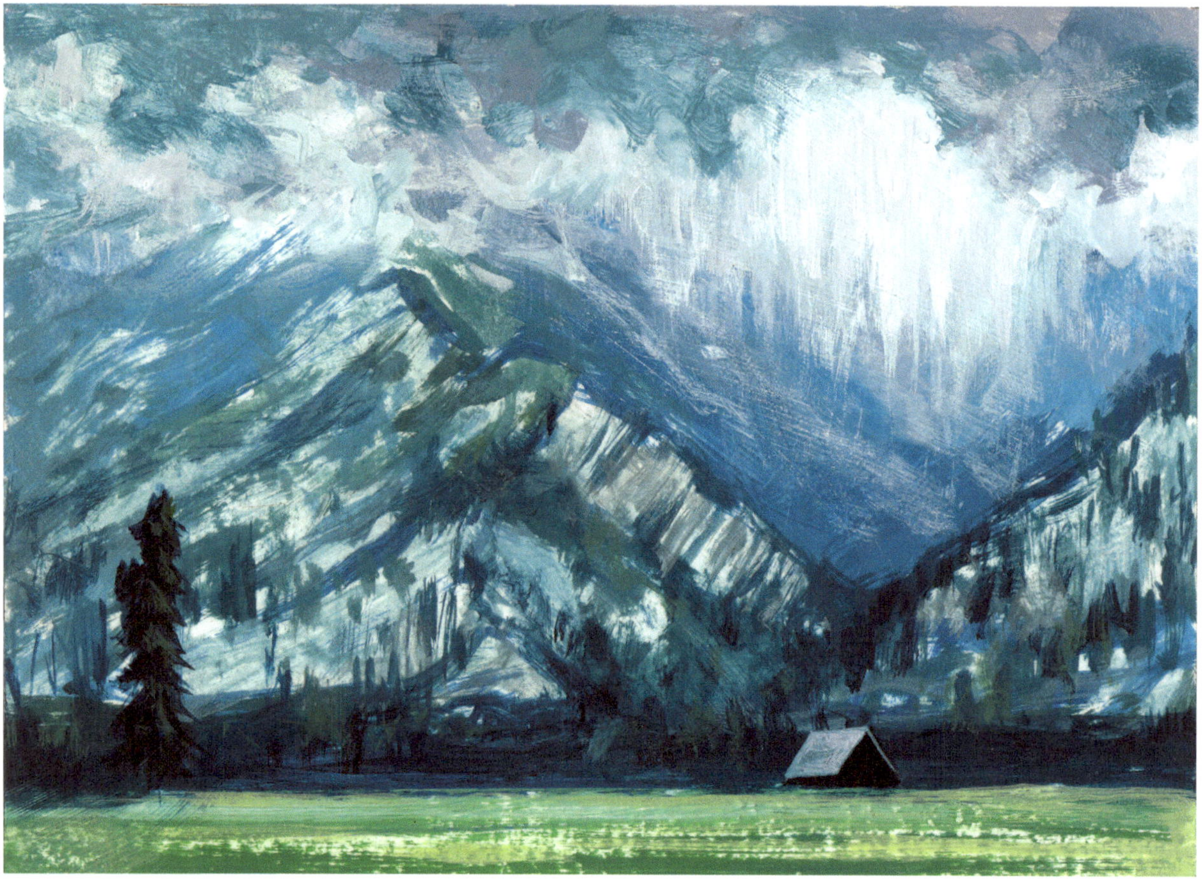

#161 Acrylic on Paper   06/10/2007

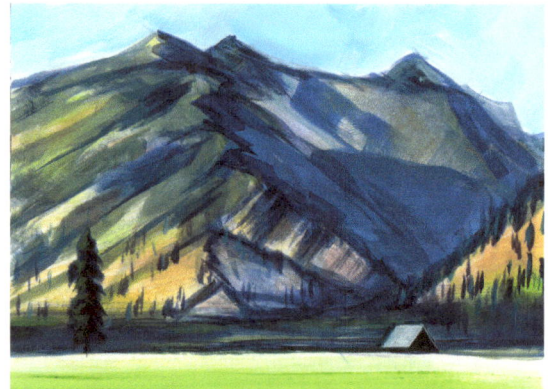

#162 Acrylic on Paper   06/11/2007

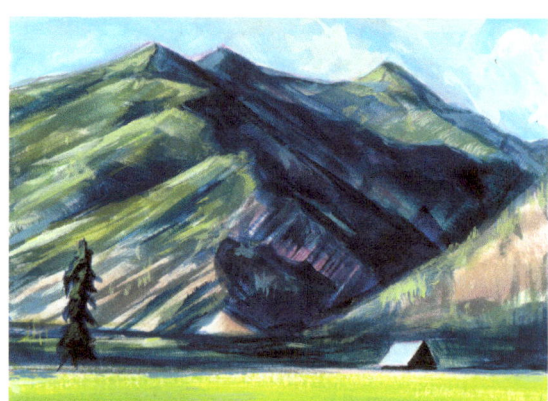

#163 Acrylic on Paper   06/12/2007

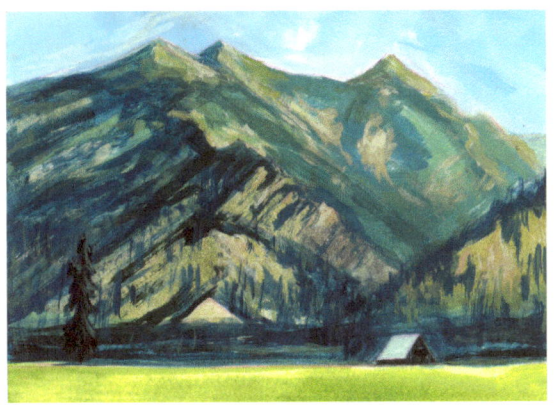

#164 Acrylic on Paper   06/13/2007

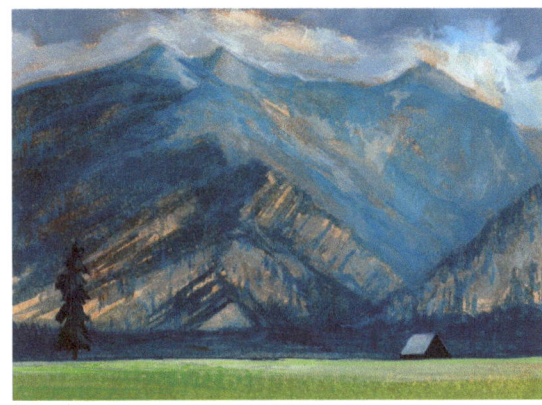

#165 Acrylic on Paper   06/14/2007

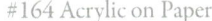

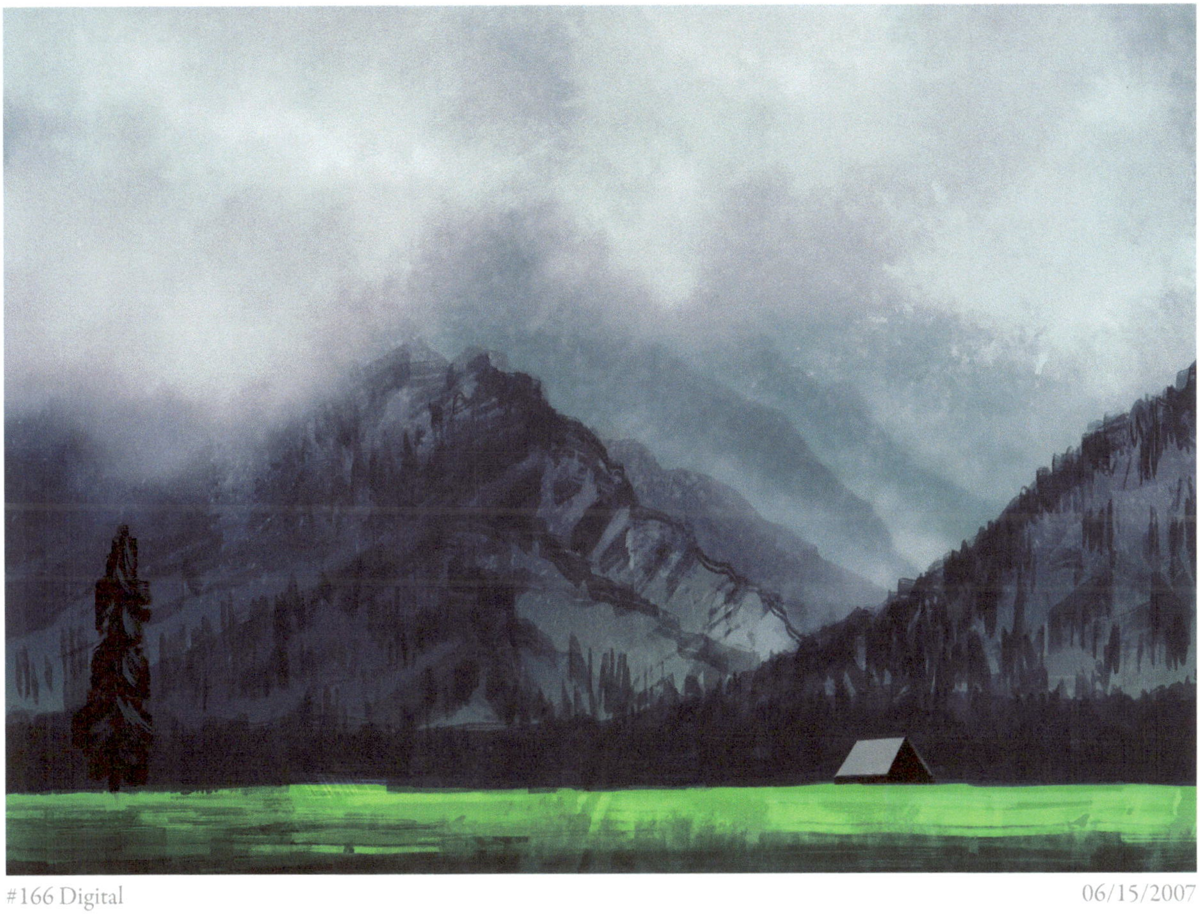

#166 Digital   06/15/2007

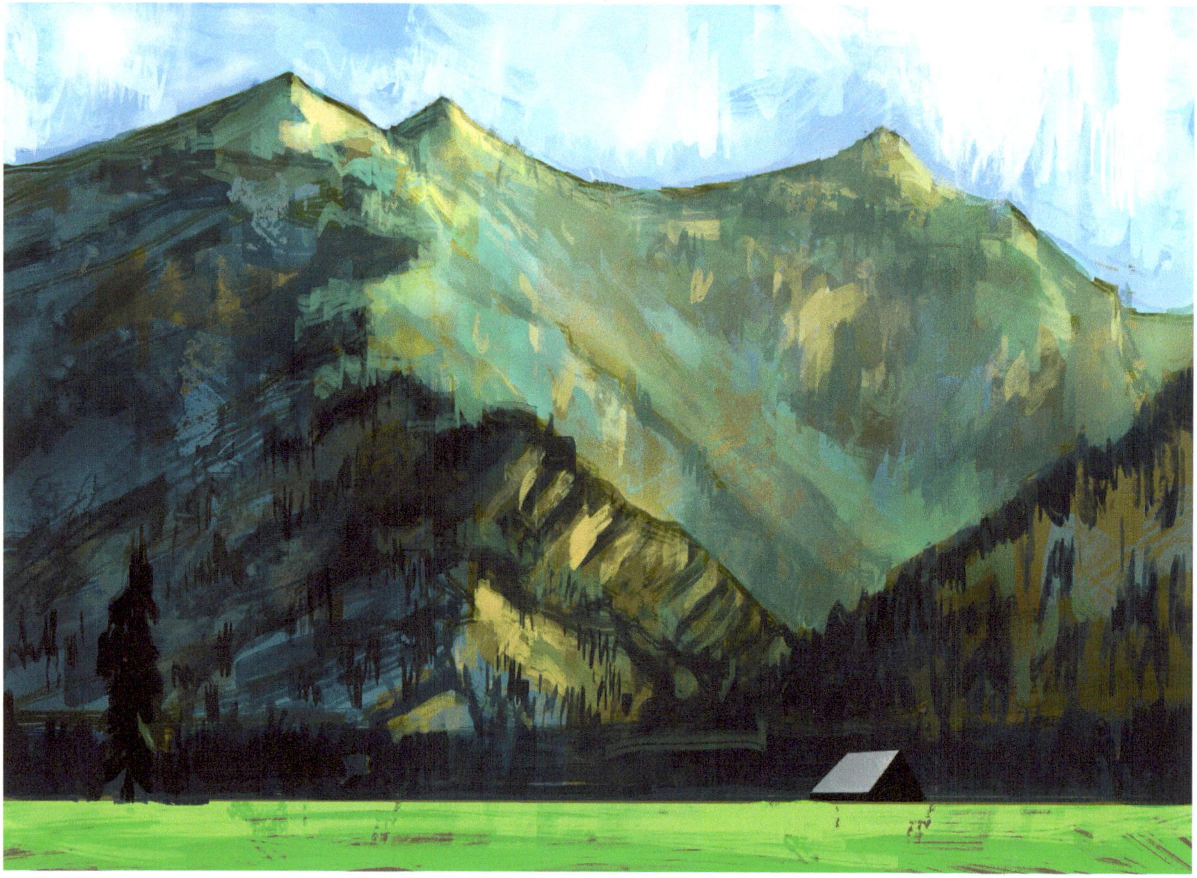

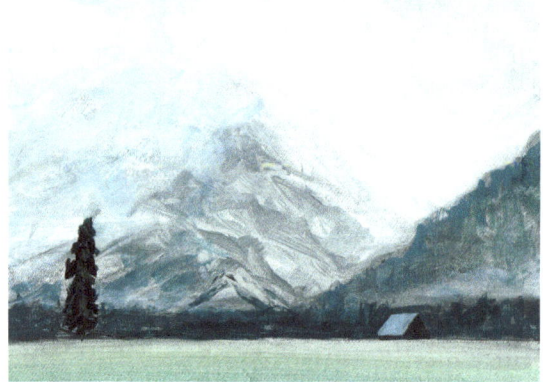

#167 Digital   06/16/2007

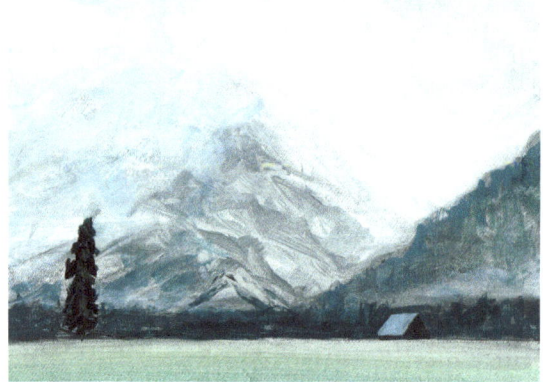

#168 Acrylic on Tyvek   06/17/2007

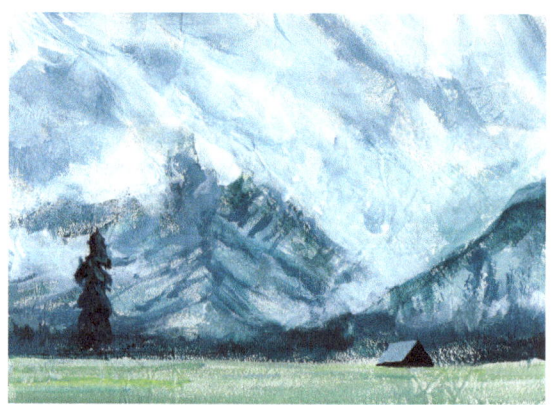

#169 Acrylic on Klondike Wrapper   06/18/2007

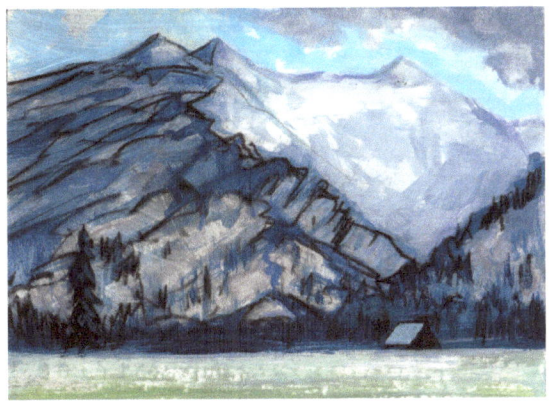

#170 Acrylic on Paper   06/19/2007

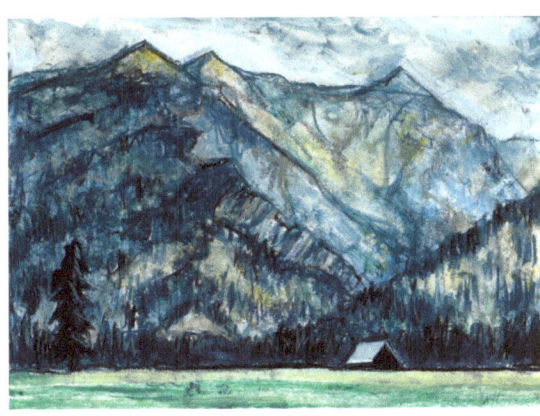

#171 Acrylic/Pastel on Paper   06/20/2007

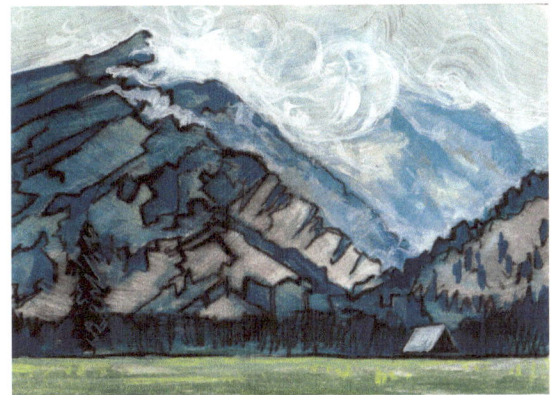

#172 Acrylic on Paper   06/21/2007

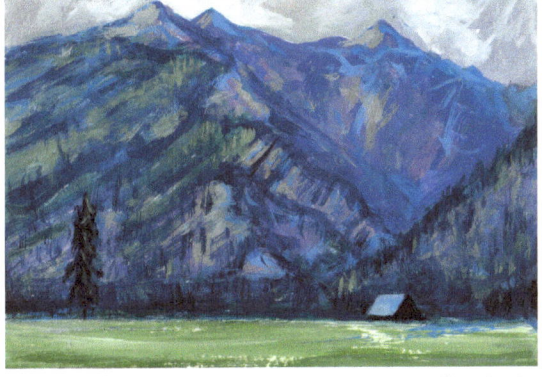

#173 Acrylic on Paper   06/22/2007

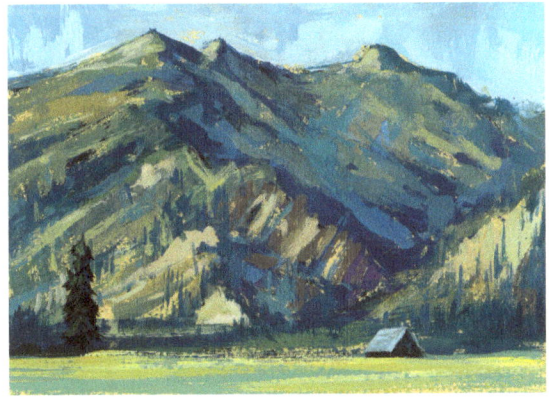

#174 Acrylic on Paper   06/23/2007

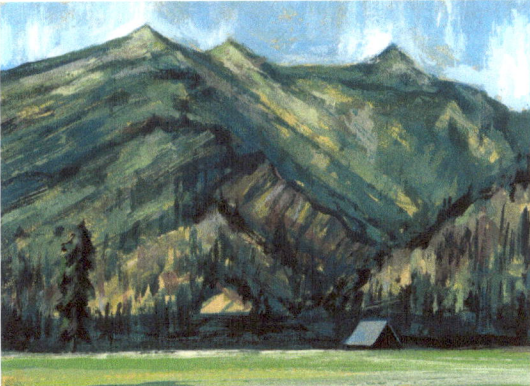

#175 Acrylic on Paper   06/24/2007

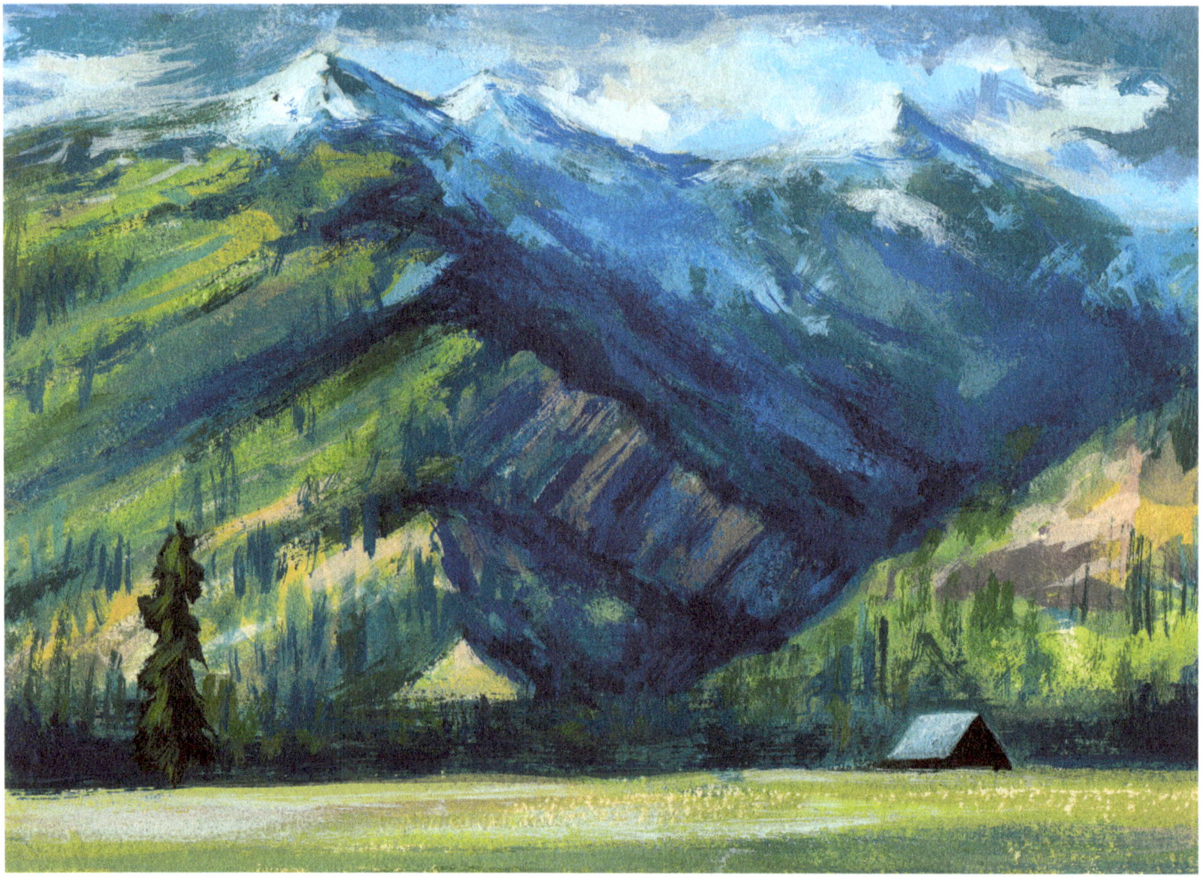

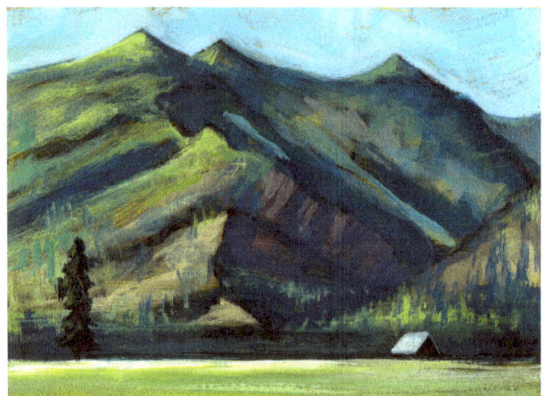

#176 Acrylic on Paper   06/25/2007

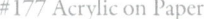

#177 Acrylic on Paper   06/26/2007

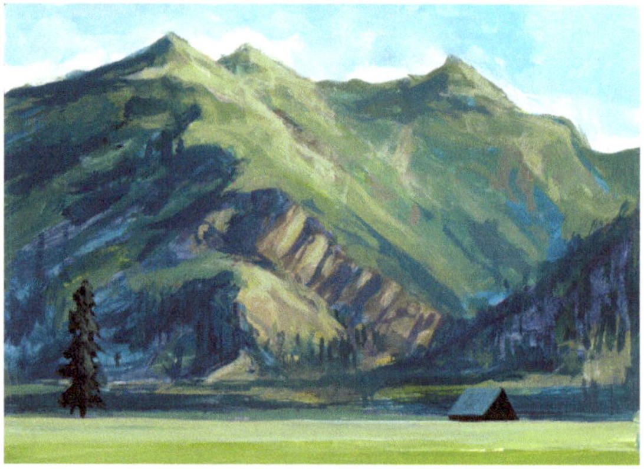

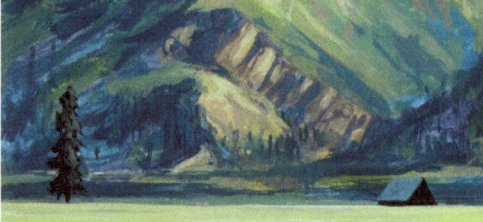

#178 Acrylic on Paper   06/27/2007

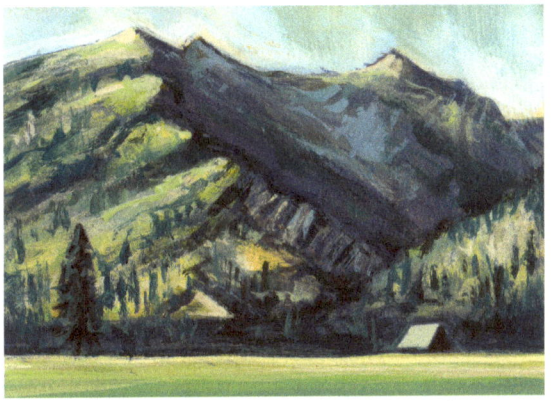

#179 Acrylic on Paper   06/28/2007

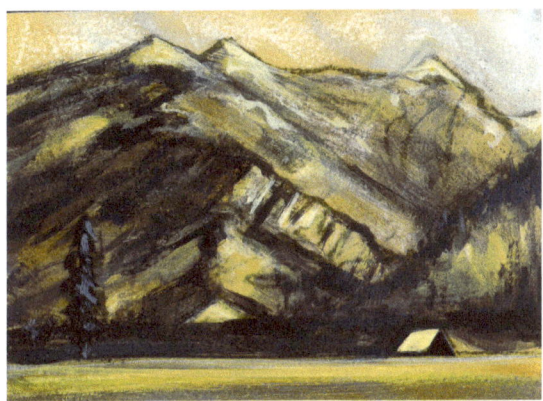

#180 Acrylic on Paper   06/29/2007

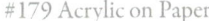

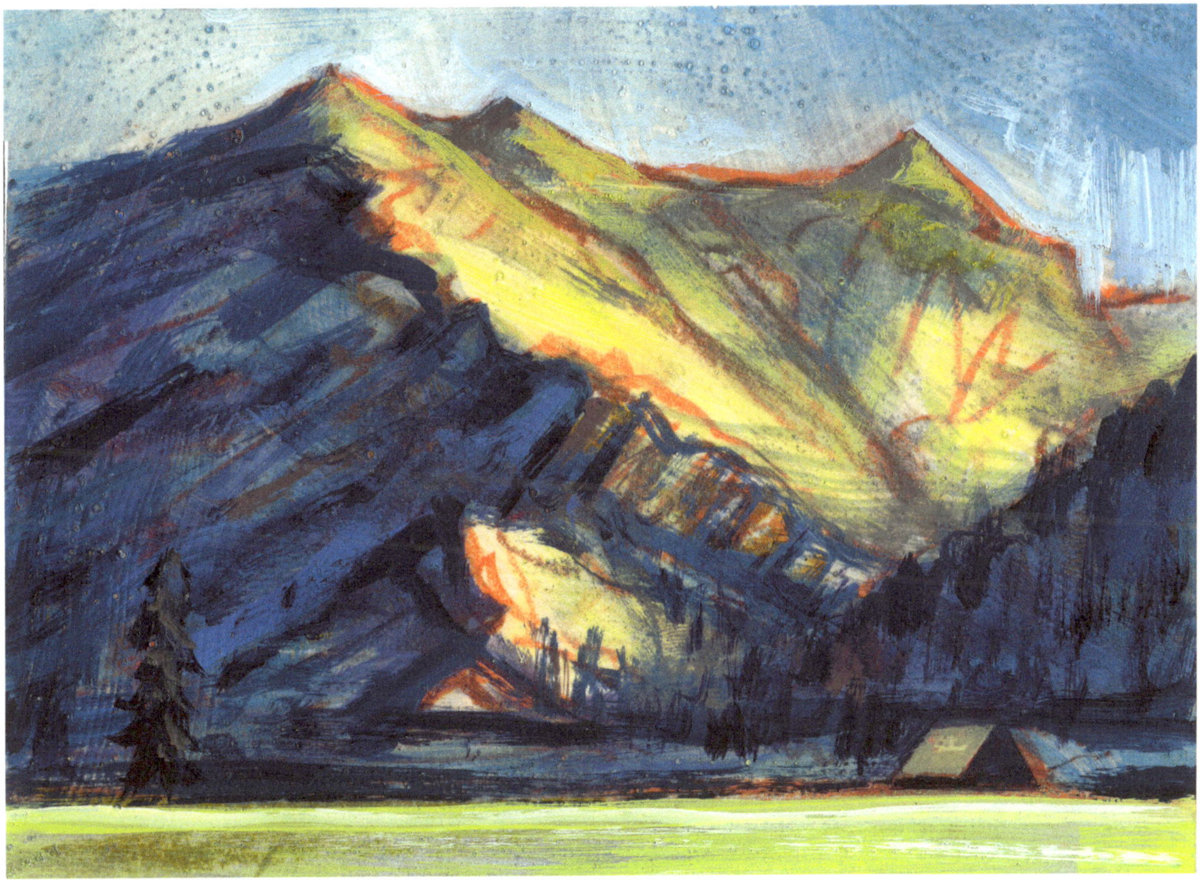

#181 Acrylic on Paper   06/30/2007

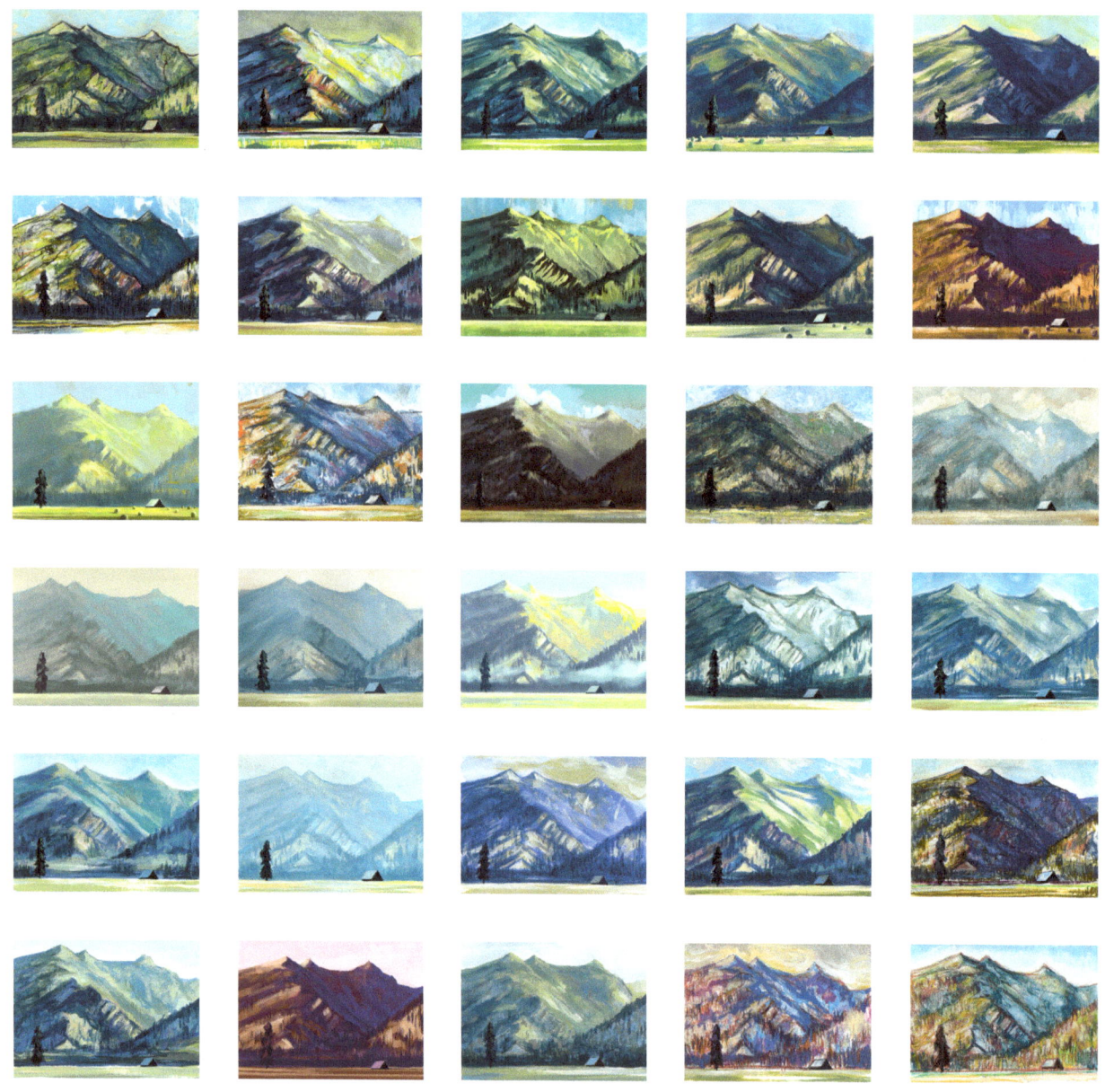

COUGAR PEAK-A-BOO
- The Art of Jared Shear -

JULY

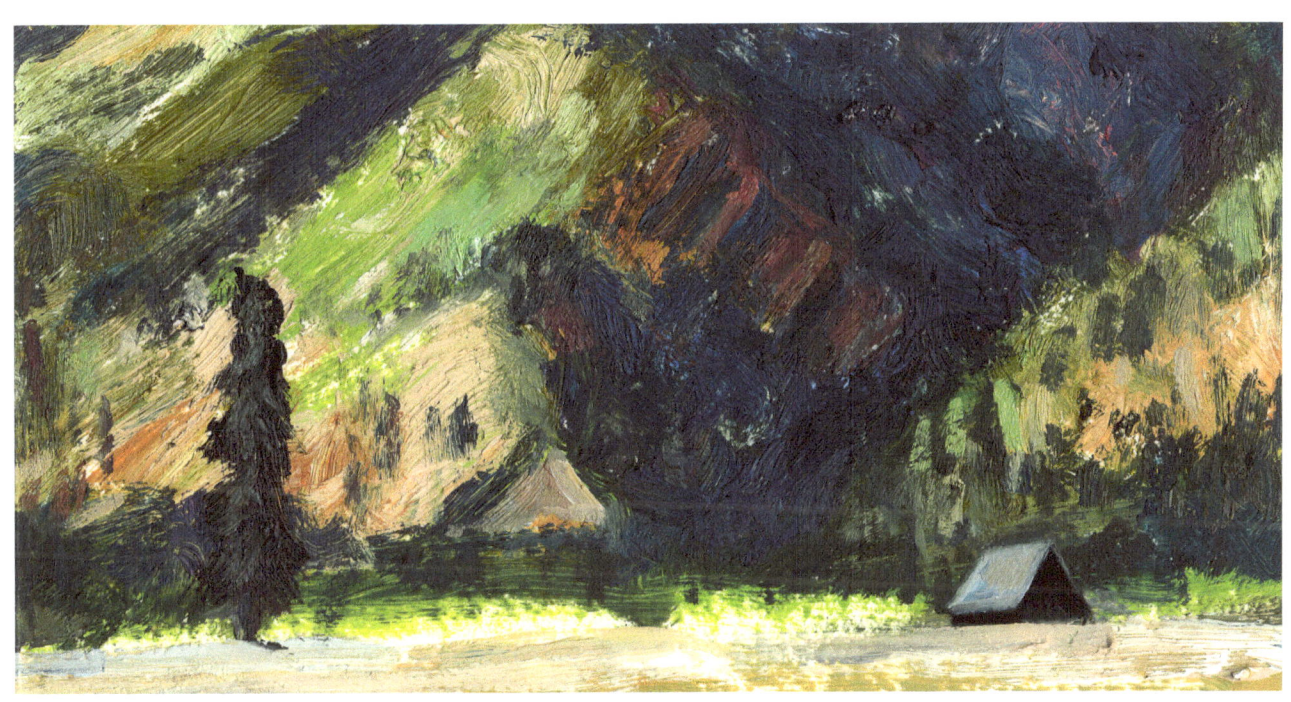

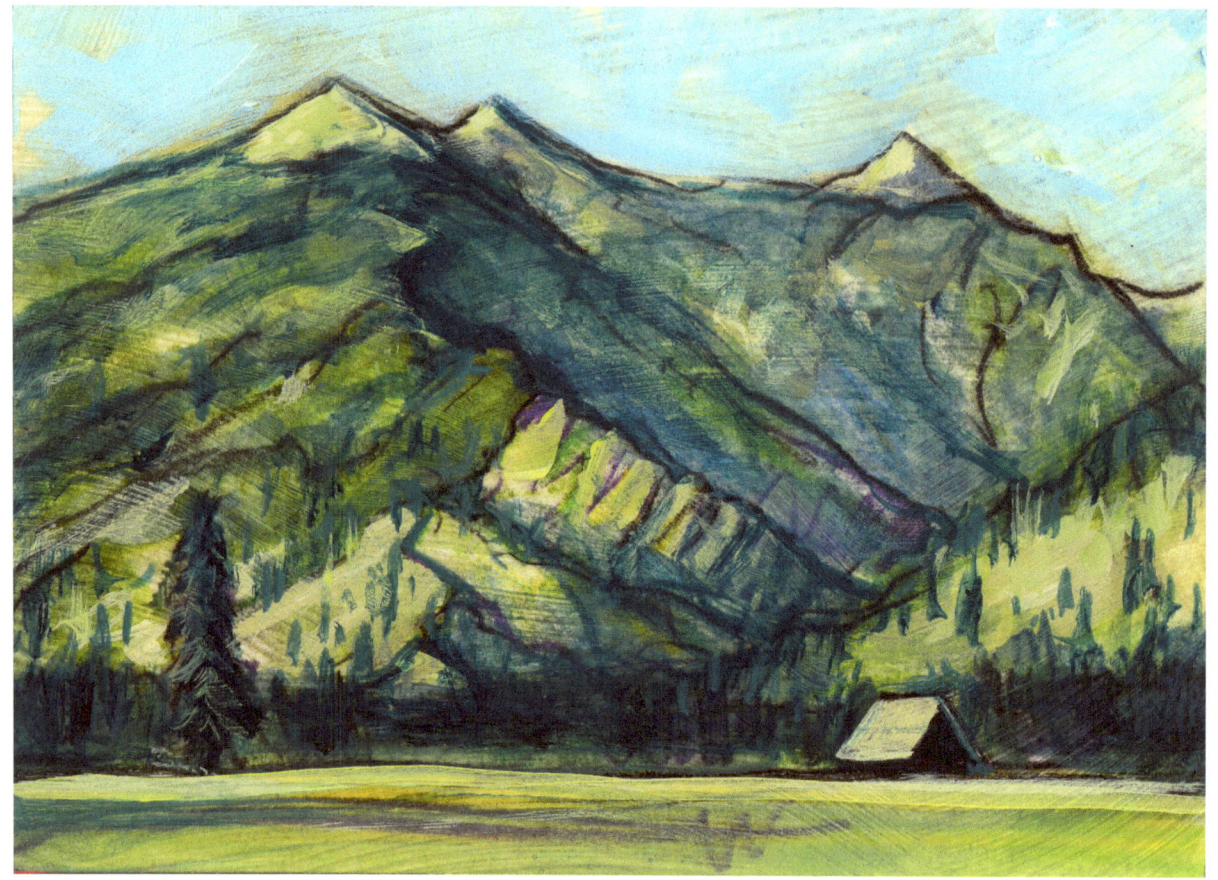

#182 Acrylic on Paper

07/01/2007

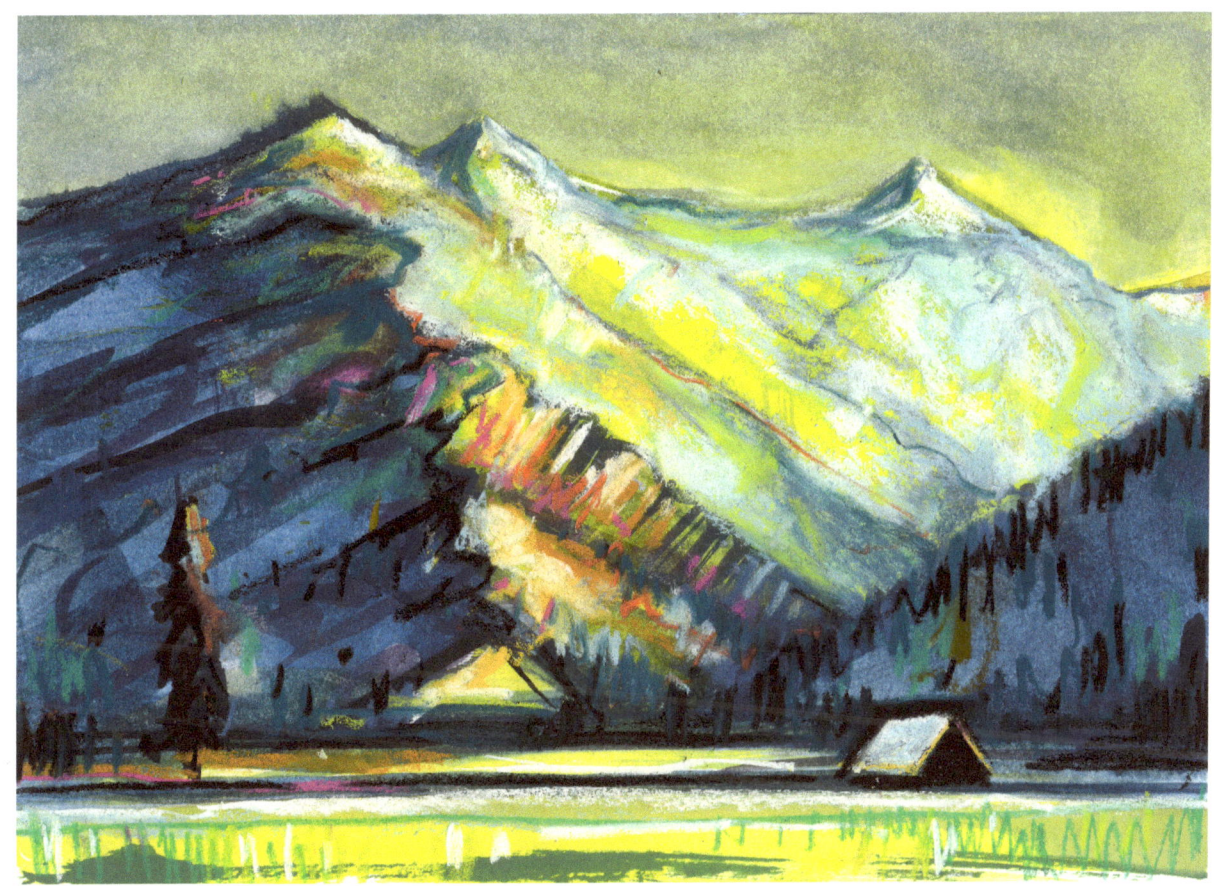

#183 Gouache/Pastel on Paper

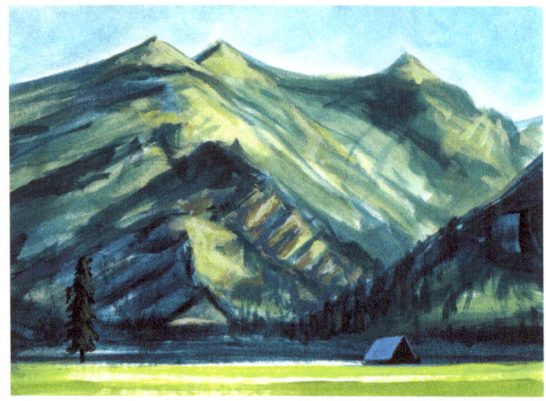

#184 Acrylic on Paper   07/03/2007

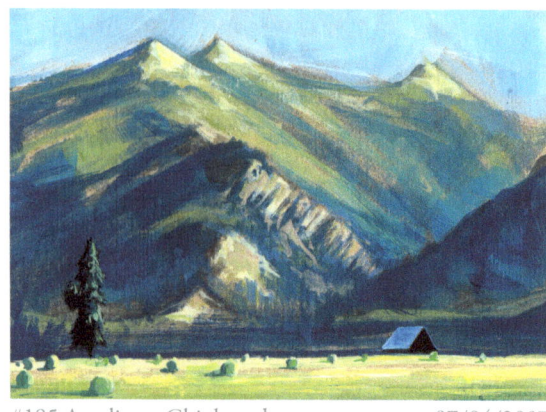

#185 Acrylic on Chipboard   07/04/2007

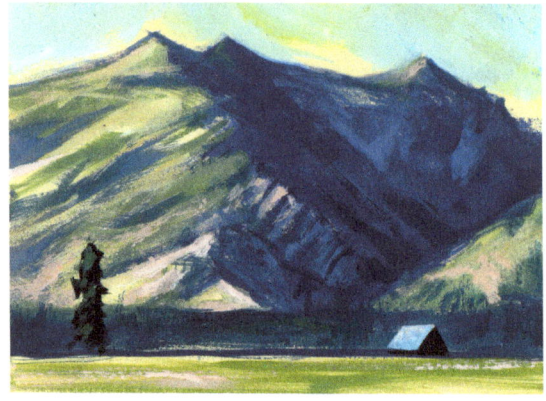

#186 Acrylic on Paper   07/05/2007

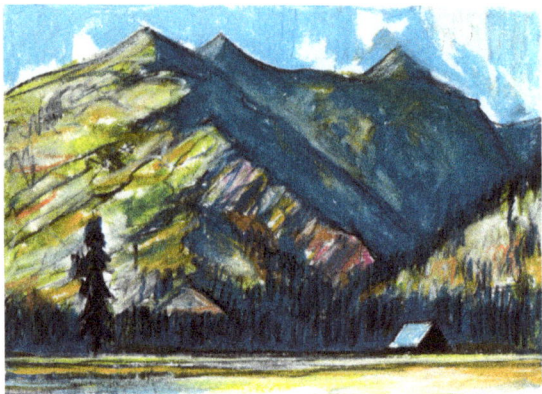

#187 Pastel on Paper   07/06/2007

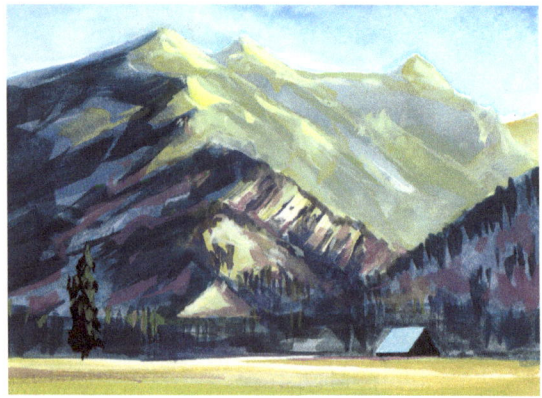

#188 Gouache on Paper   07/07/2007

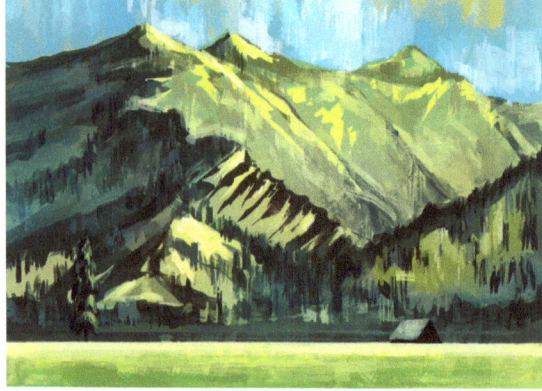

#189 Digital   07/08/2007

COUGAR PEAK-A-BOO
- The Art of Jared Shear -

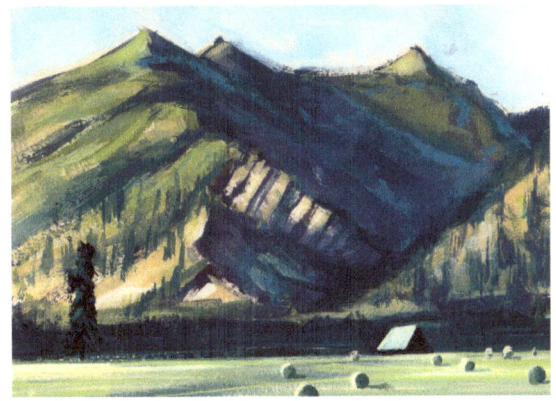

#190 Acrylic on Paper   07/09/2007

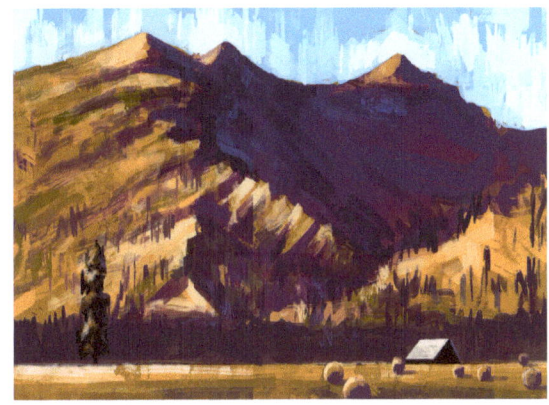

#191 Digital   07/10/2007

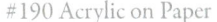

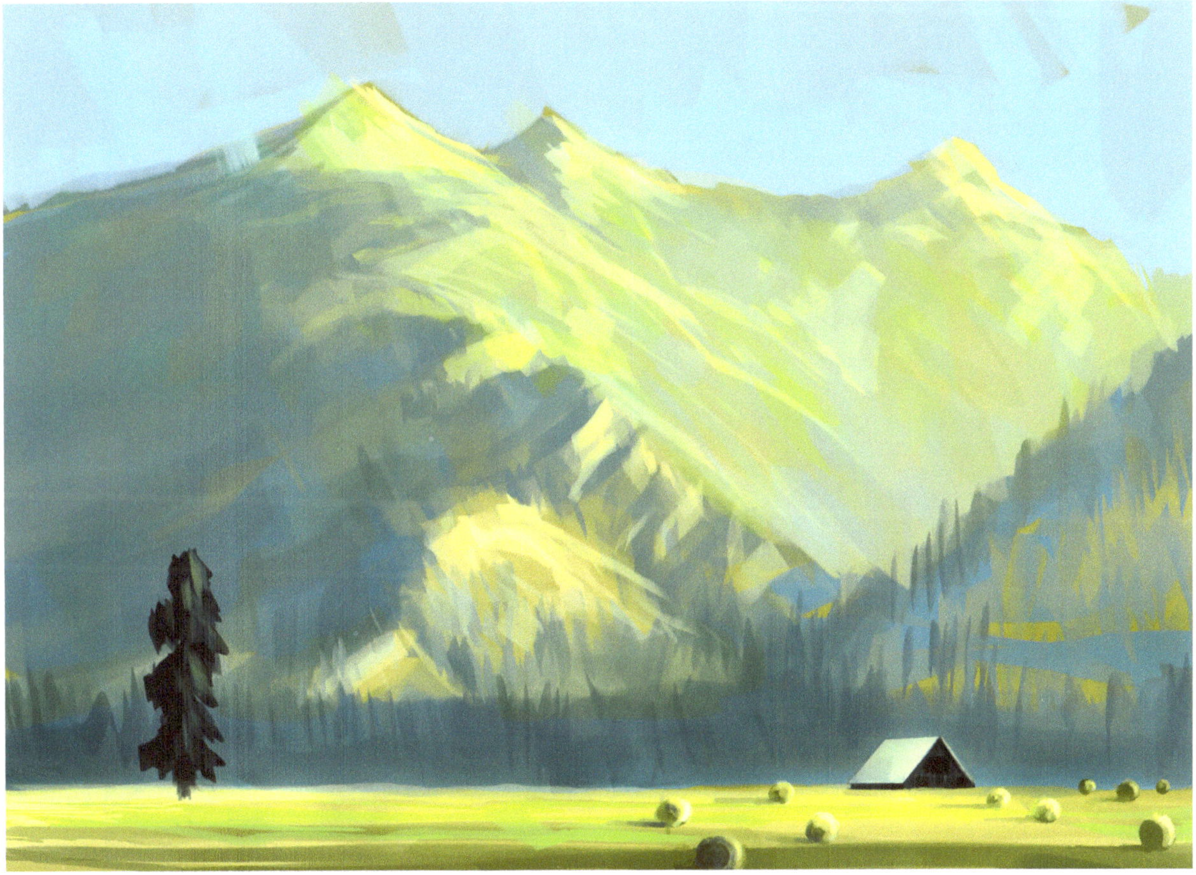

#192 Digital   07/11/2007

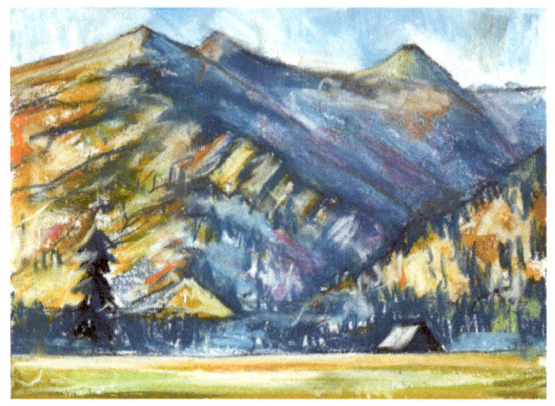

#193 Pastel on Paper — 07/12/2007

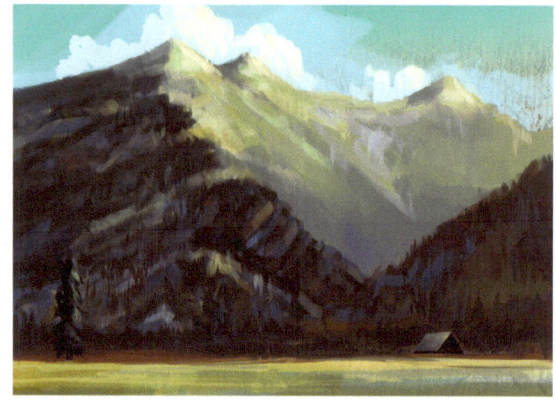

#194 Digital — 07/13/2007

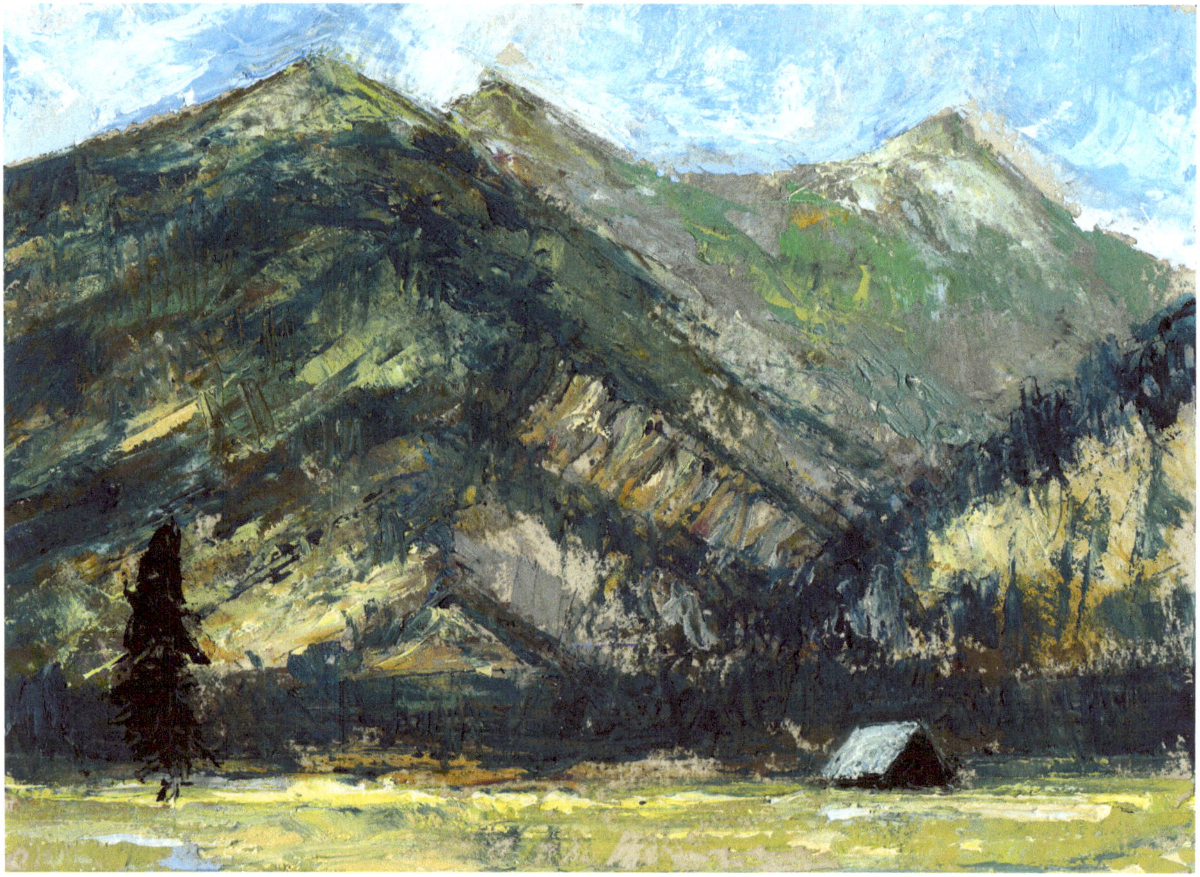

#195 Oil on Paper — 07/14/2007

COUGAR PEAK-A-BOO
- The Art of Jared Shear -

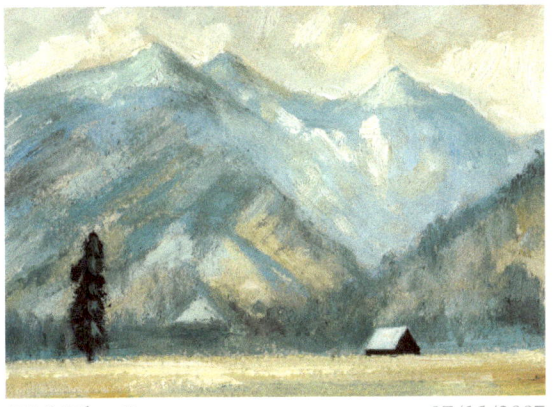

#196 Oil on Paper   07/15/2007

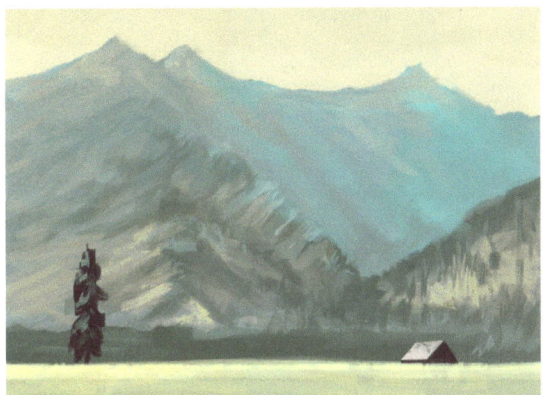

#197 Digital   07/16/2007

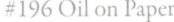

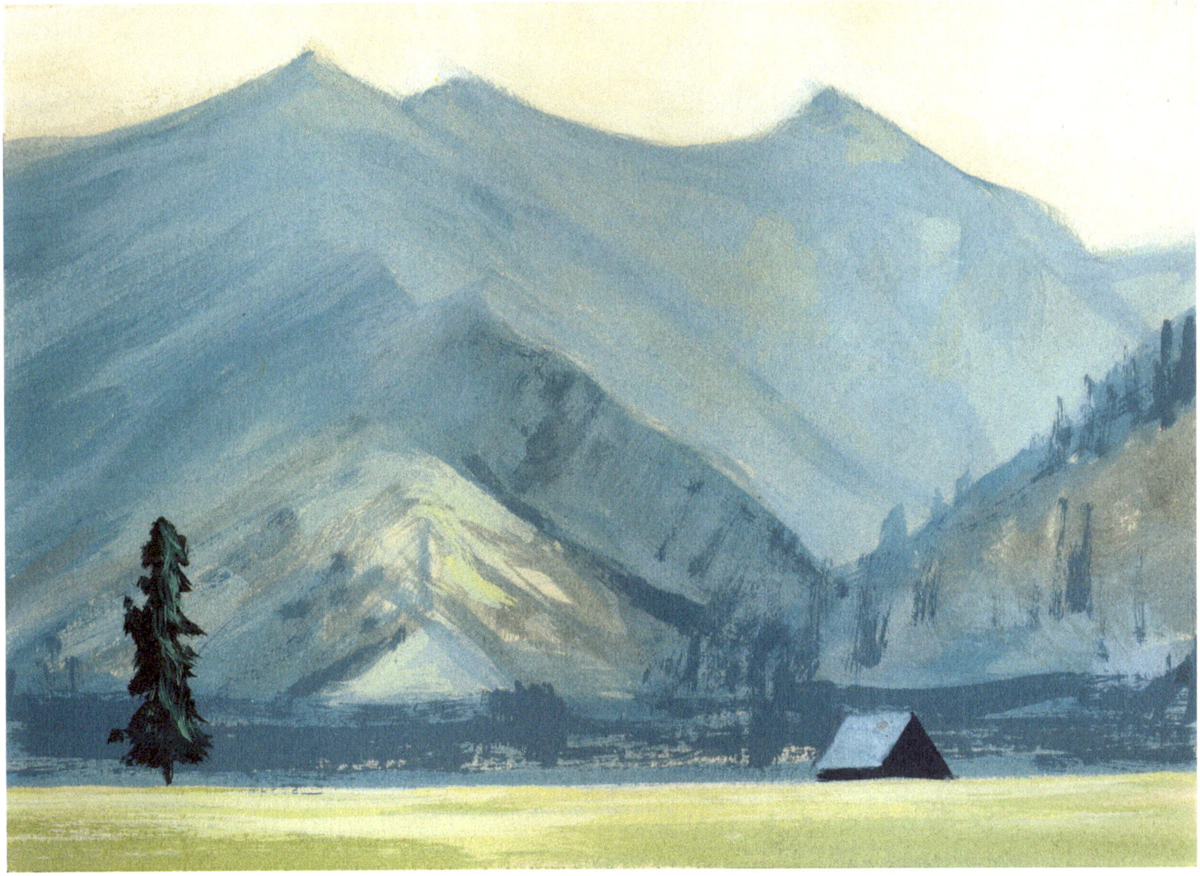

#198 Acrylic on Paper   07/17/2007

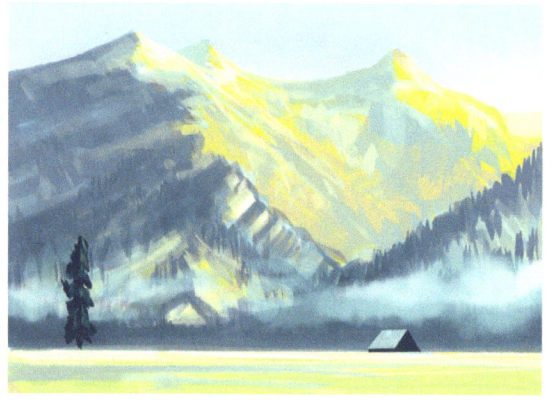

#199 Digital   07/18/2007

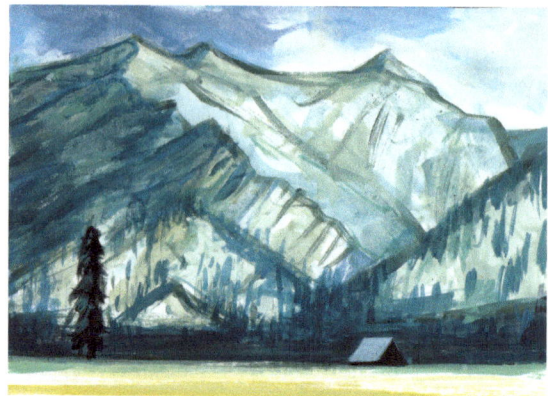

#200 Acrylic on Paper   07/19/2007

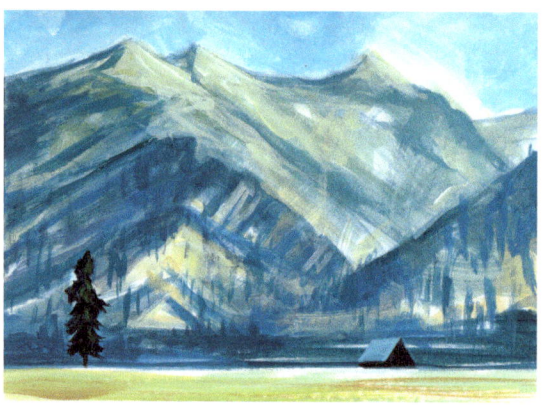

#201 Acrylic on Paper   07/20/2007

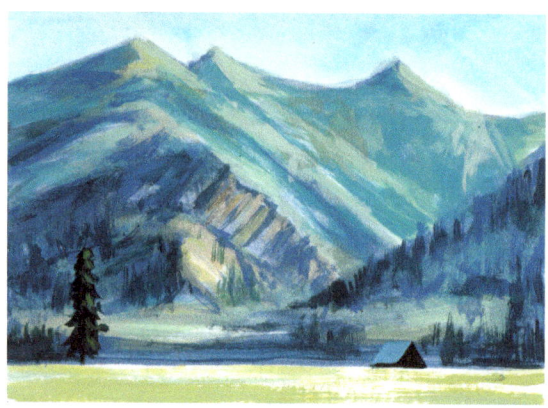

#202 Acrylic on Paper   07/21/2007

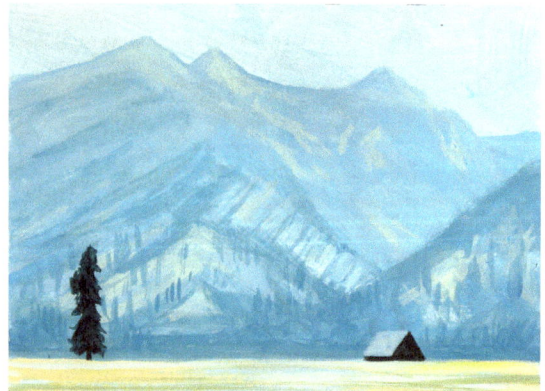

#203 Acrylic on Paper   07/22/2007

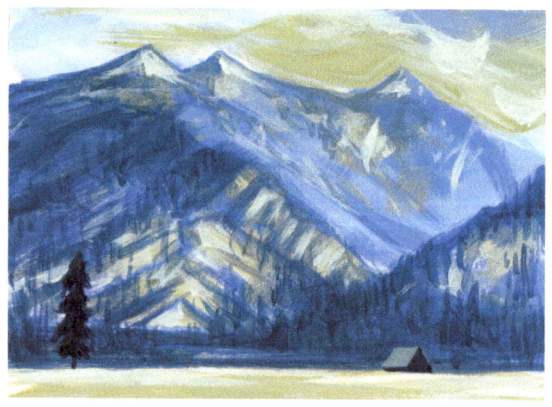

#204 Acrylic on Paper   07/23/2007

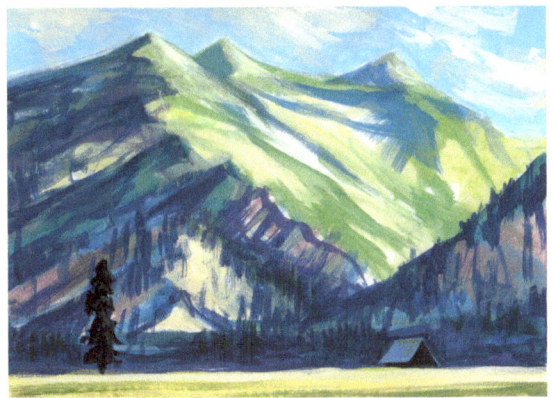

#205 Acrylic on Paper   07/24/2007

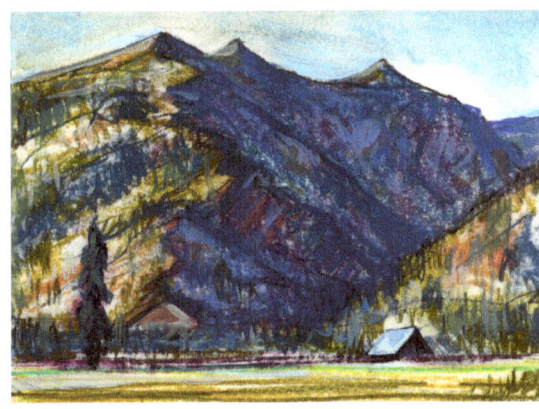

#206 Pastel/Acrylic on Paper   07/25/2007

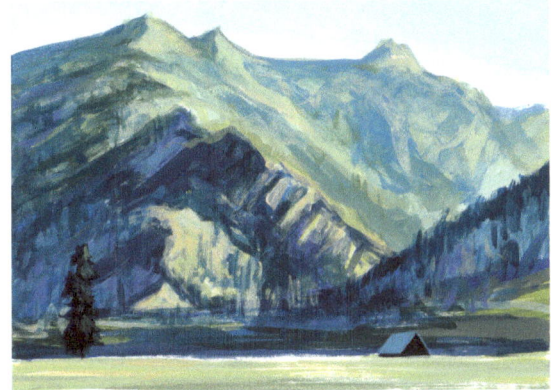

#207 Acrylic on Paper   07/26/2007

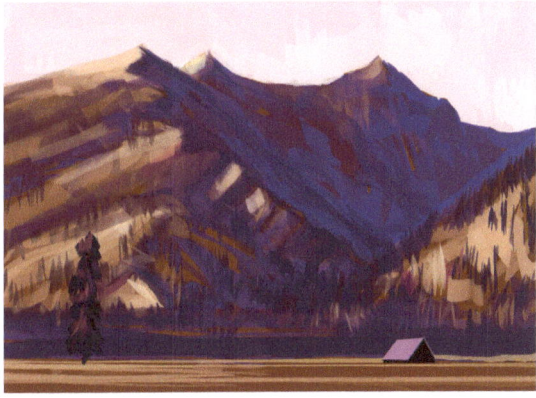

#208 Digital   07/27/2007

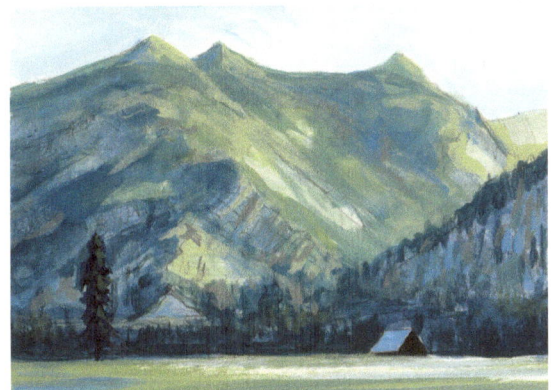

#209 Acrylic on Paper   07/28/2007

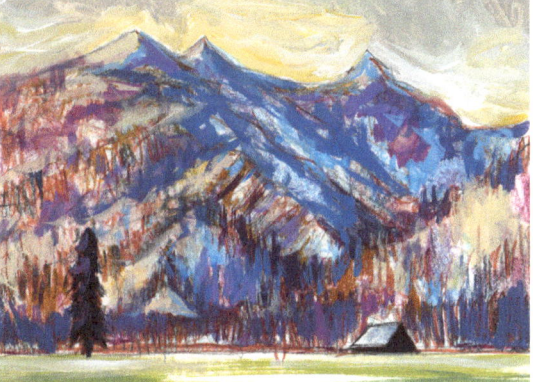

#210 Pastel/Acrylic on Paper   07/29/2007

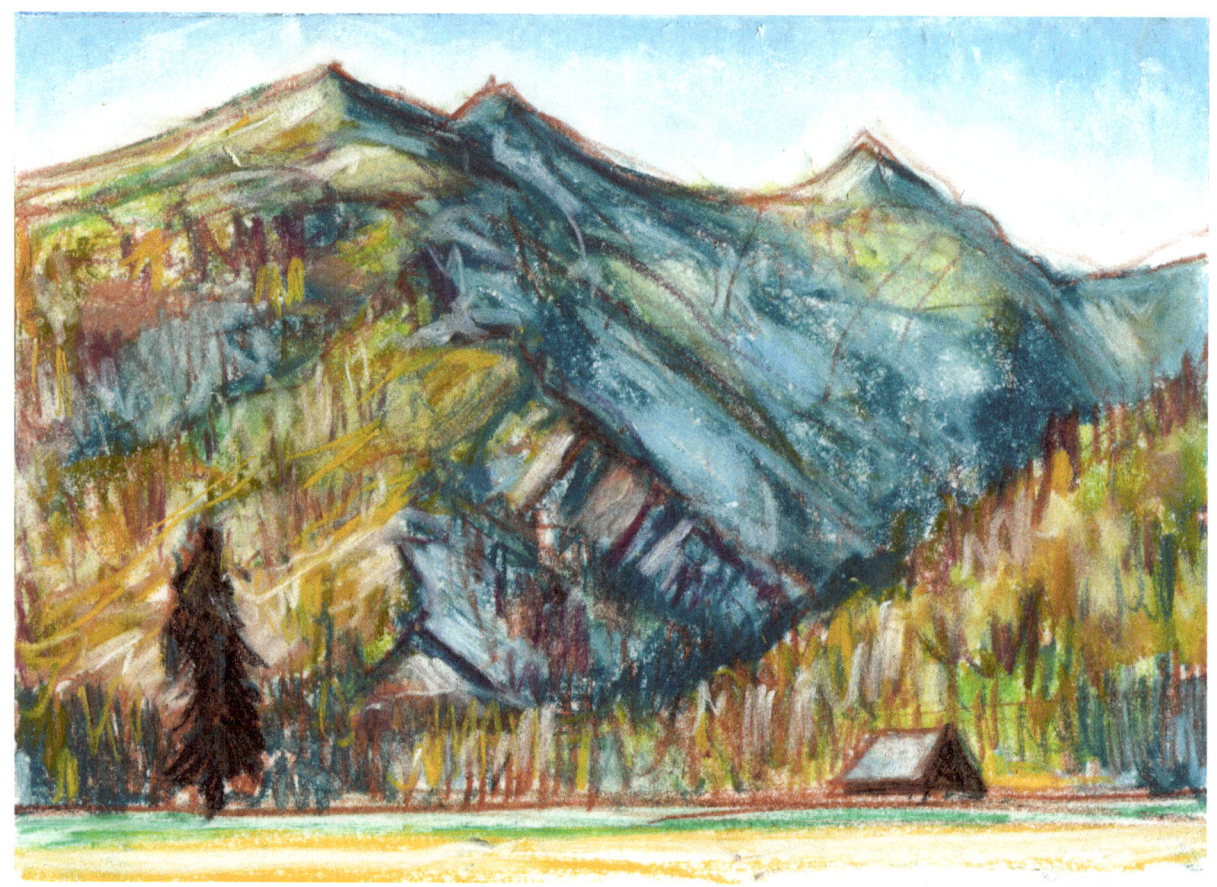

#211 Pastel on Paper

07/30/2007

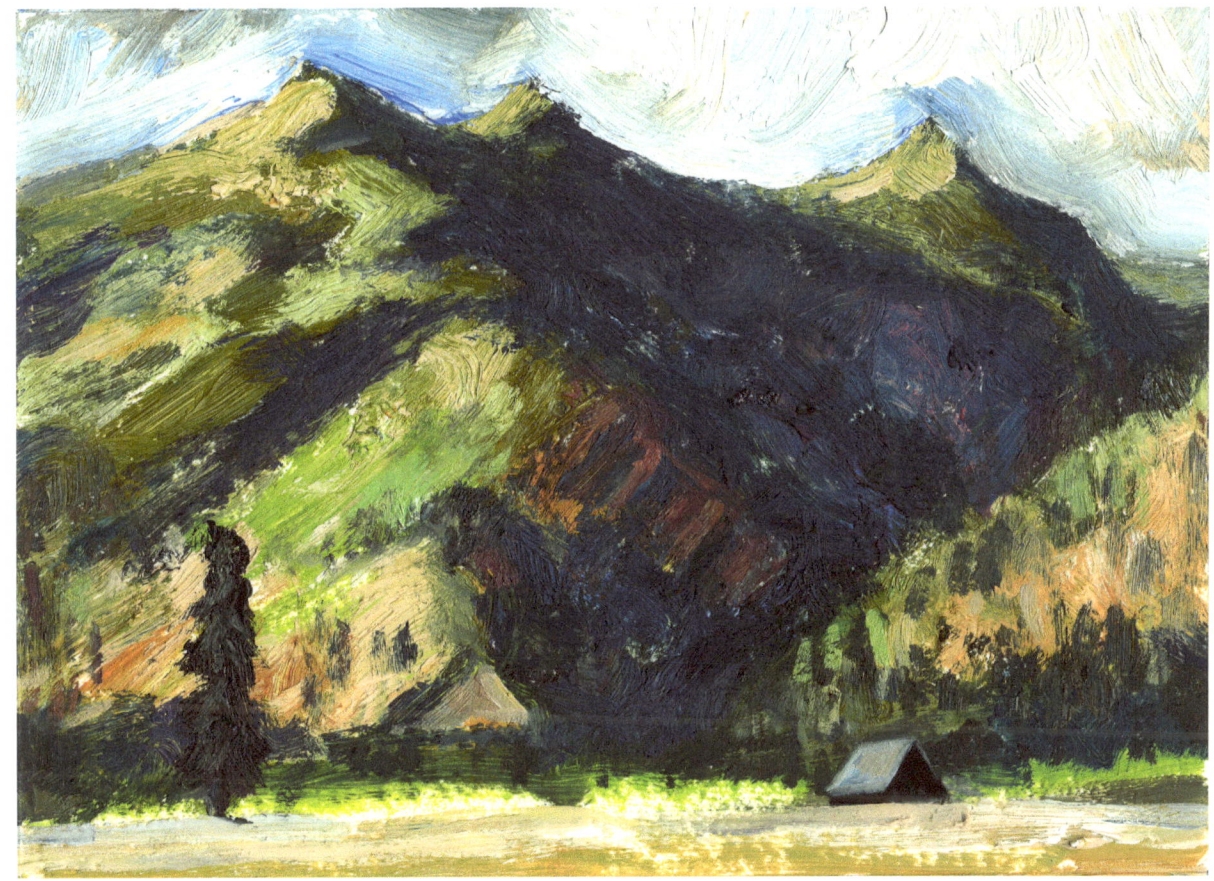

#212 Oil on Paper

07/31/2007

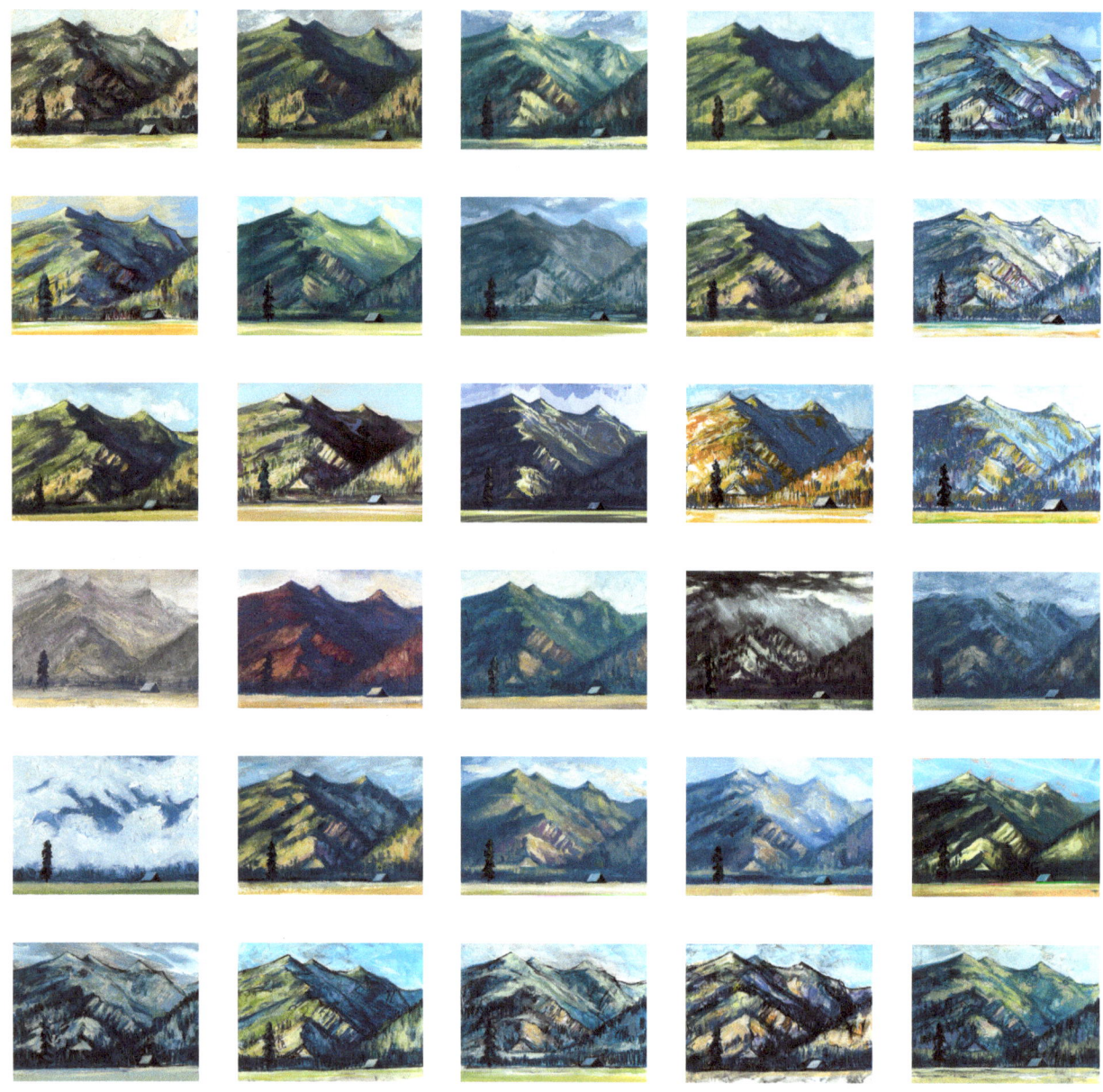

COUGAR PEAK-A-BOO
- The Art of Jared Shear -

AUGUST

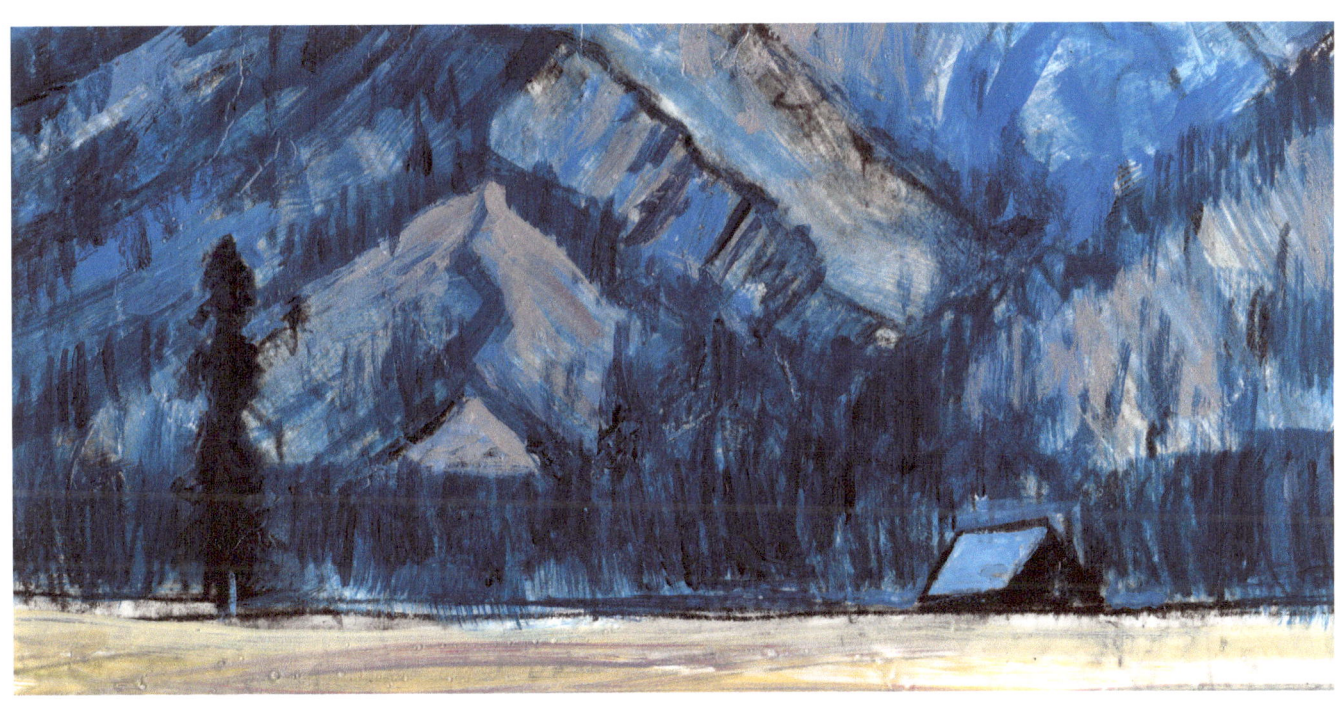

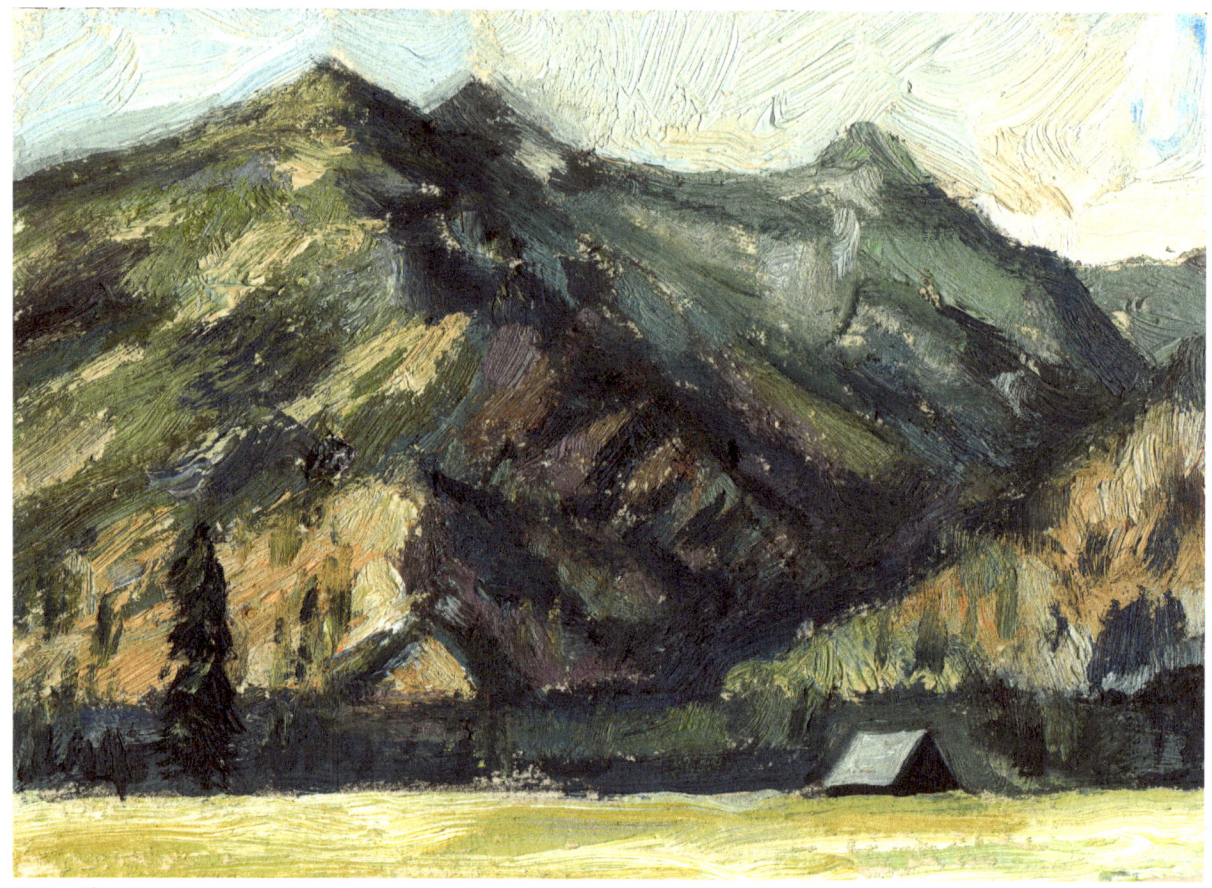

#213 Oil on Paper   08/01/2007

COUGAR PEAK-A-BOO
- The Art of Jared Shear -

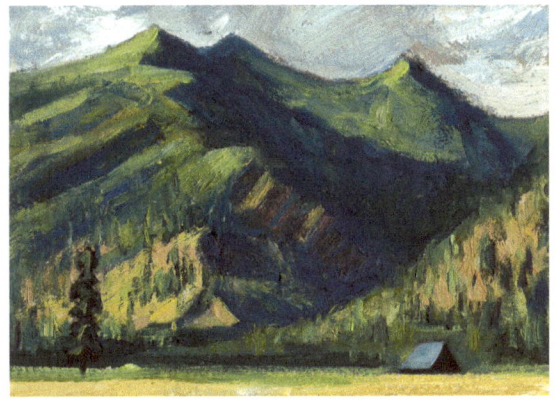

#214 Oil on Paper   08/02/2007

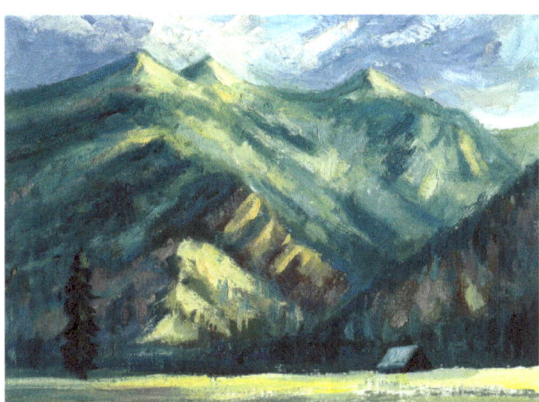

#215 Oil on Paper   08/03/2007

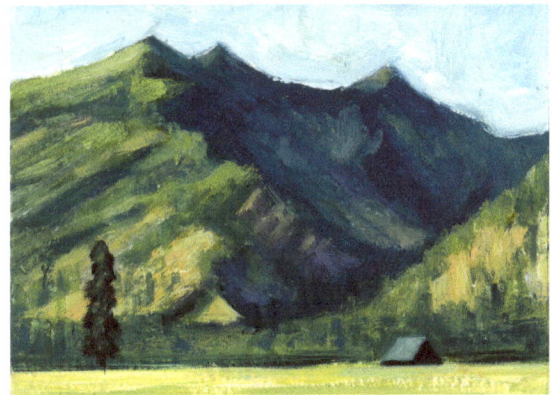

#216 Oil on Paper   08/04/2007

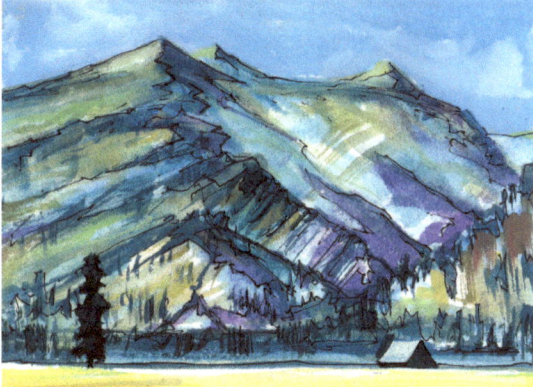

#217 Watercolor/Gouache on Paper   08/05/2007

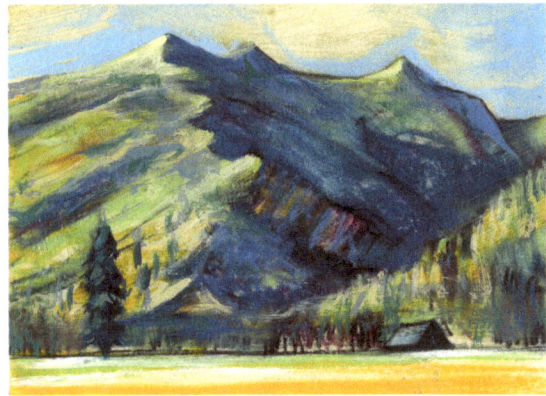

#218 Pastel/Acrylic on Paper   08/06/2007

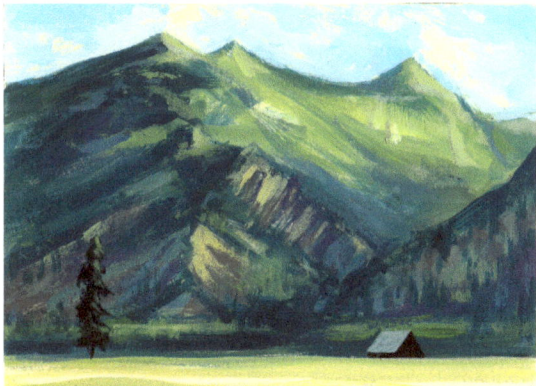

#219 Acrylic on Paper   08/07/2007

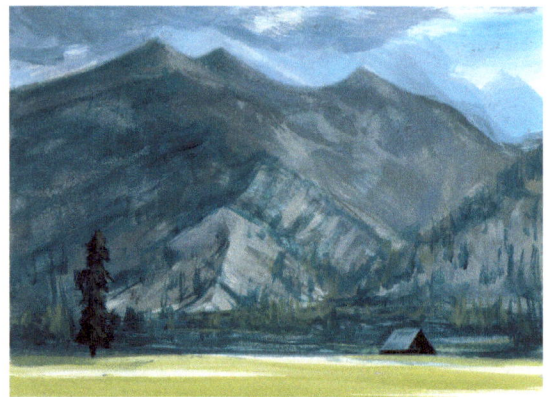

#220 Acrylic on Paper   08/08/2007

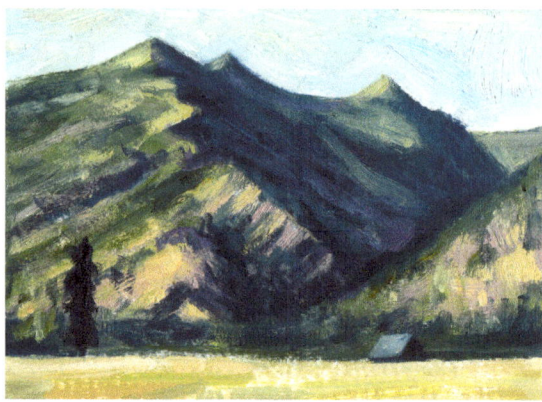

#221 Oil on Paper   08/09/2007

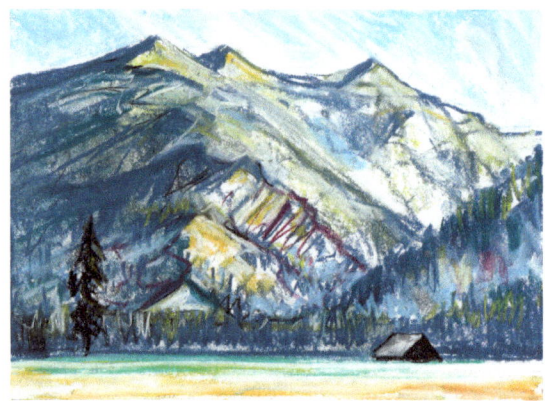

#222 Pastel on Paper   08/10/2007

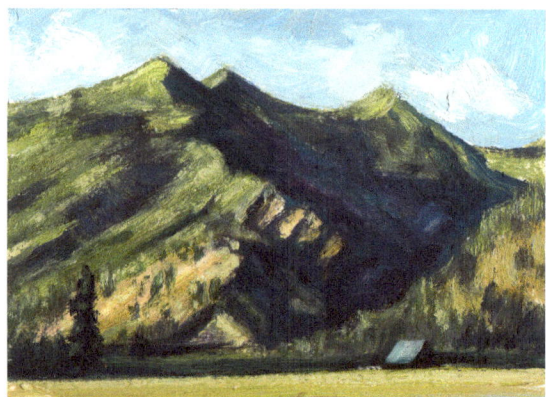

#223 Oil on Paper   08/11/2007

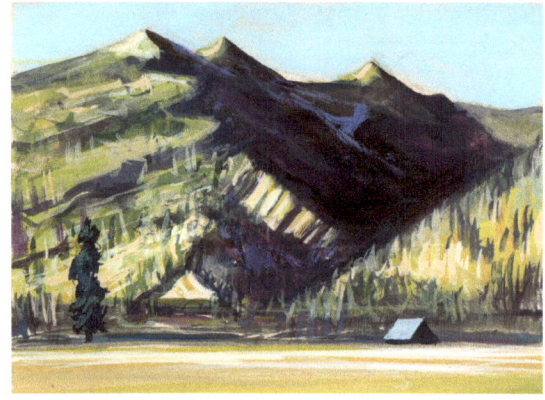

#224 Gouache on Paper   08/12/2007

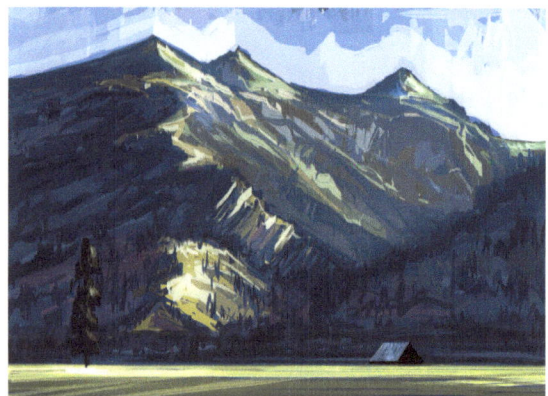

#225 Digital   08/13/2007

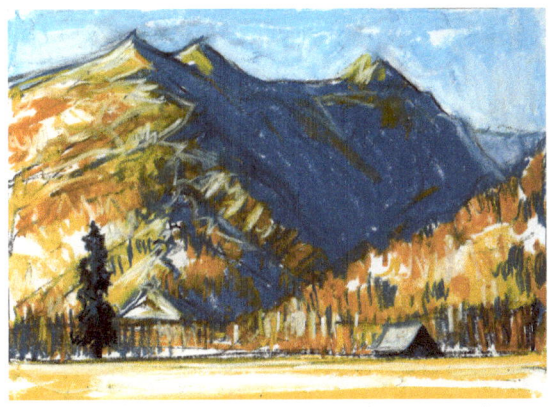

#226 Digital   08/14/2007

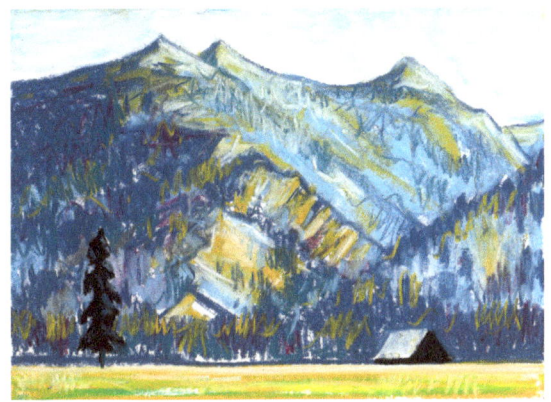

#227 Acrylic on Paper   08/15/2007

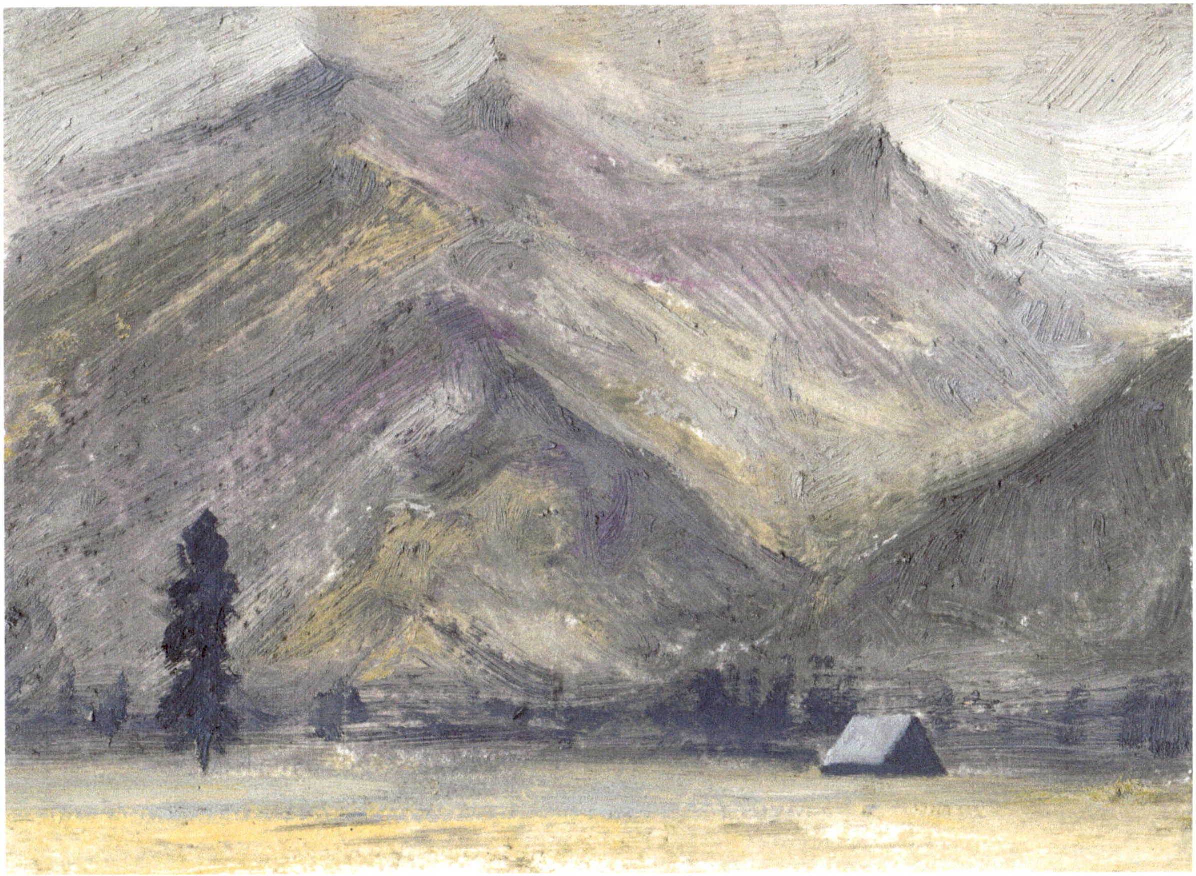

#228 Oil on Paper   08/16/2007

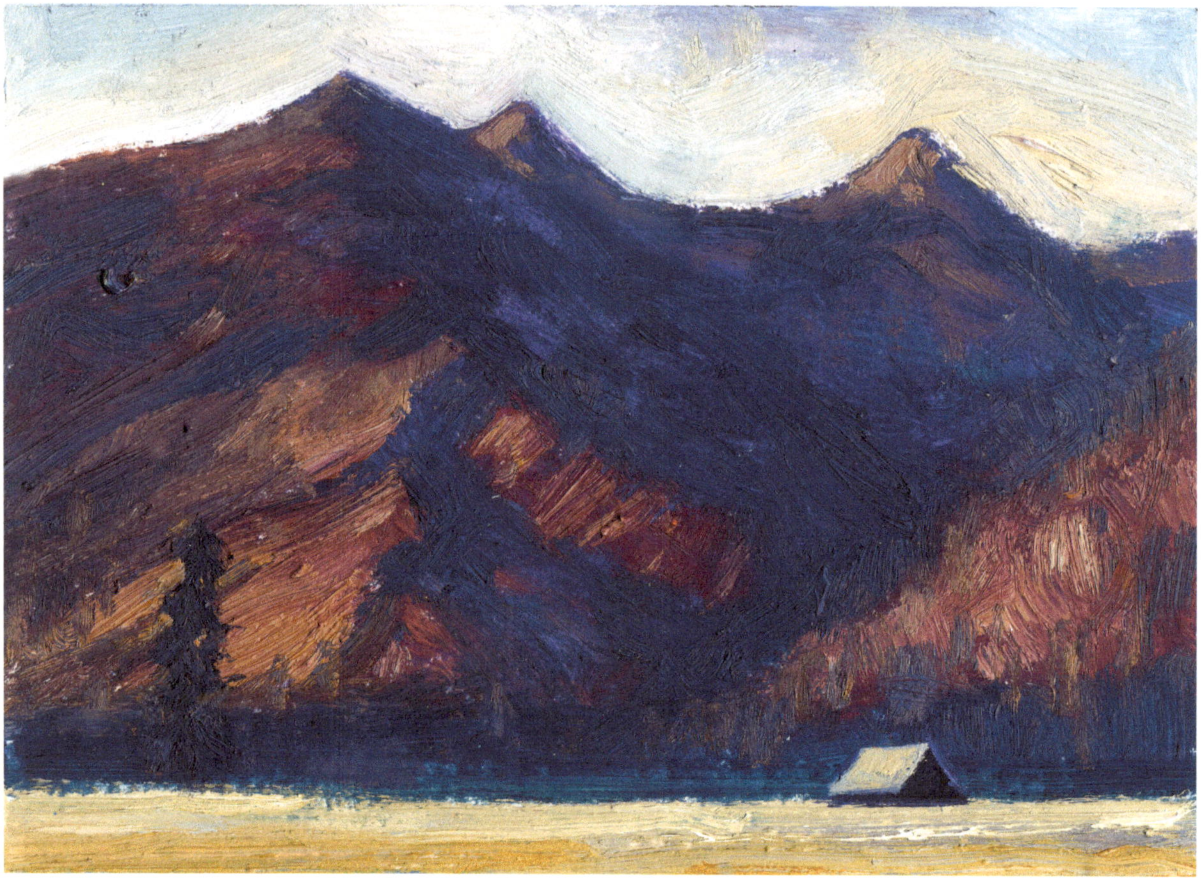

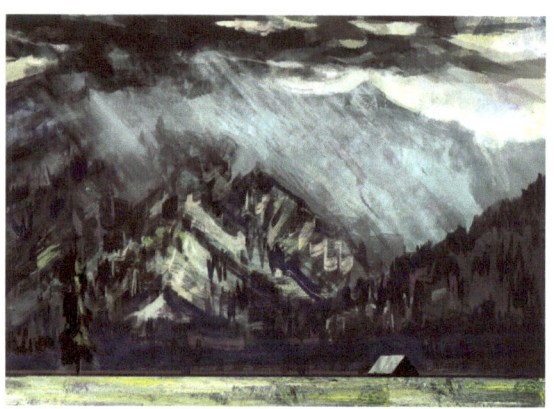

#229 Oil on Paper   08/17/2007

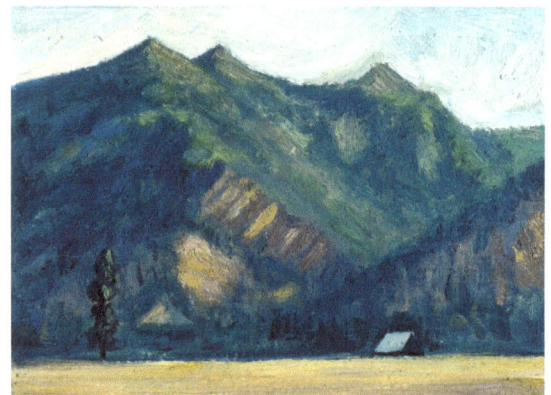

#230 Oil on Paper   08/18/2007

#231 Digital   08/19/2007

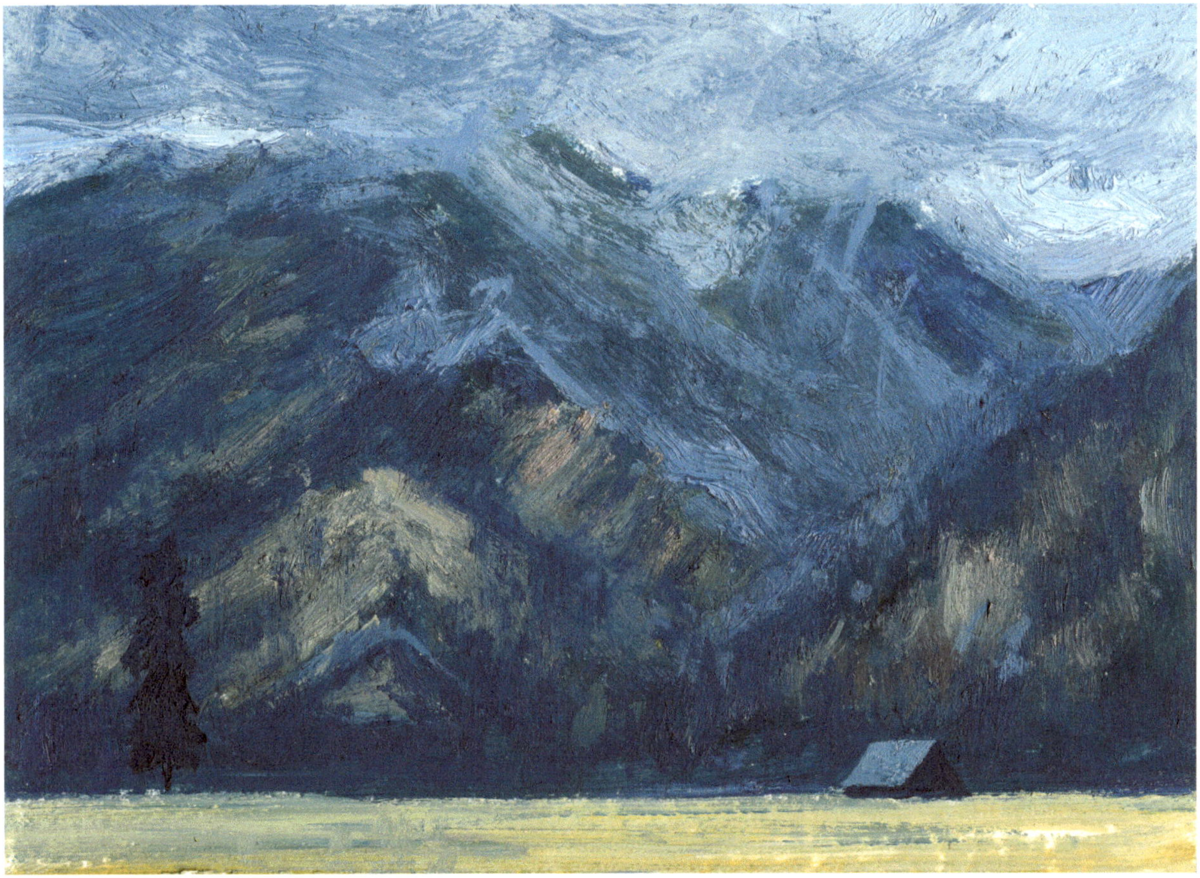

#232 Oil on Paper   08/20/2007

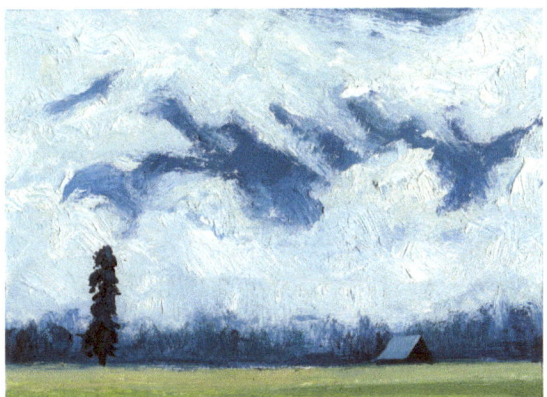

#233 Oil on Paper   08/21/2007

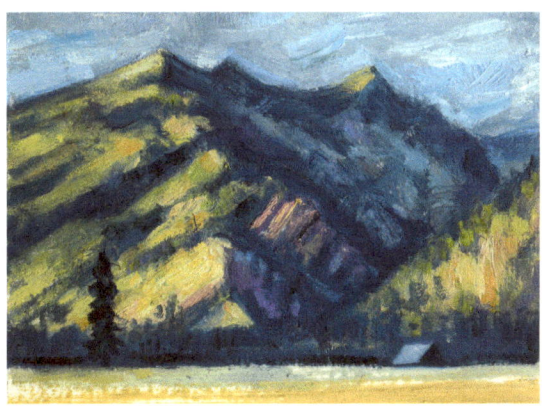

#234 Oil on Paper   08/22/2007

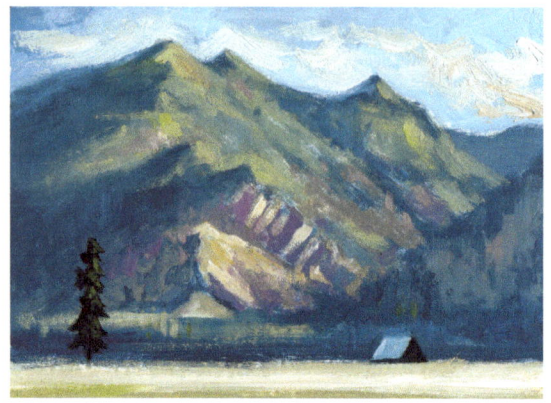

#235 Oil on Paper   08/23/2007

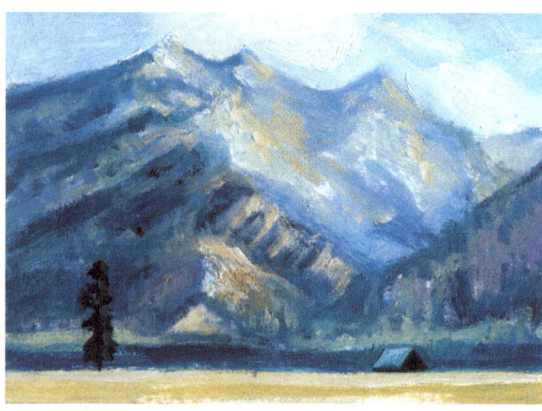

#236 Oil on Paper   08/24/2007

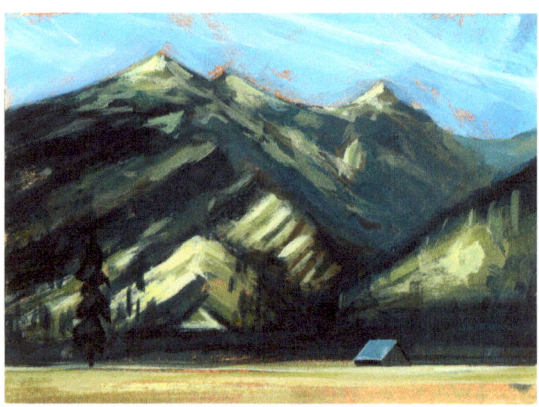

#237 Acrylic on Paper   08/25/2007

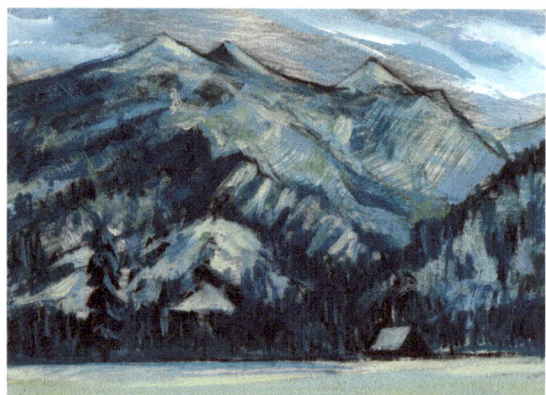

#238 Acrylic on Paper   08/26/2007

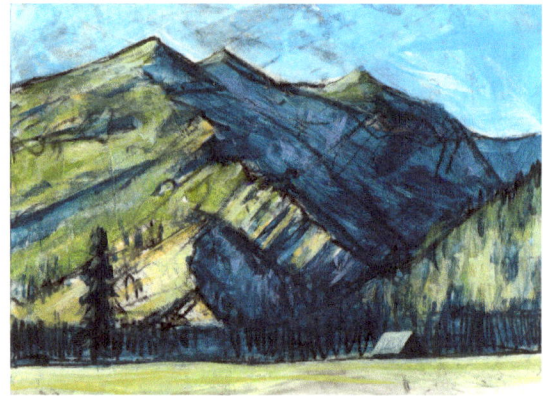

#239 Acrylic on Paper   08/27/2007

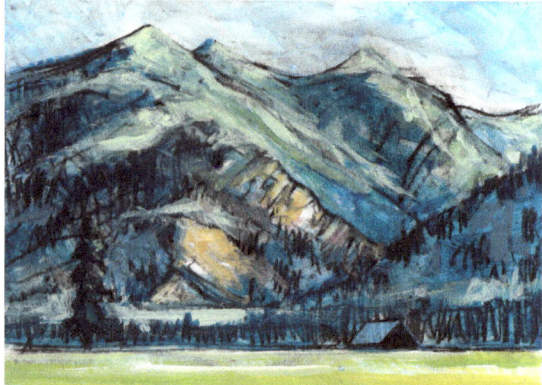

#240 Acrylic on Paper   08/28/2007

COUGAR PEAK-A-BOO
- The Art of Jared Shear -

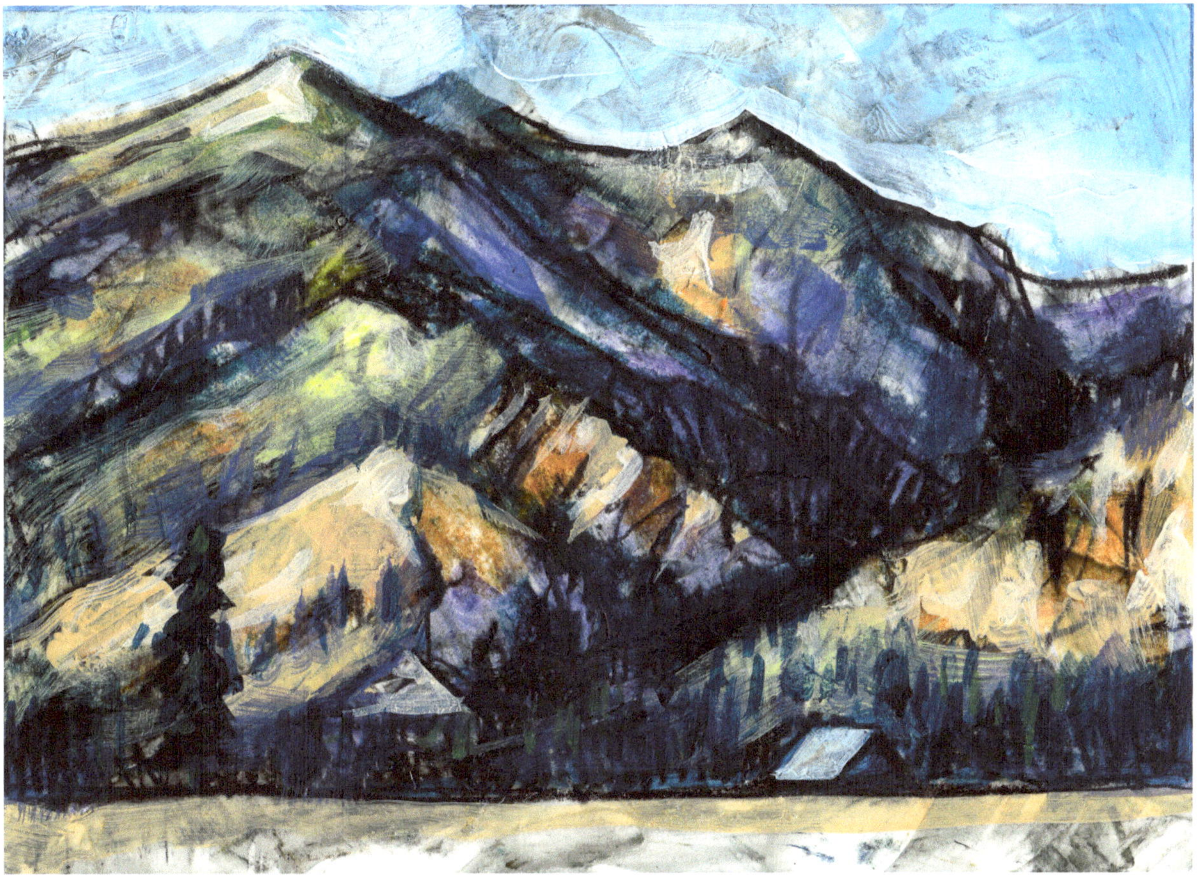

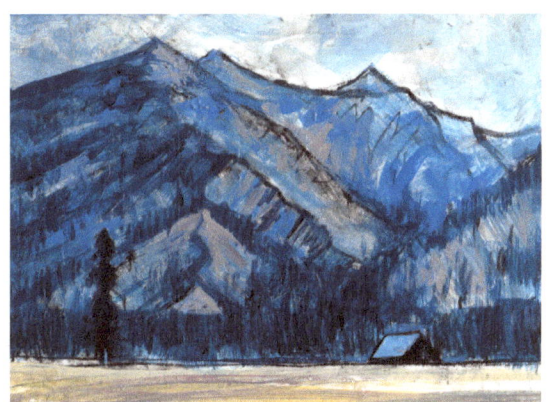

#241 Acrylic on Paper   08/29/2007

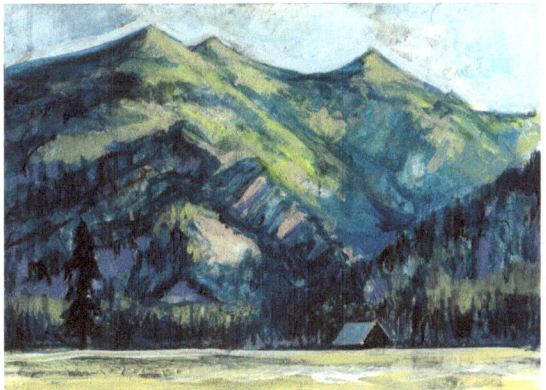

#242 Acrylic on Paper   08/30/2007

#243 Acrylic on Paper   08/31/2007

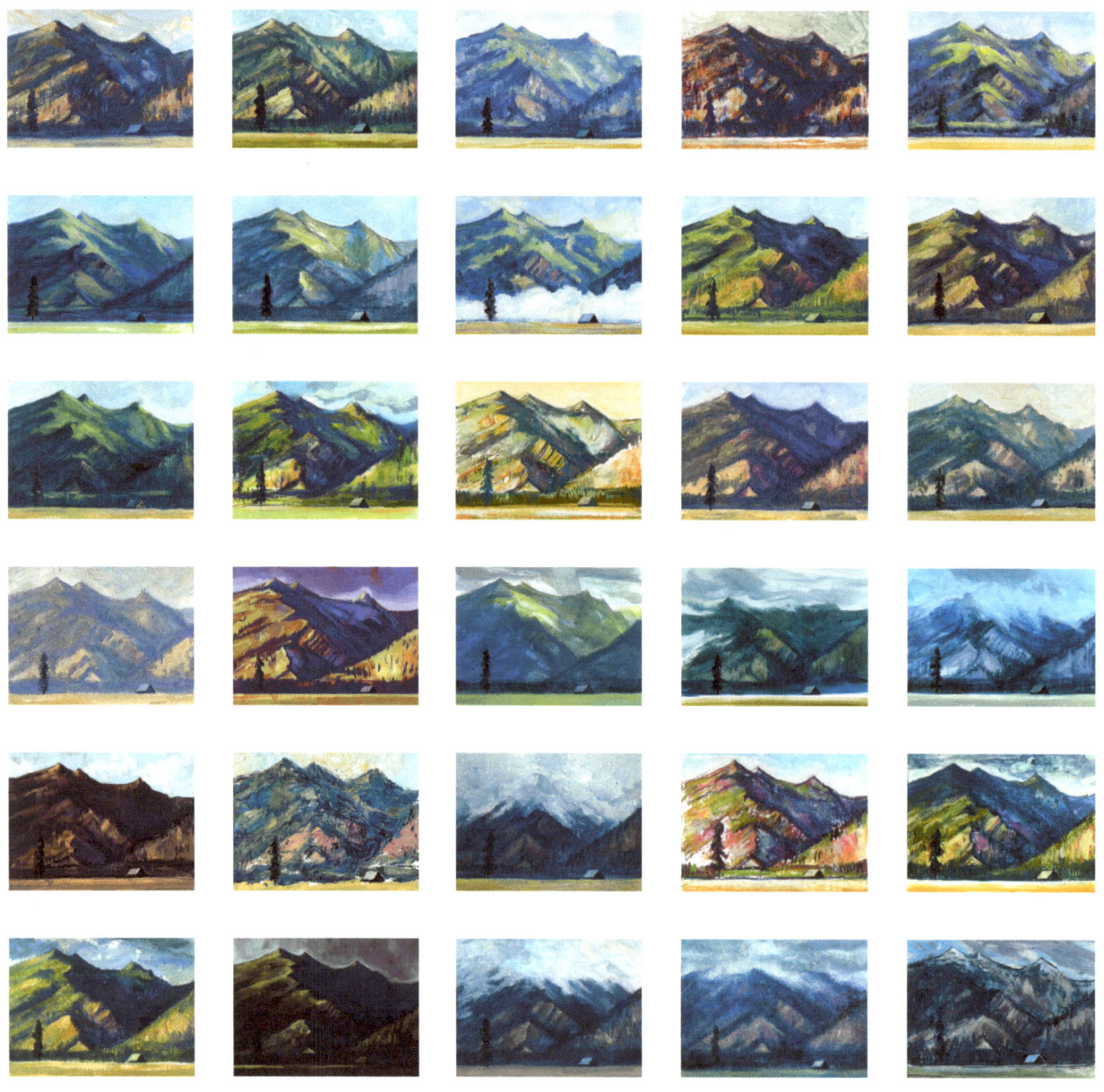

COUGAR PEAK-A-BOO
- The Art of Jared Shear -

SEPTEMBER

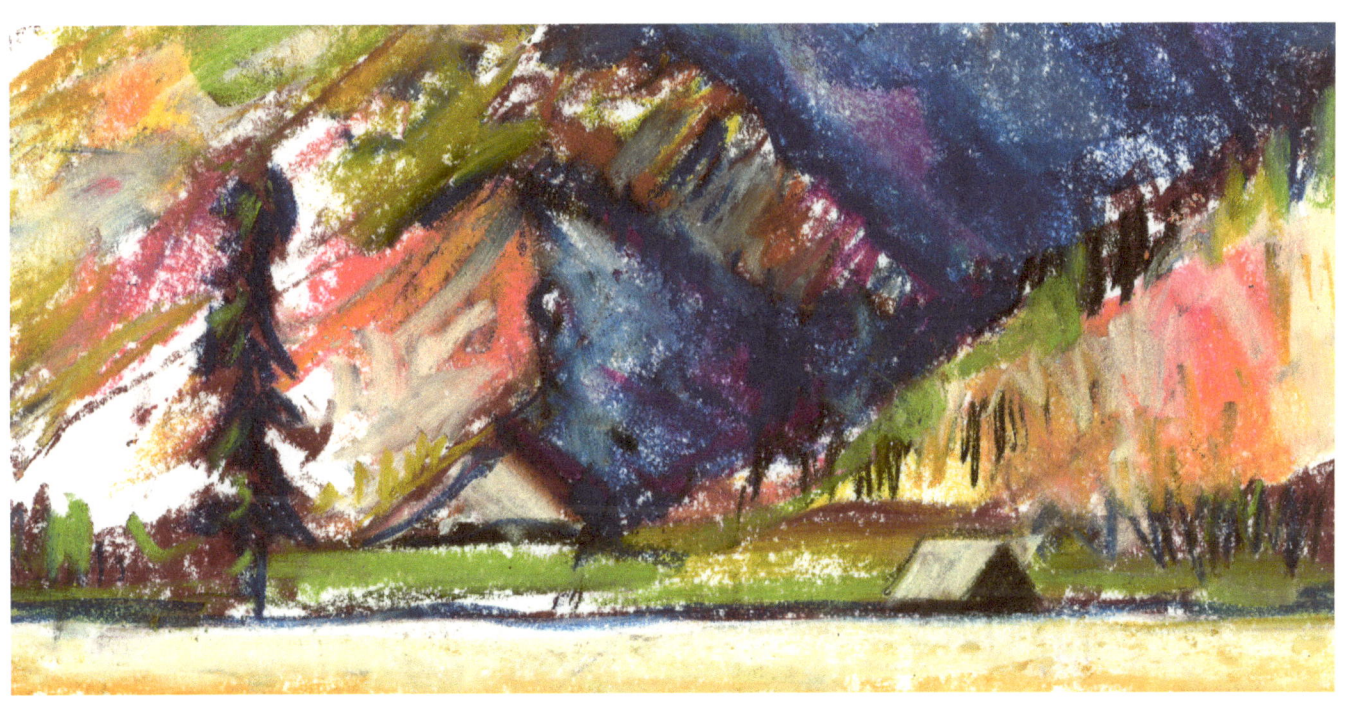

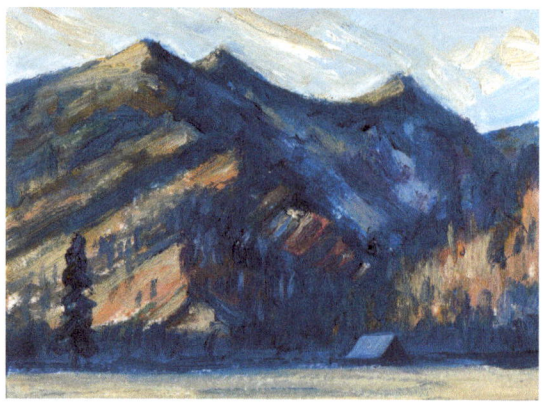

#244 Oil on Paper   09/01/2007

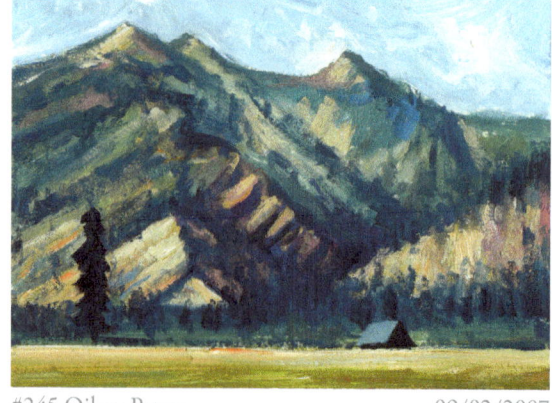

#245 Oil on Paper   09/02/2007

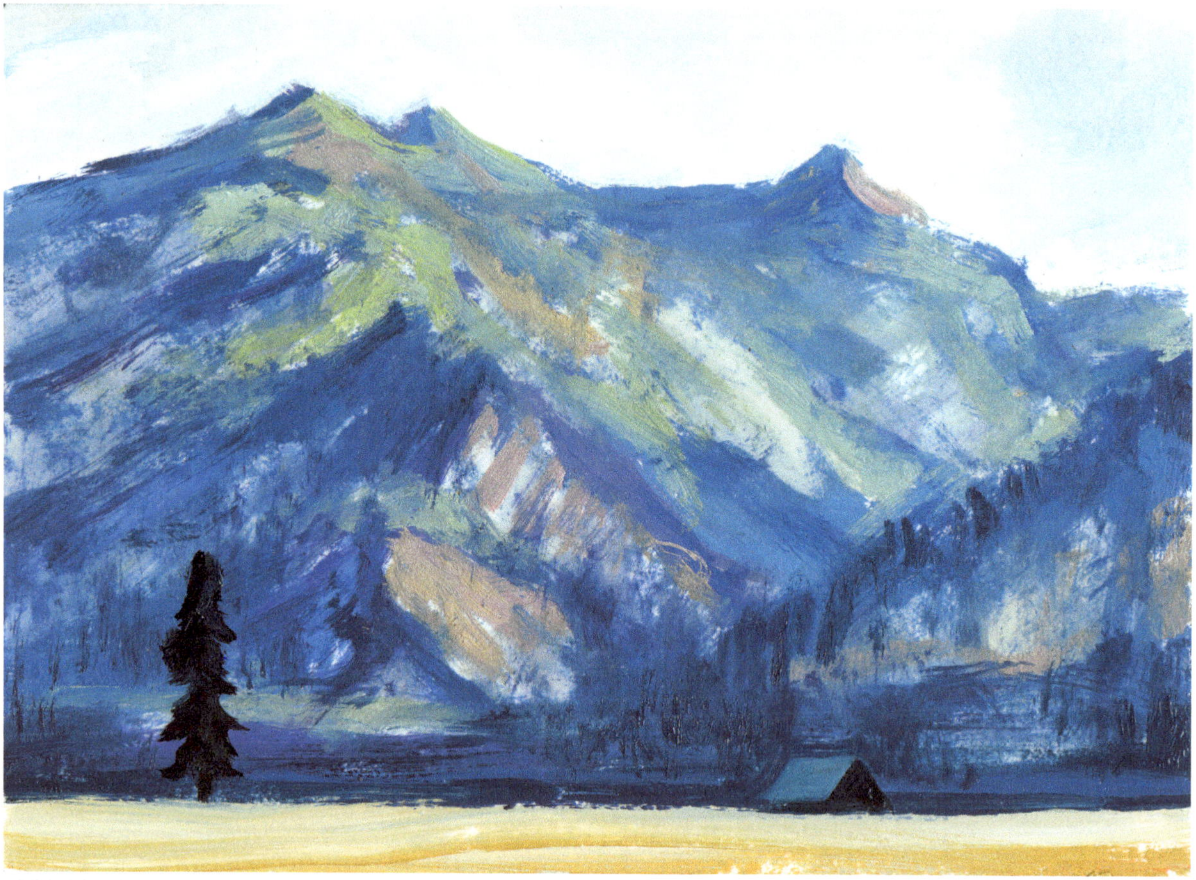

#246 Oil on Paper   09/03/2007

COUGAR PEAK-A-BOO
- The Art of Jared Shear -

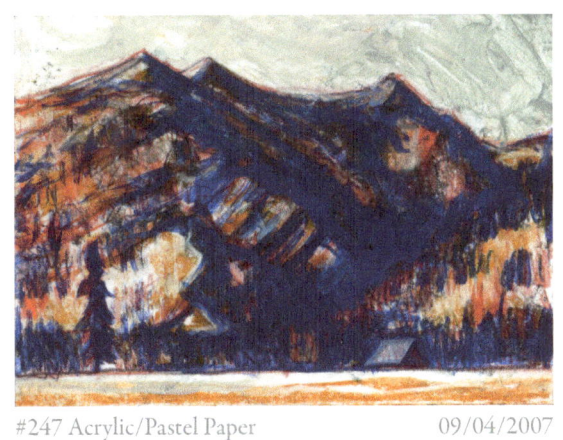

#247 Acrylic/Pastel Paper   09/04/2007

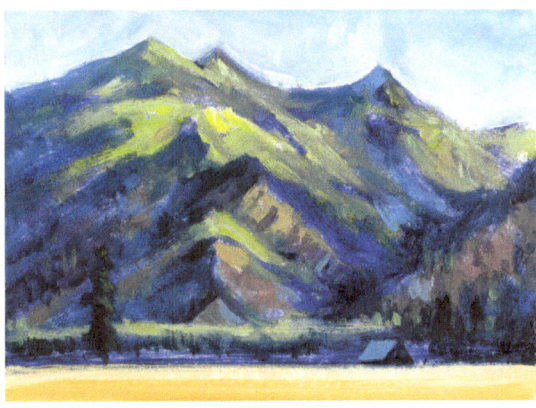
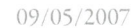

#248 Oil on Paper   09/05/2007

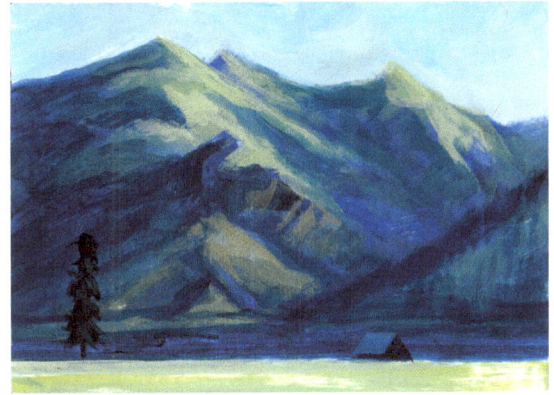

#249 Acrylic on Paper   09/06/2007

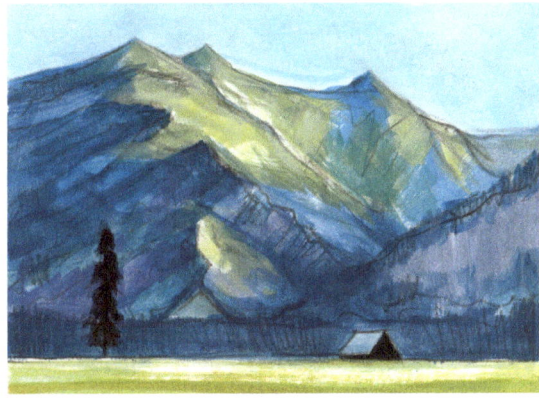

#250 Acrylic on Paper   09/07/2007

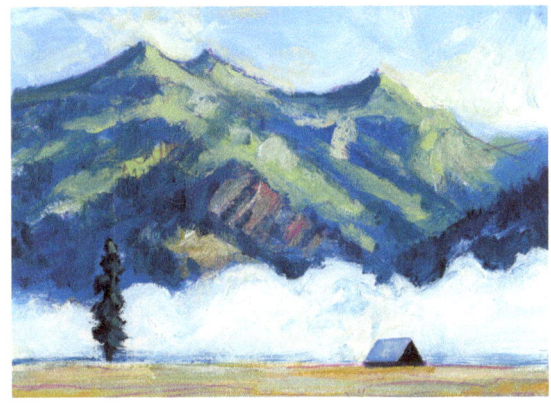

#251 Oil on Paper   09/08/2007

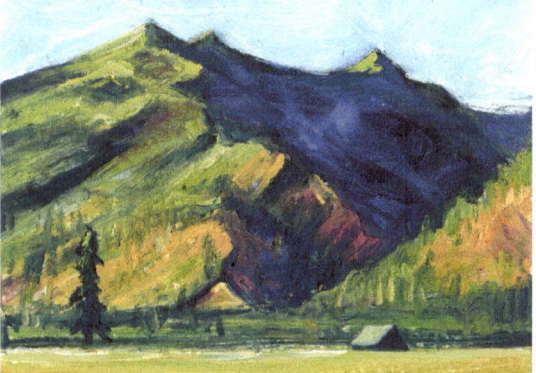

#252 Oil on Paper   09/09/2007

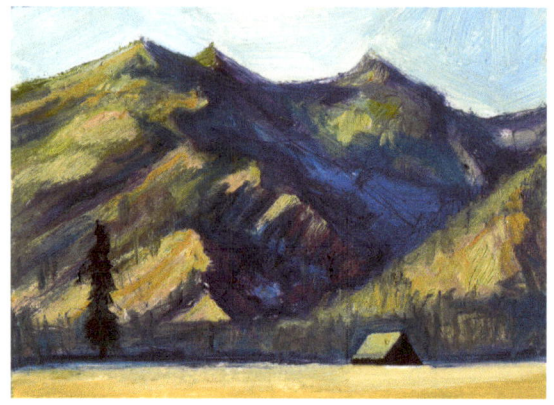

#253 Oil on Paper   09/10/2007

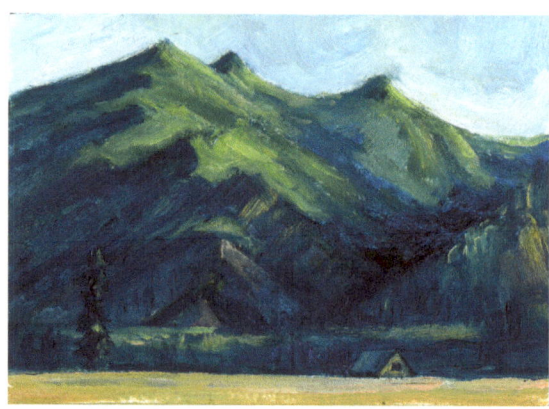

#254 Oil on Paper   09/11/2007

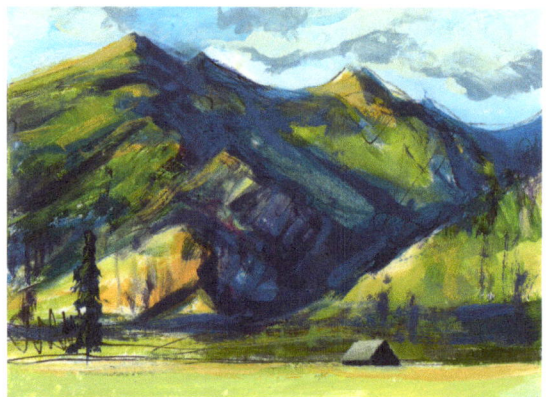

#255 Acrylic on Paper   09/12/2007

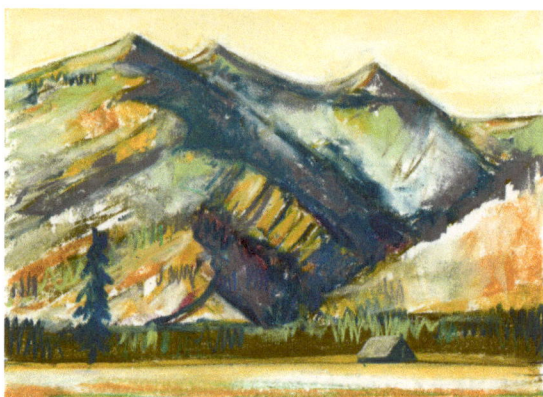

#256 Pastel on Paper   09/13/2007

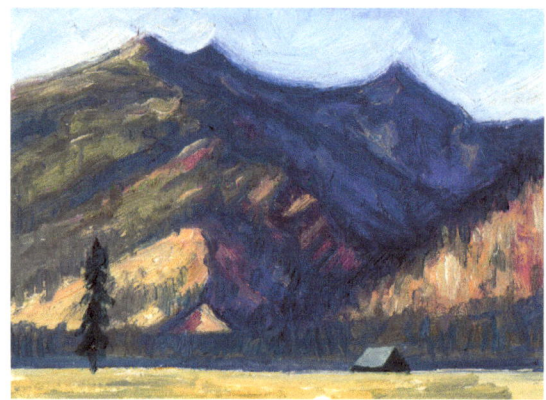

#257 Oil on Paper   09/14/2007

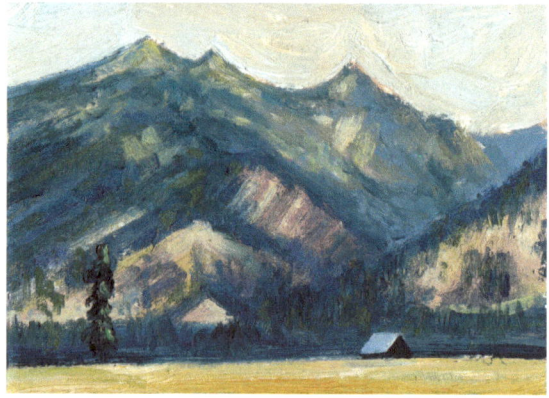

#258 Oil on Paper   09/15/2007

COUGAR PEAK-A-BOO
- The Art of Jared Shear -

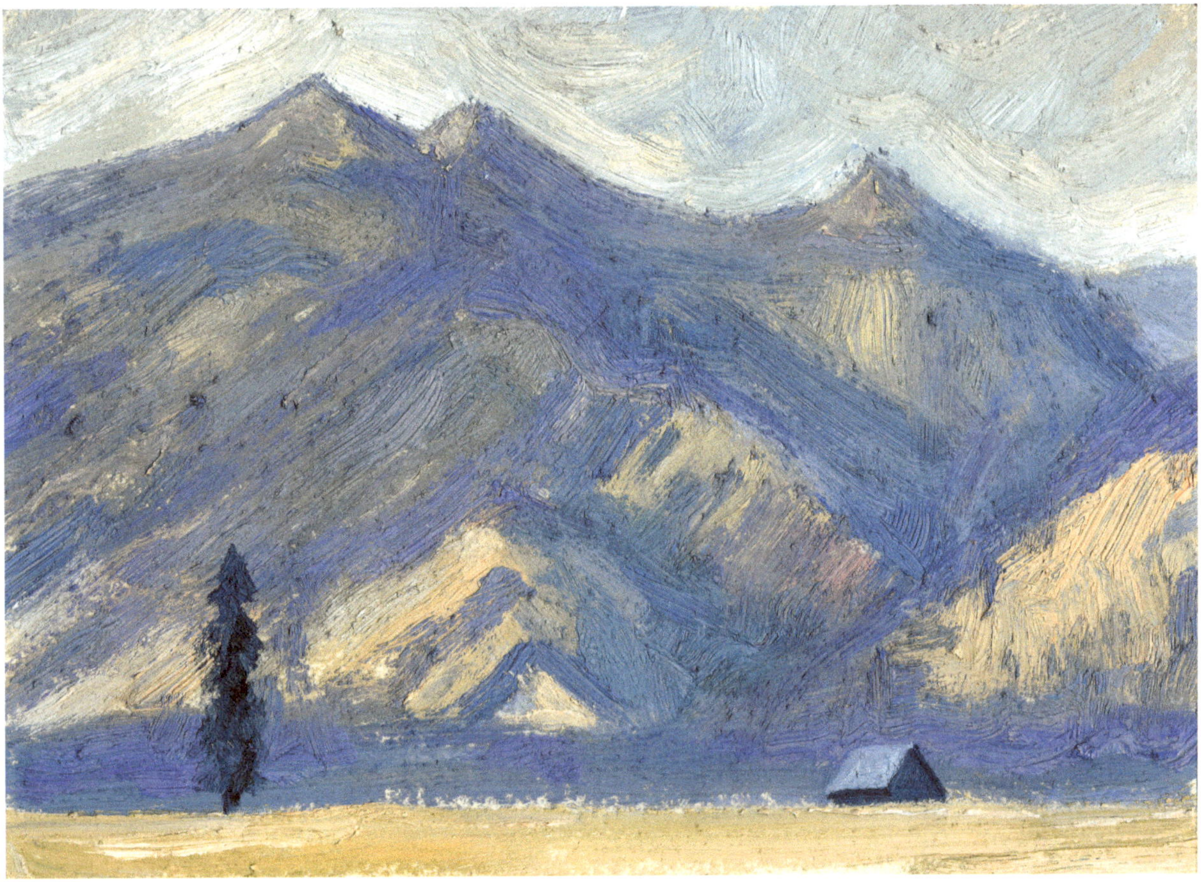

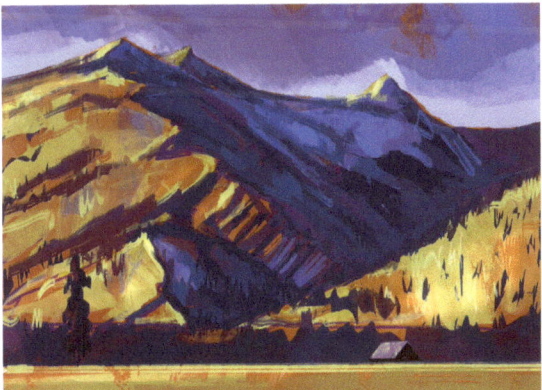

#259 Oil on Paper   09/16/2007

#260 Digital   09/17/2007

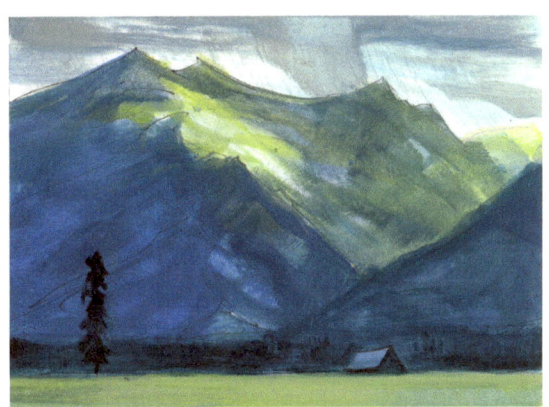

#261 Acrylic on Paper   09/18/2007

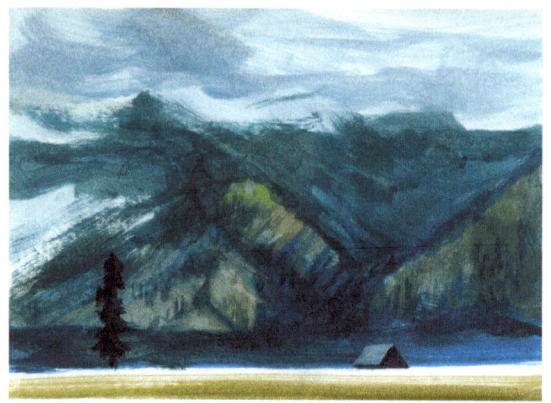

#262 Acrylic on Paper   09/19/2007

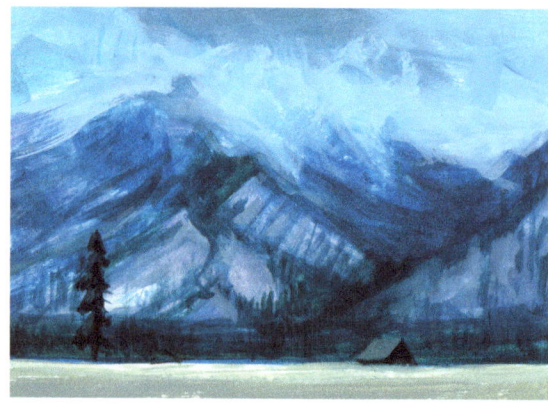

#263 Acrylic on Paper   09/20/2007

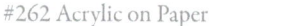

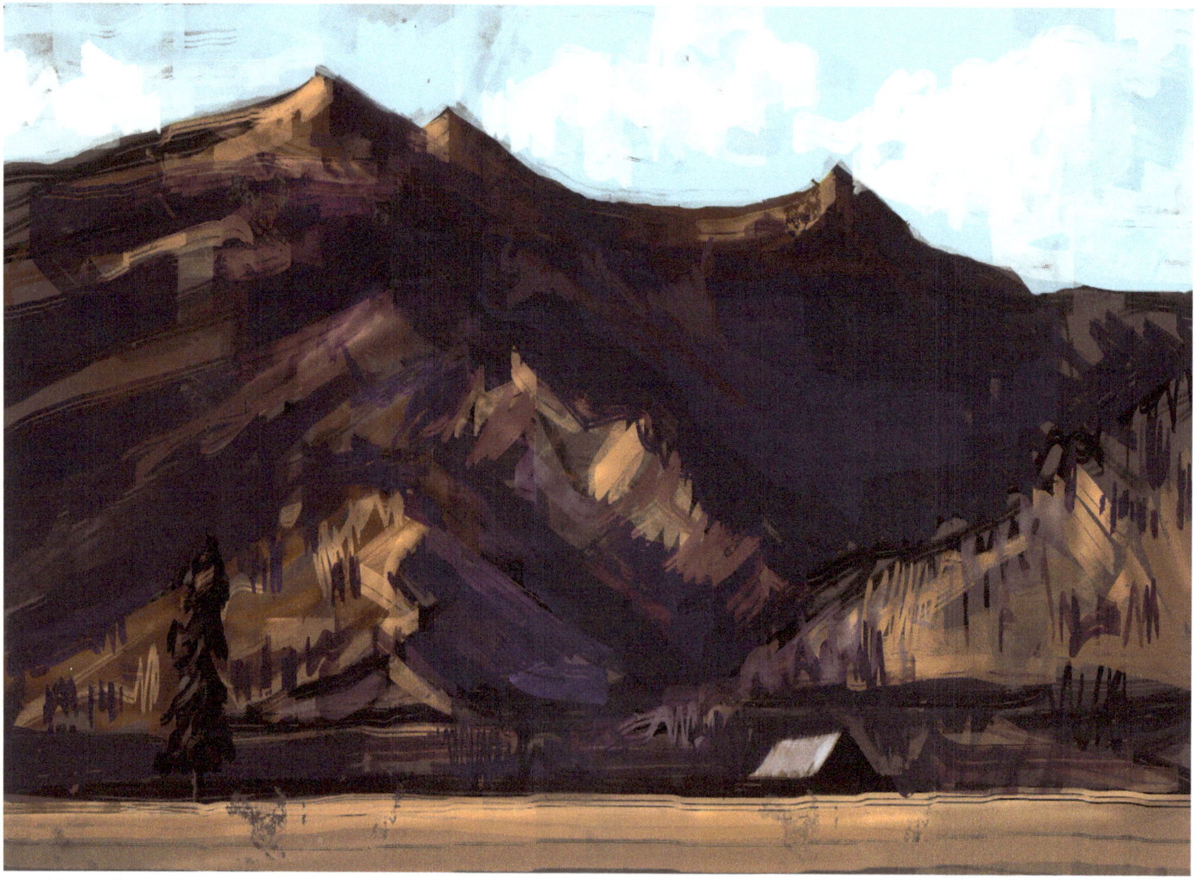

#264 Digital   09/21/2007

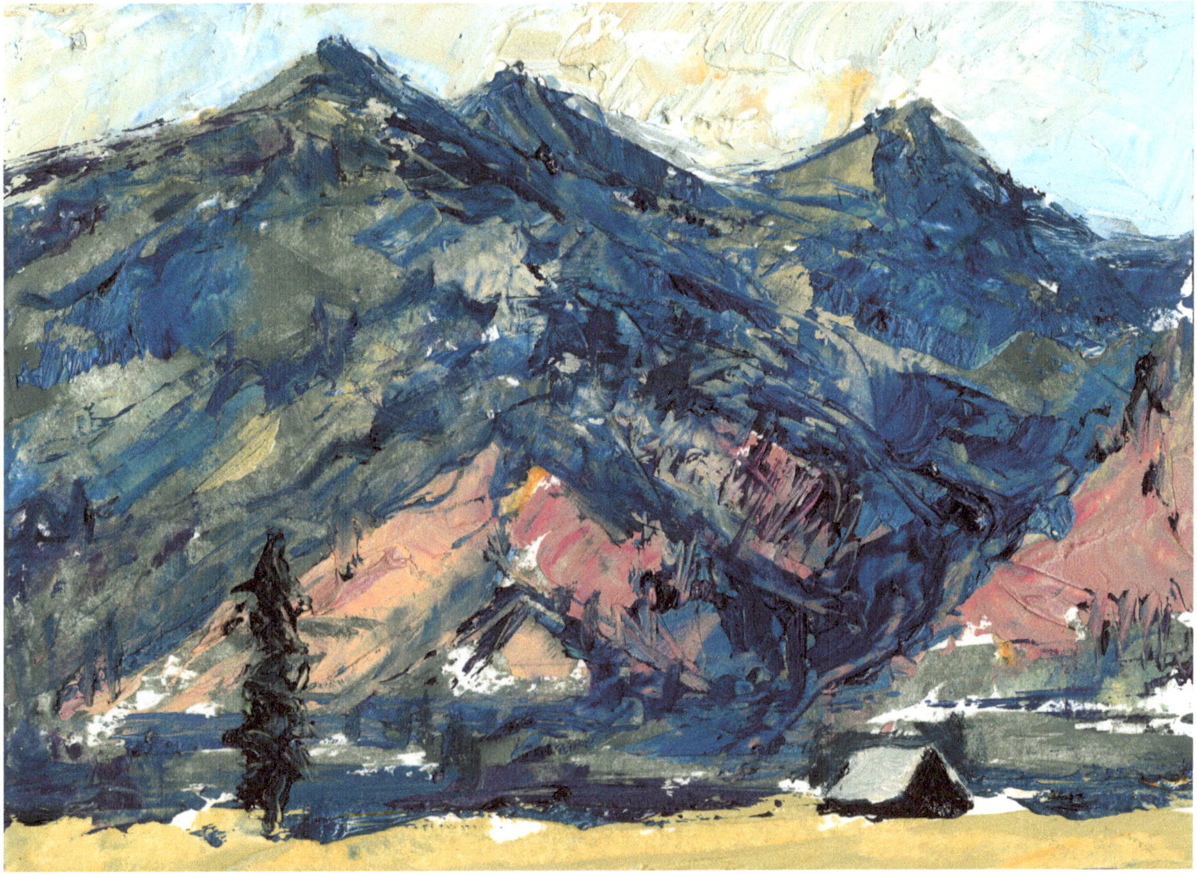

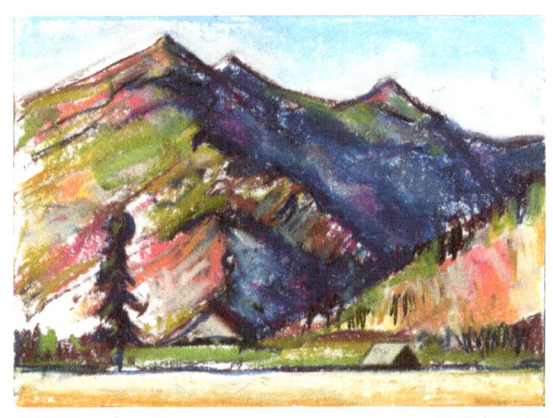

#265 Oil on Paper

09/22/2007

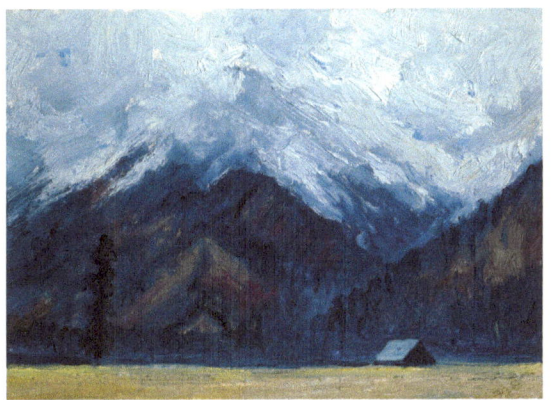

#266 Oil on Paper   09/23/2007

#267 Pastel on Paper   09/24/2007

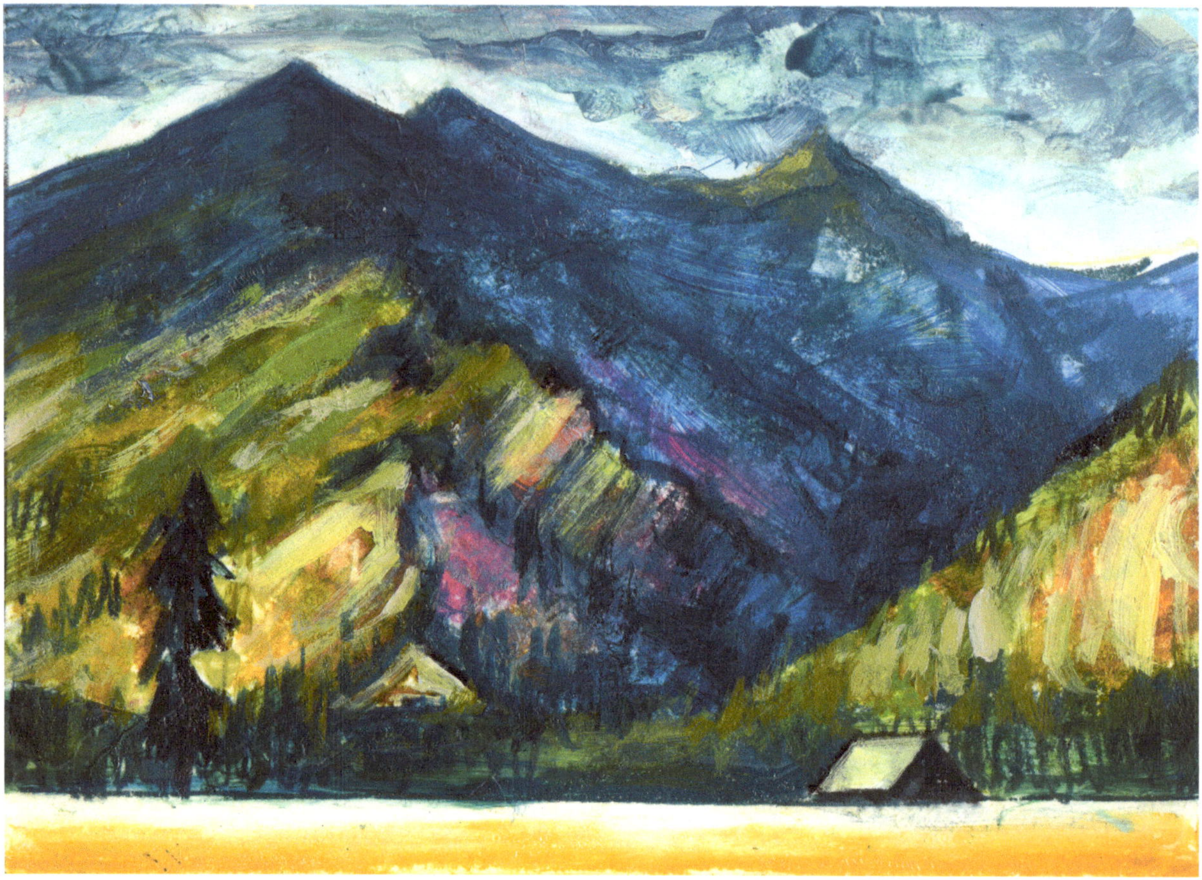

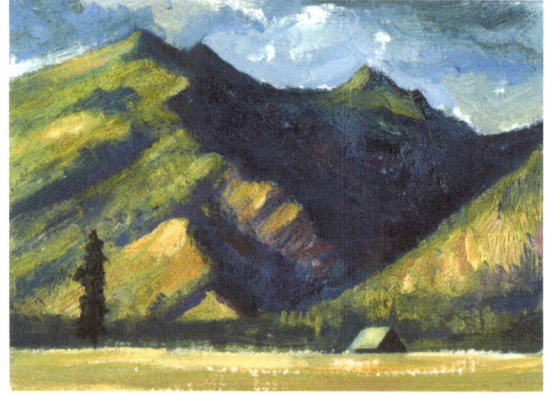

#268 Pastel/Acrylic on Paper   09/25/2007

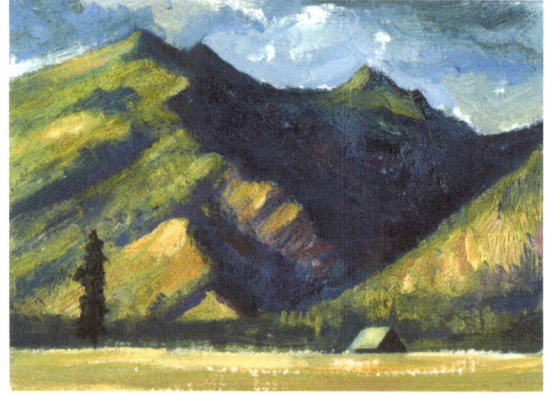

#269 Oil on Paper   09/26/2007

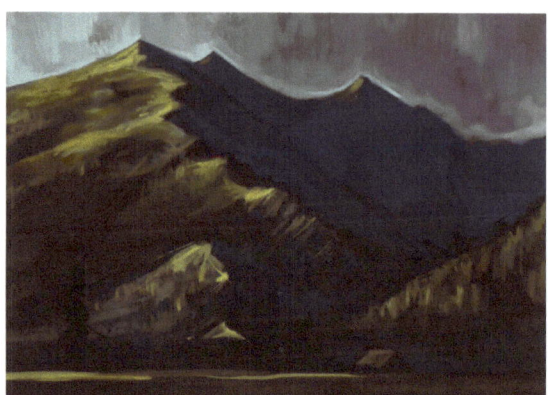

#270 Digital   09/27/2007

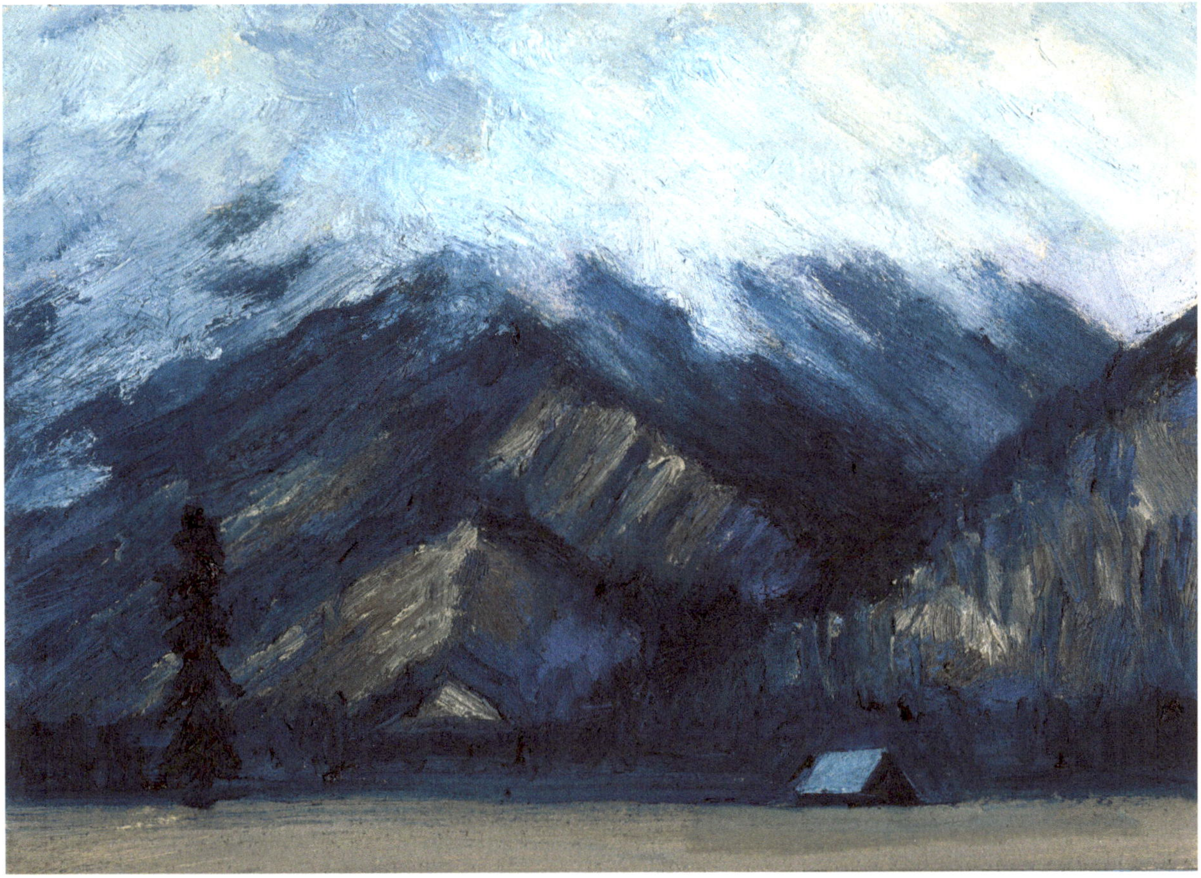

#271 Oil on Paper   09/28/2007

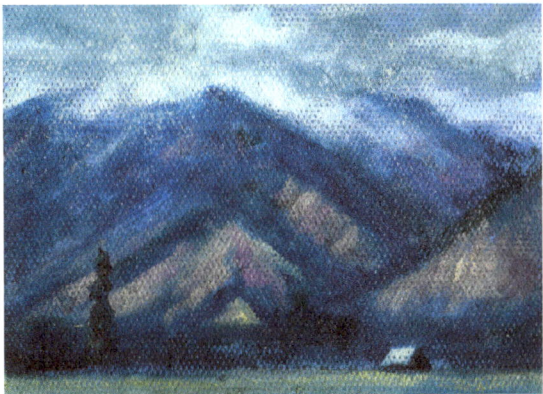

#272 Oil on Tyvek   09/29/2007

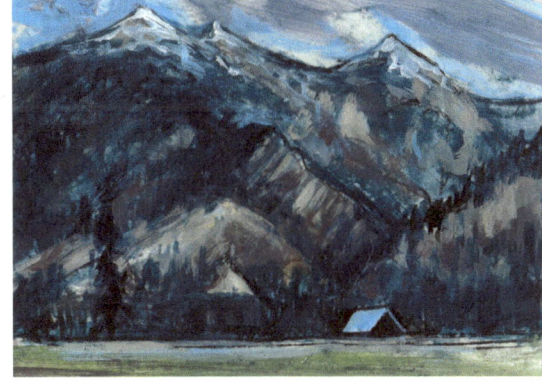

#273 Acrylic on Paper   09/30/2007

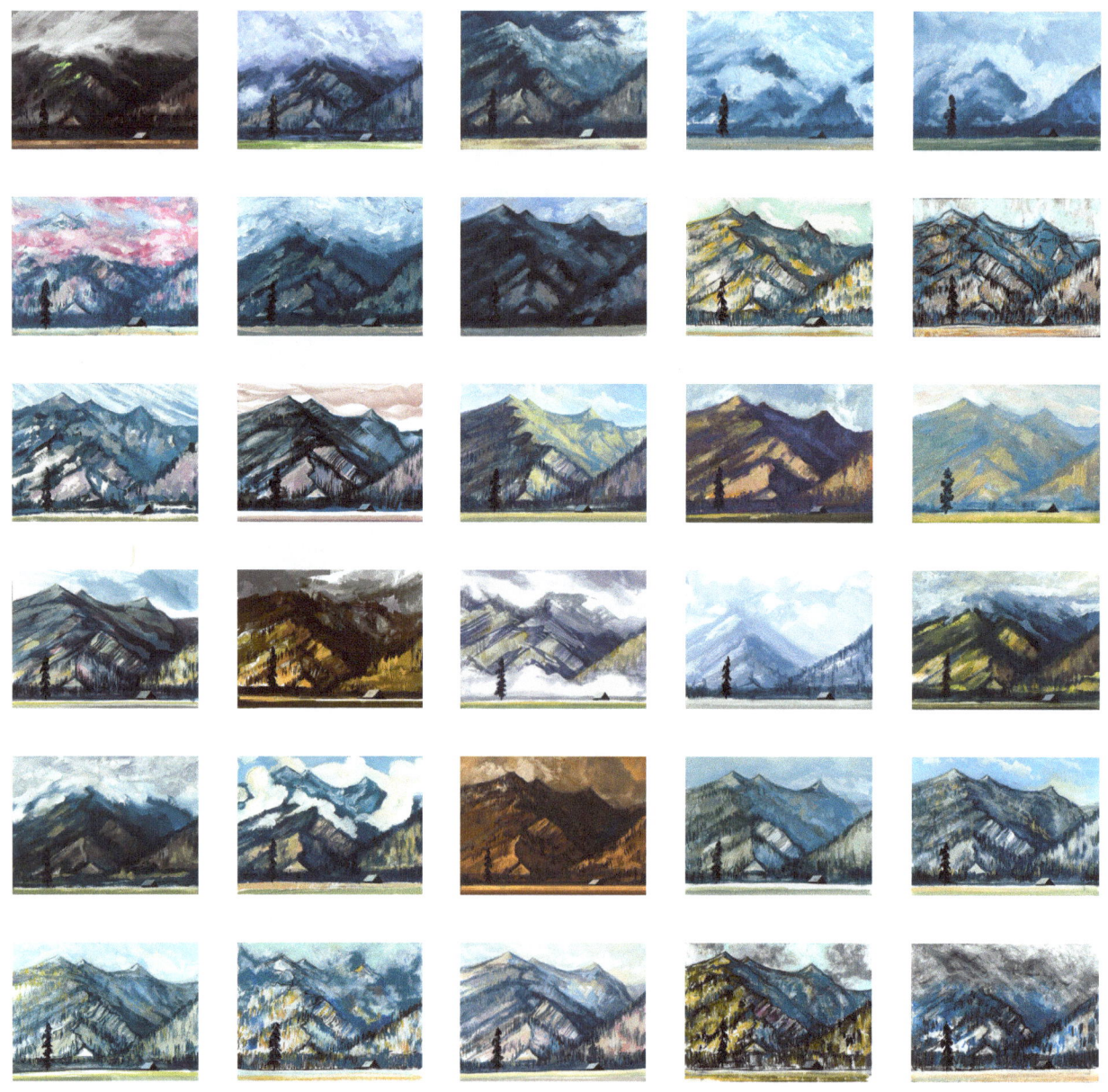

COUGAR PEAK-A-BOO
- The Art of Jared Shear -

OCTOBER

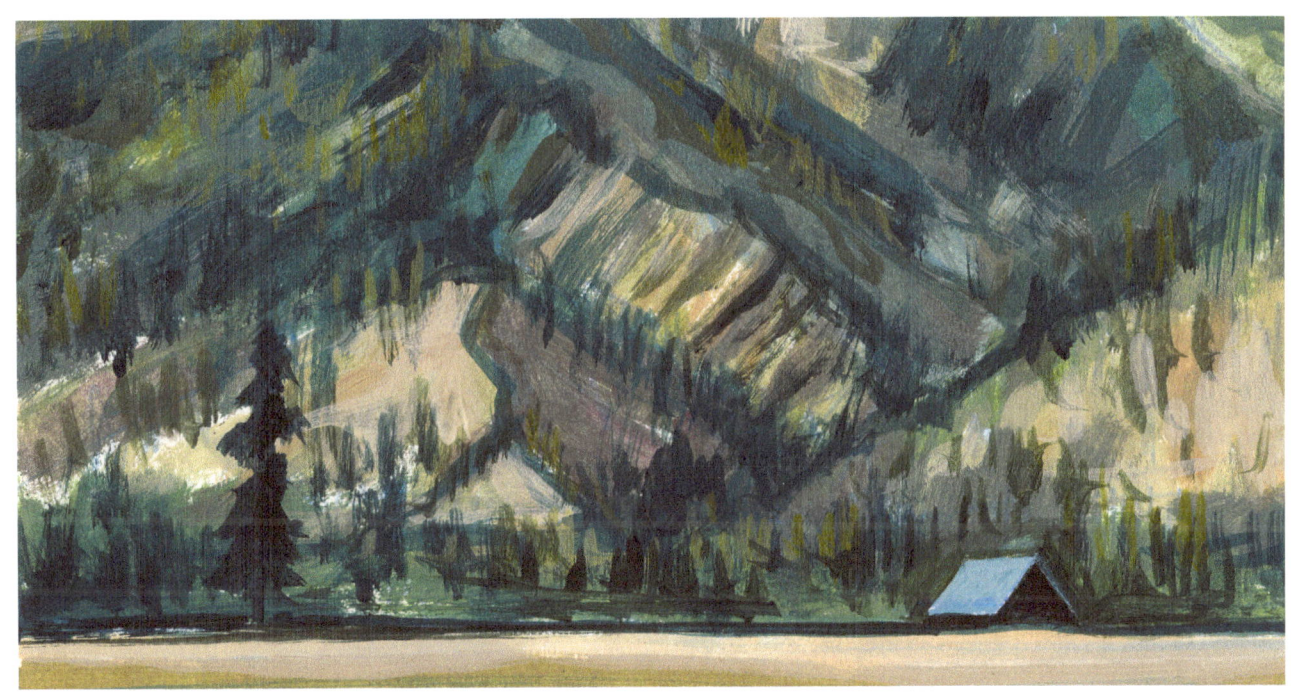

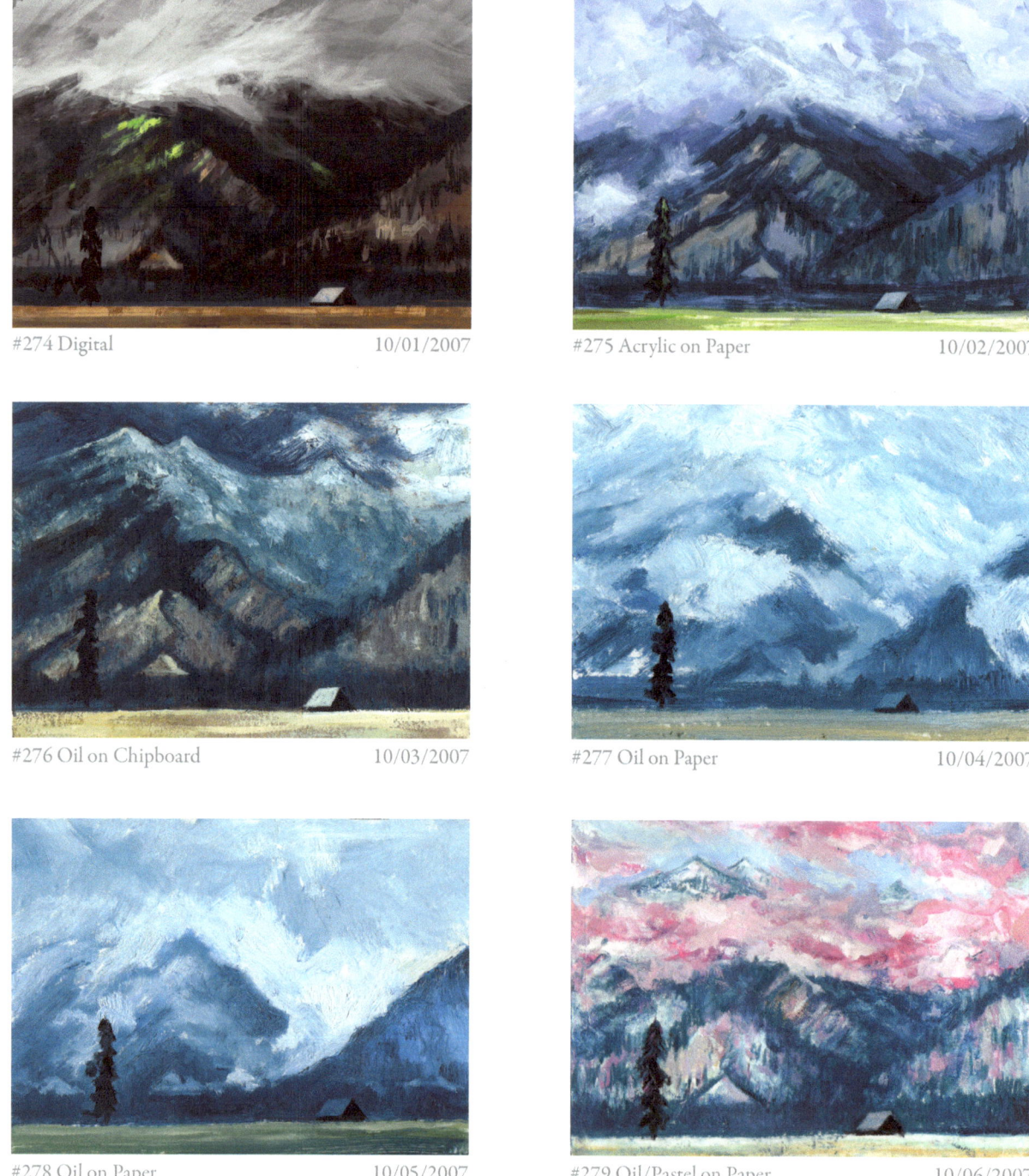

#274 Digital   10/01/2007

#275 Acrylic on Paper   10/02/2007

#276 Oil on Chipboard   10/03/2007

#277 Oil on Paper   10/04/2007

#278 Oil on Paper   10/05/2007

#279 Oil/Pastel on Paper   10/06/2007

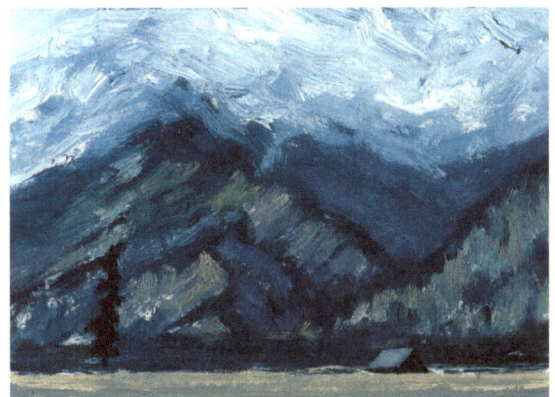

#280 Oil on Paper   10/07/2007

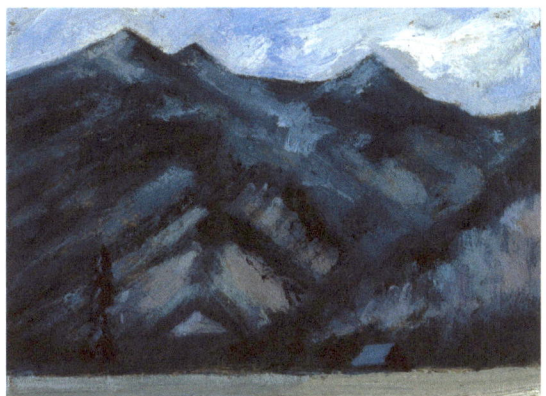

#281 Oil on Chipboard   10/08/2007

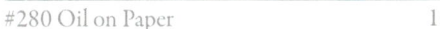

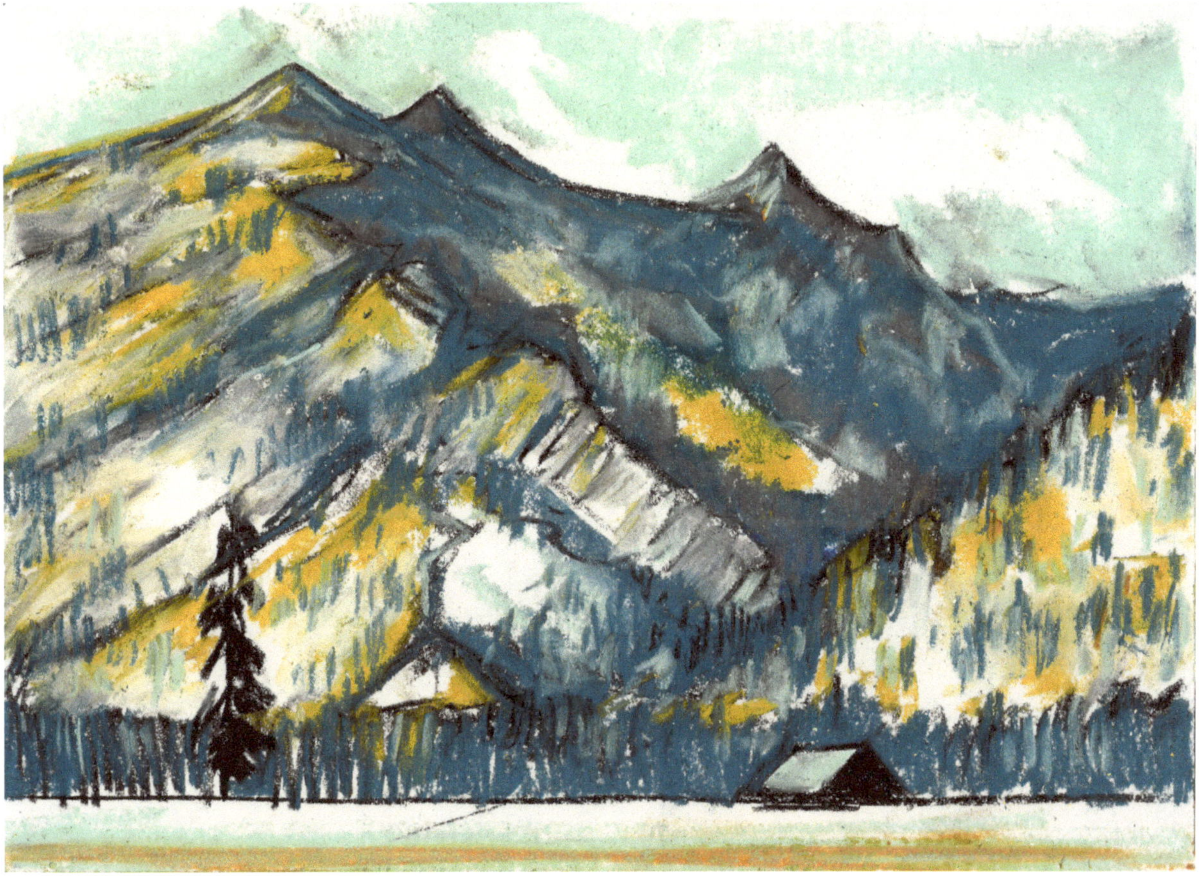

#282 Pastel on Paper   10/09/2007

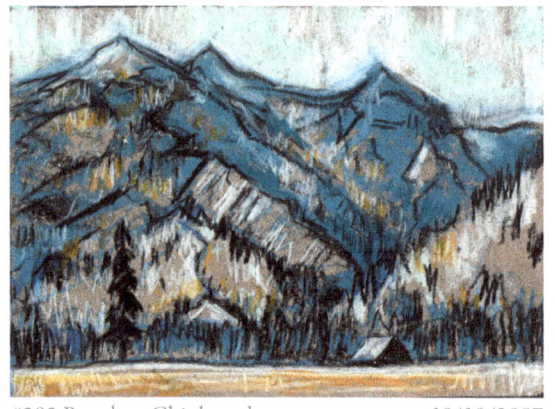

#283 Pastel on Chipboard 10/10/2007

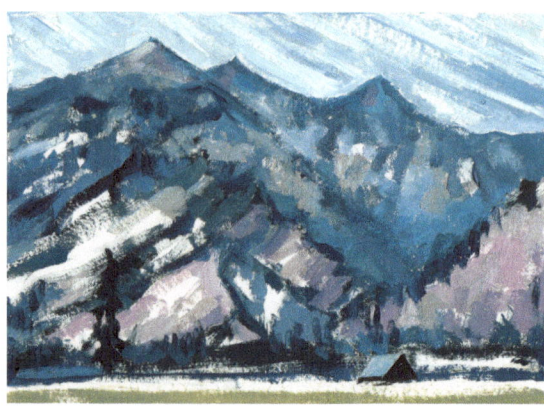

#284 Oil on Paper 10/11/2007

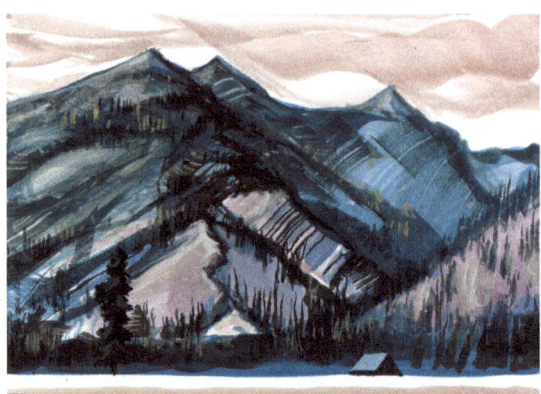

#285 Gouache on Illustration Board 10/12/2007

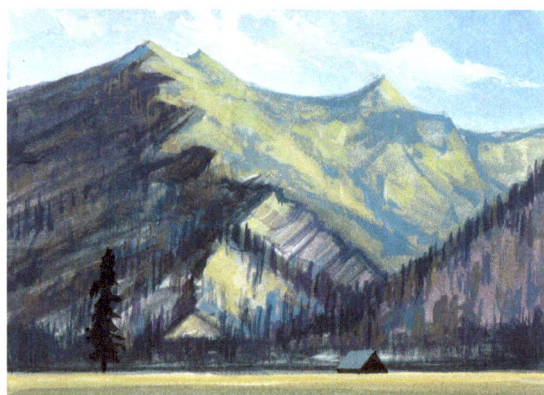

#286 Gouache on Illustration Board 10/13/2007

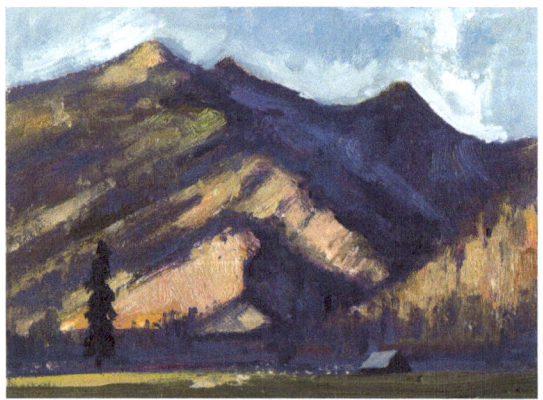

#287 Oil on Paper 10/14/2007

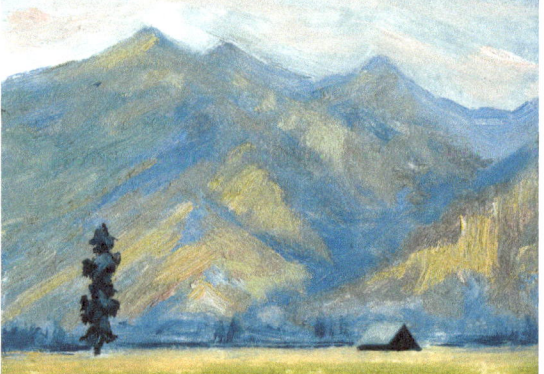

#288 Oil on Paper 10/15/2007

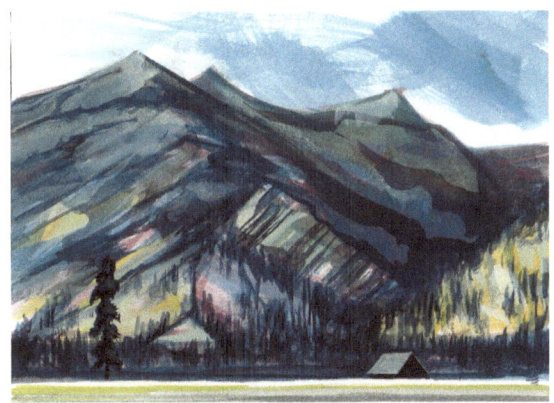

#289 Gouache on Illustration Board   10/16/2007

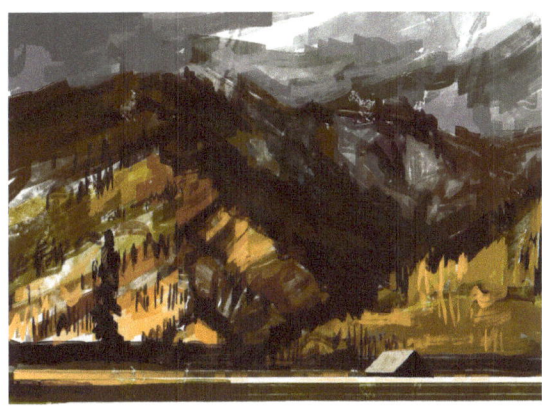

#290 Digital   10/17/2007

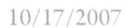

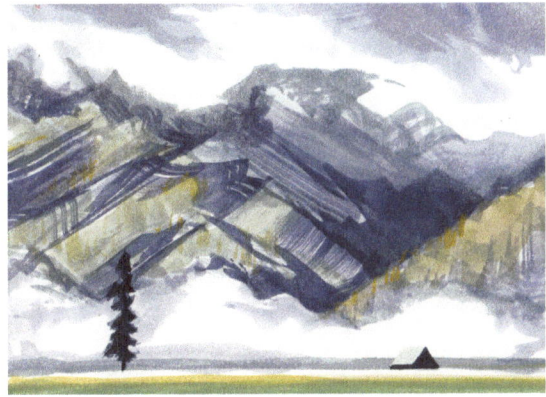

#291 Gouache on Illustration Board   10/18/2007

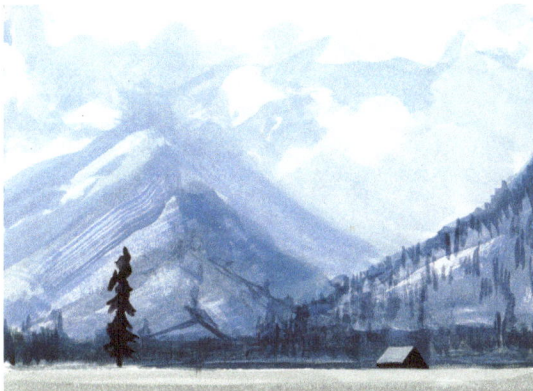

#292 Gouache on Illustration Board   10/19/2007

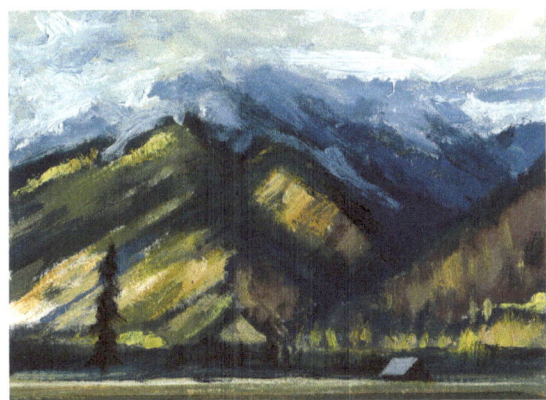

#293 Oil on Illustration Board   10/20/2007

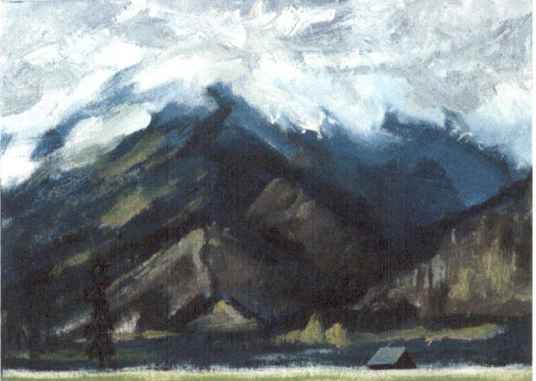

#294 Oil on Illustration Board   10/21/2007

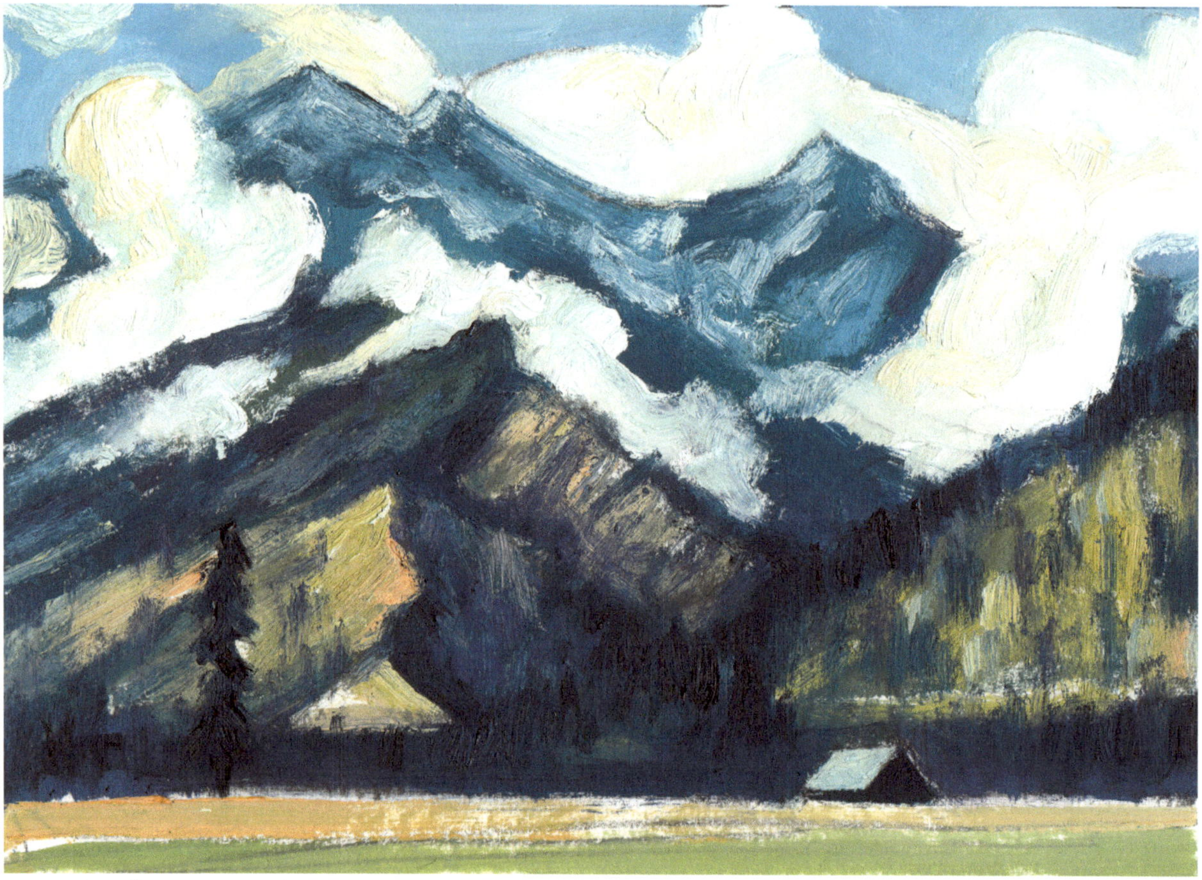

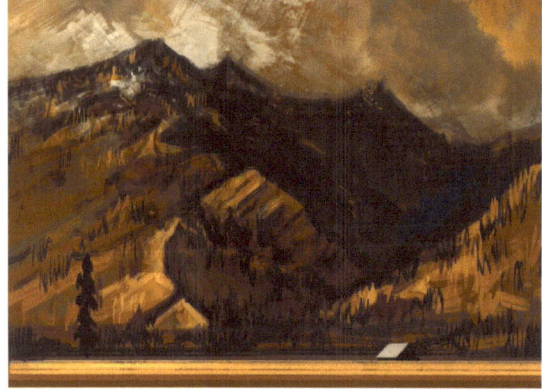

#295 Oil on Illustration Board   10/22/2007

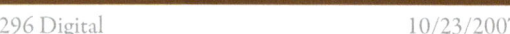

#296 Digital   10/23/2007   #297 Gouache on Illustration Board   10/24/2007

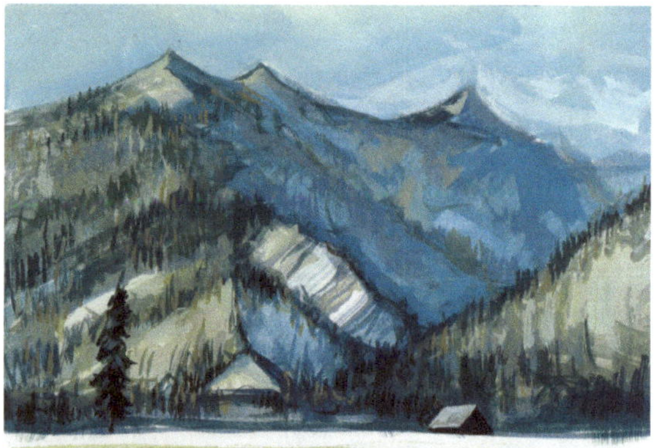

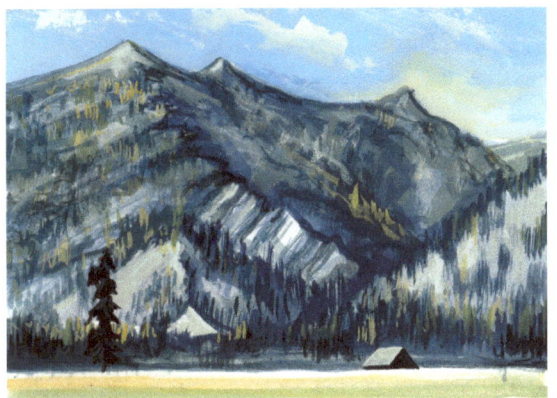

#298 Gouache on Paper   10/25/2007

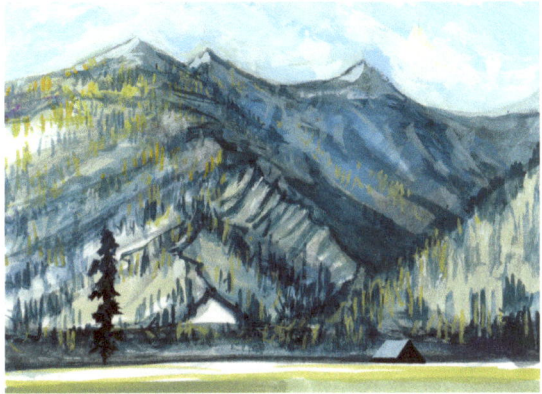

#299 Gouache on Illustration Board   10/26/2007

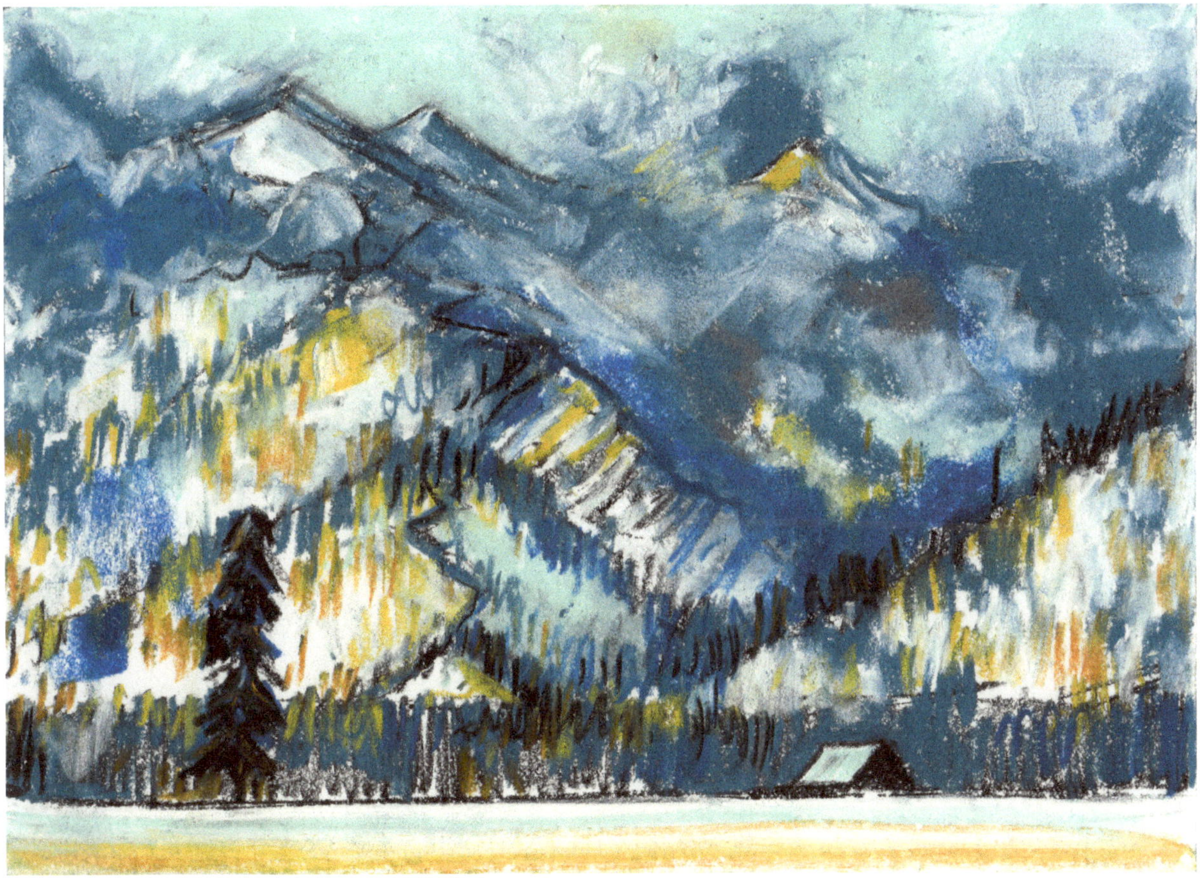

#300 Pastel on Paper   10/27/2007

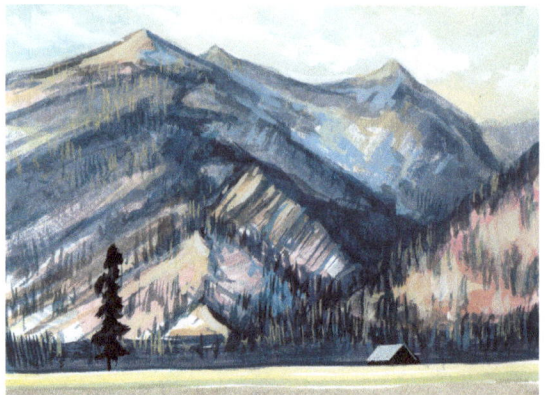

#301 Gouache on Illustration Board   10/28/2007

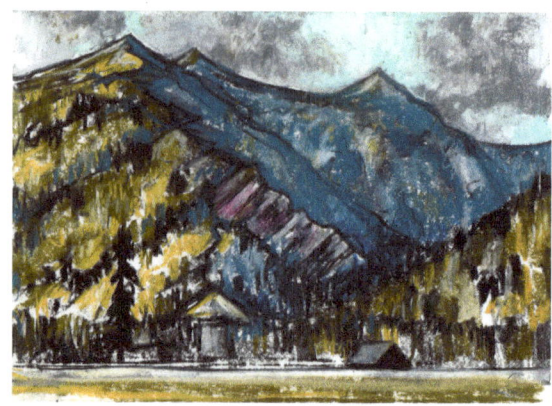

#302 Pastel on Paper   10/29/2007

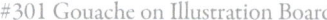

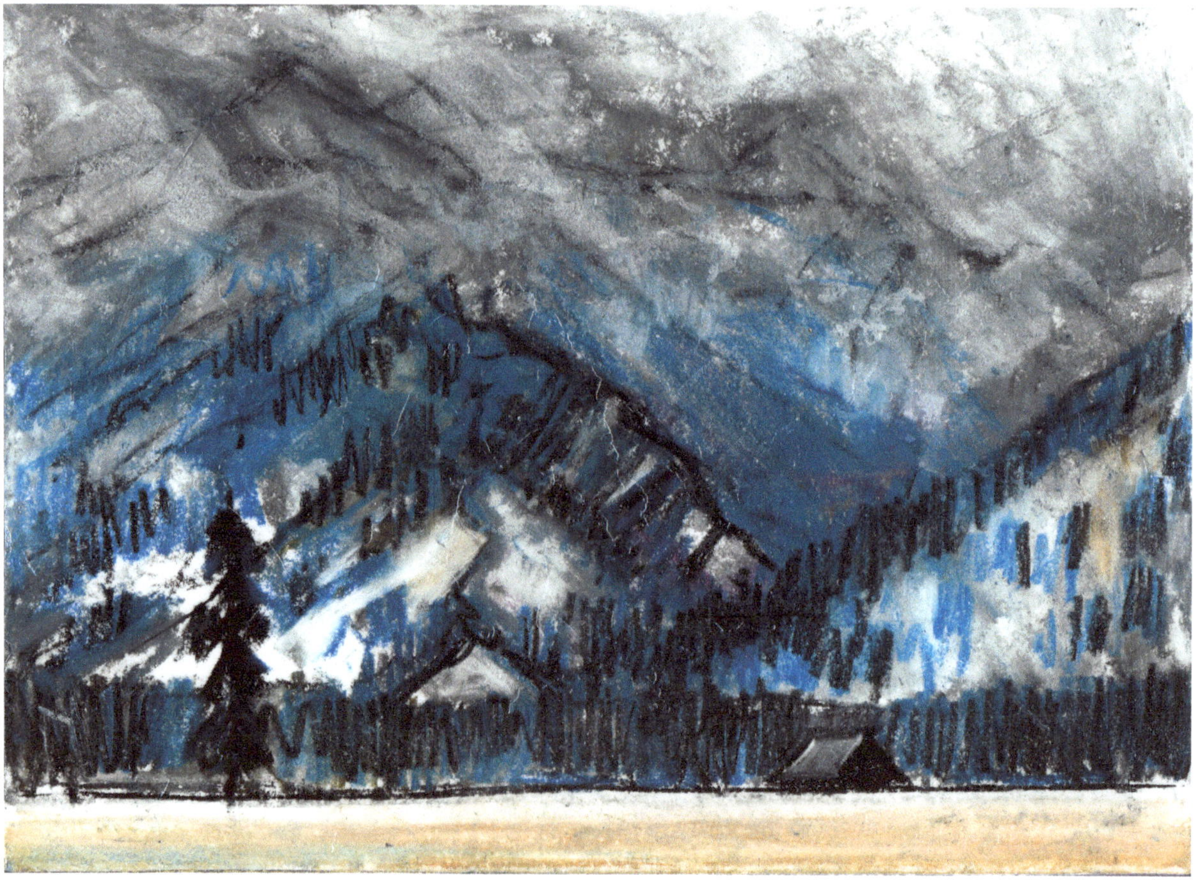

#303 Pastel on Paper   10/30/2007

COUGAR PEAK-A-BOO
- The Art of Jared Shear -

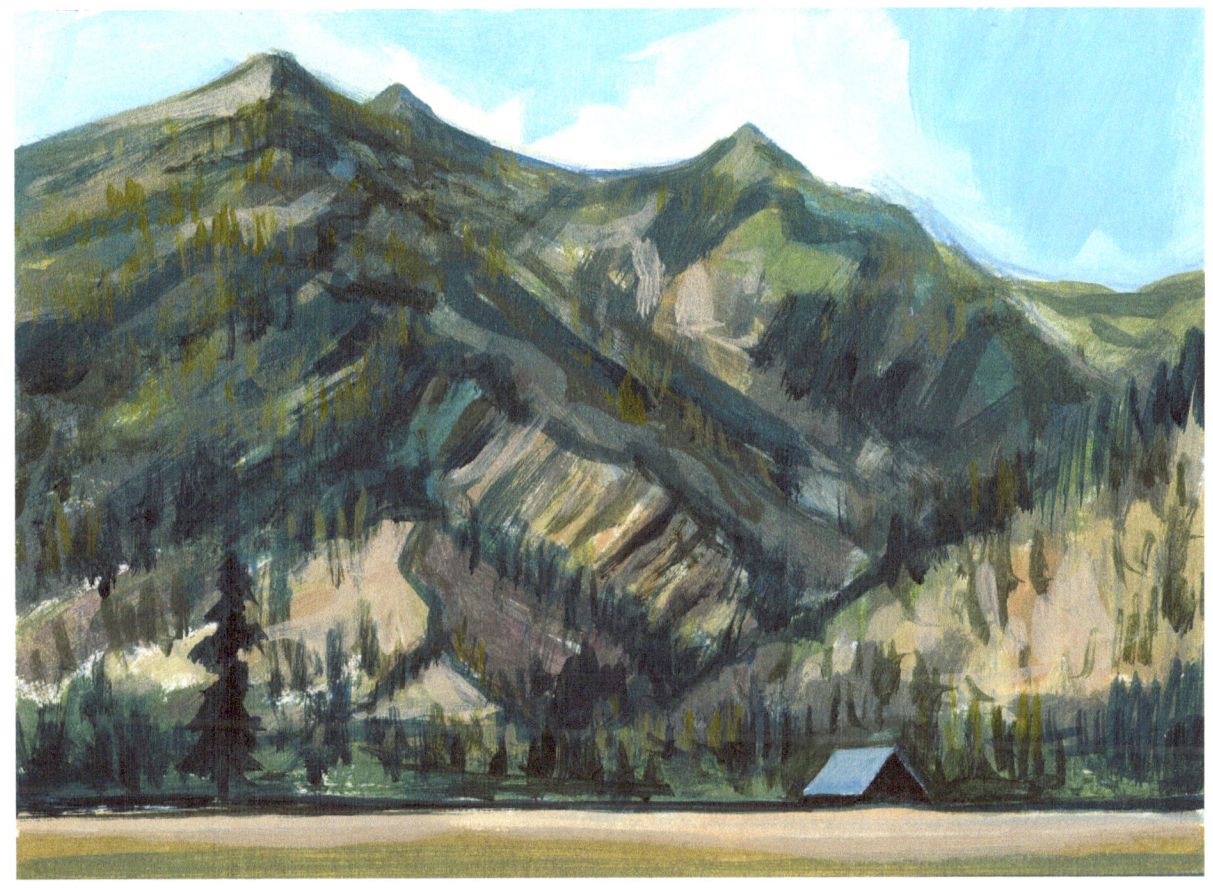

#304 Acrylic on Paper

10/31/2007

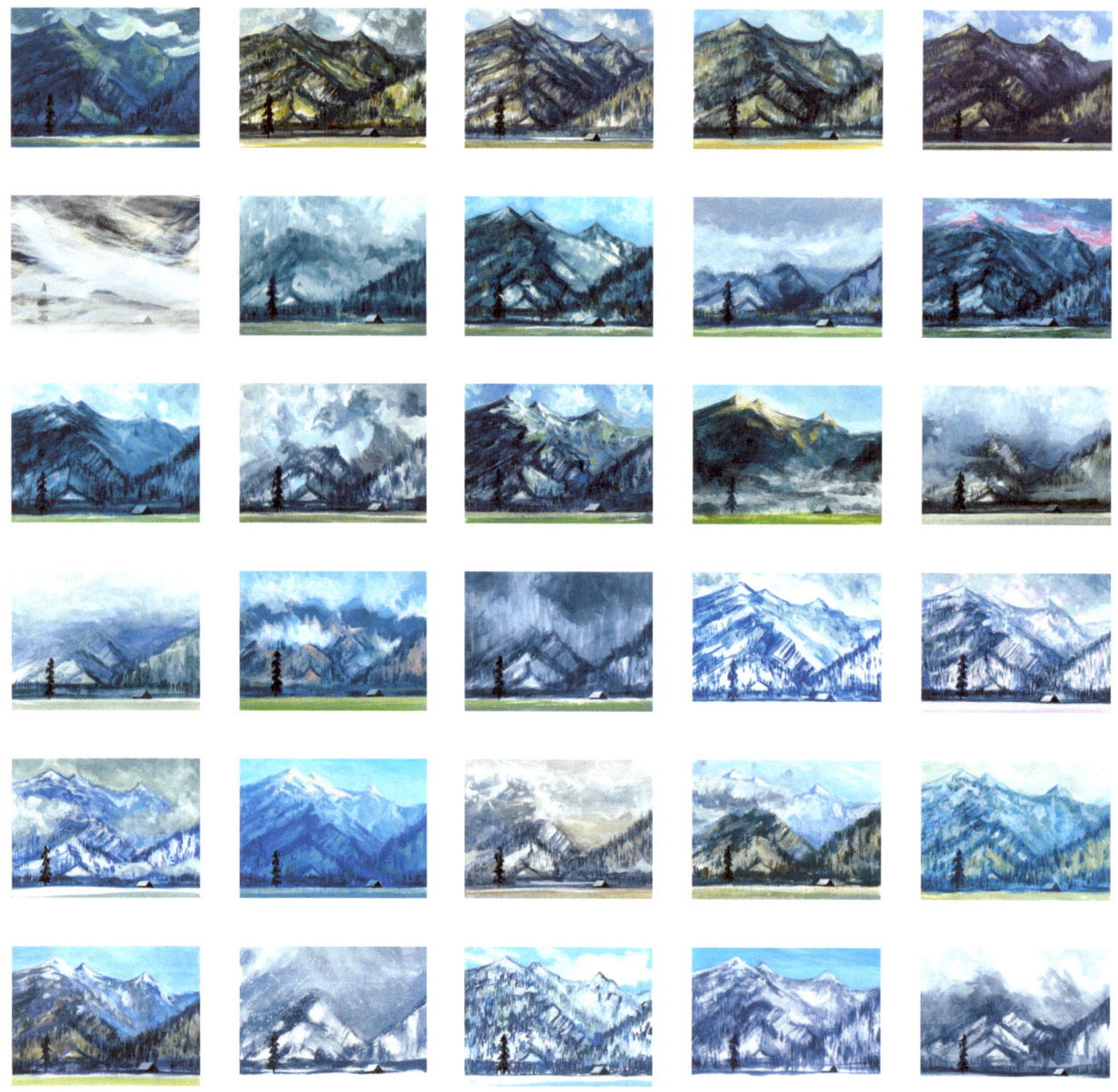

COUGAR PEAK-A-BOO
- The Art of Jared Shear -

NOVEMBER

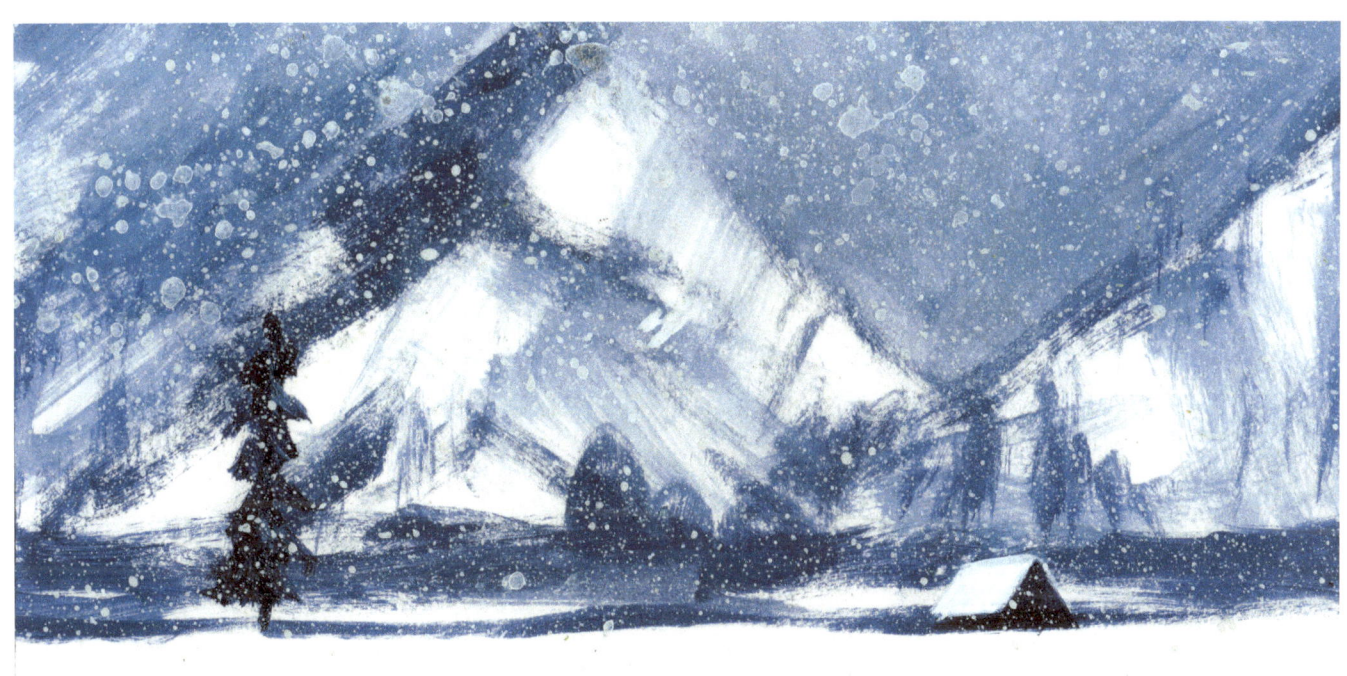

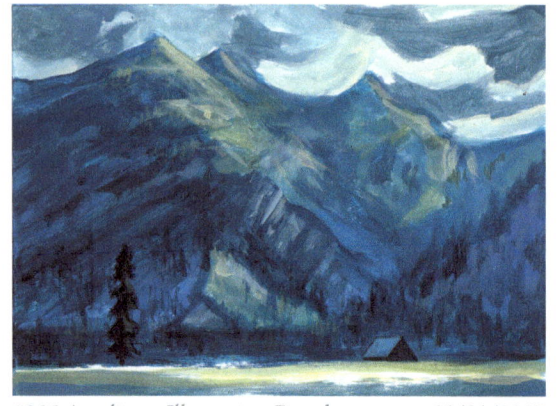

#305 Acrylic on Illustration Board   11/01/2007

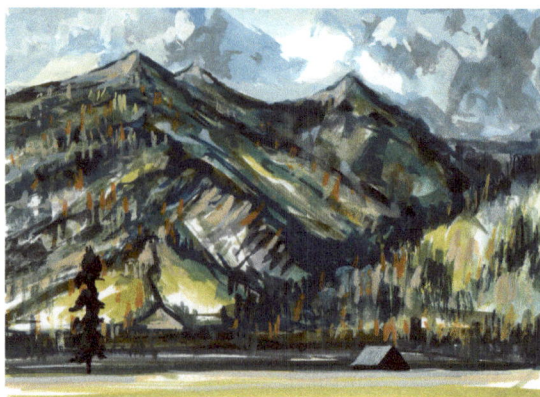

#306 Gouache on Paper   11/02/2007

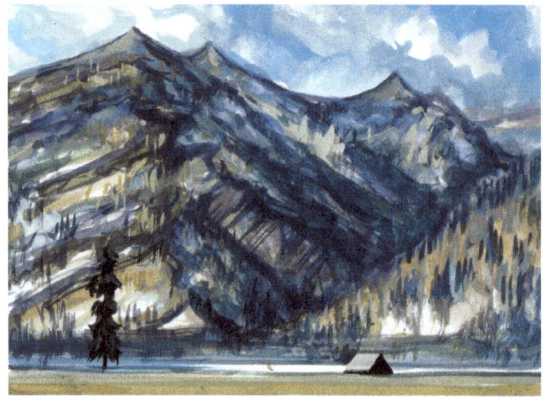

#307 Gouache on Paper   11/03/2007

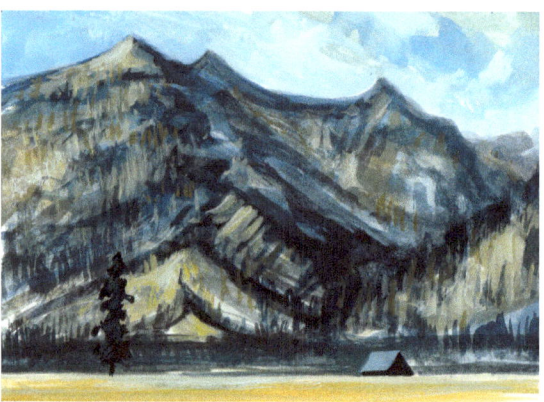

#308 Gouache on Paper   11/04/2007

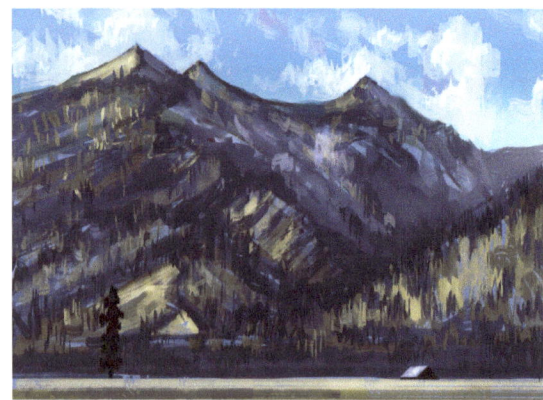

#309 Digital   11/05/2007

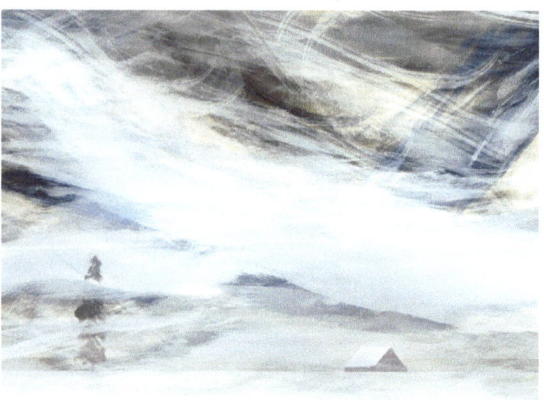

#310 Digital   11/06/2007

COUGAR PEAK-A-BOO
- The Art of Jared Shear -

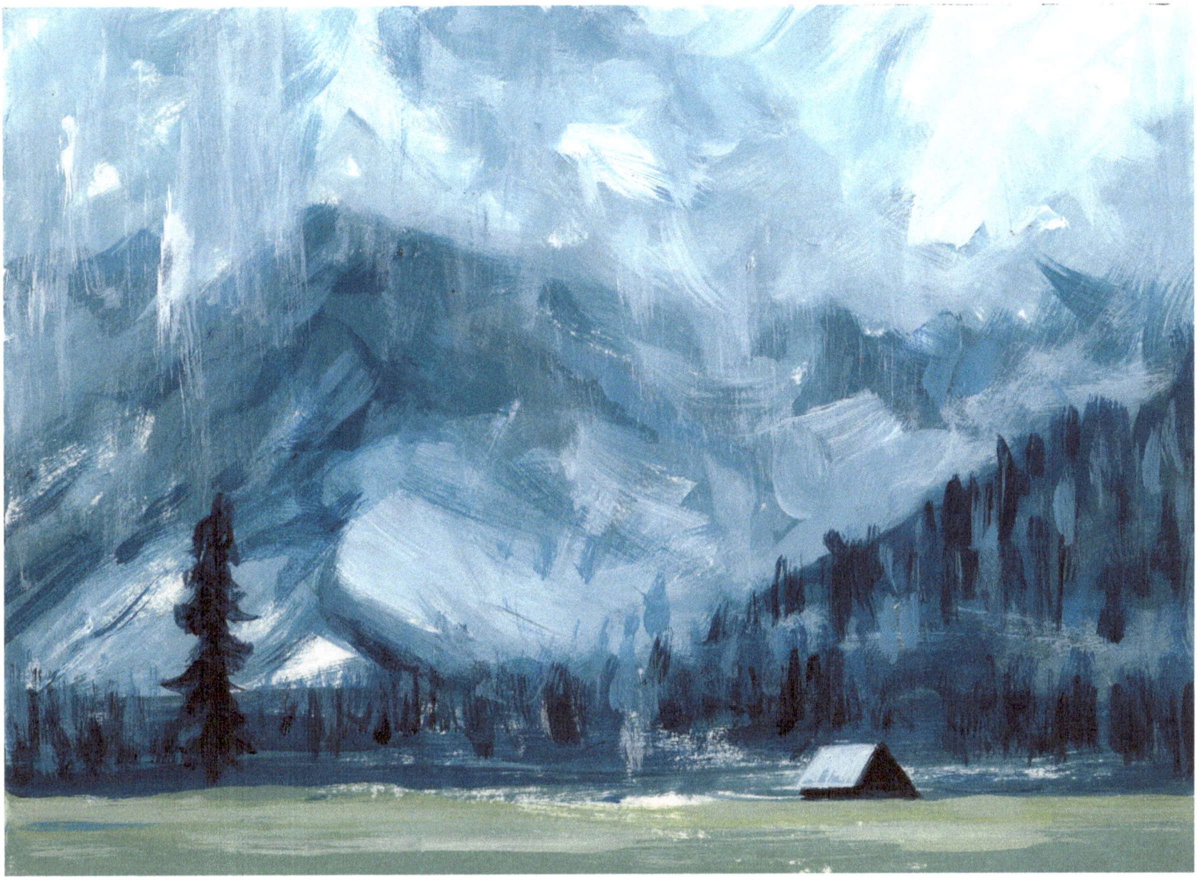

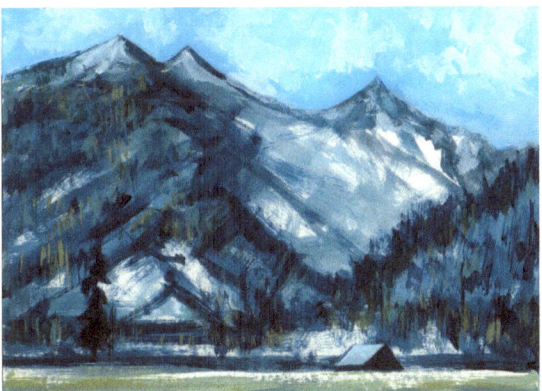

#311 Acrylic on Paper   11/07/2007

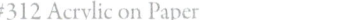

#312 Acrylic on Paper   11/08/2007

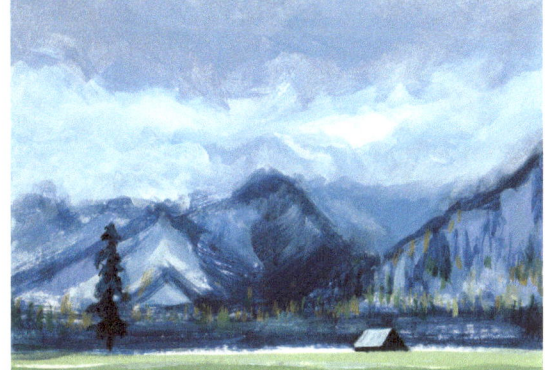

#313 Acrylic on Paper   11/09/2007

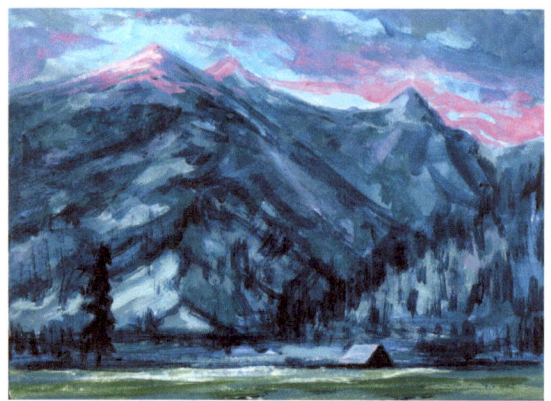

#314 Acrylic on Paper   11/10/2007

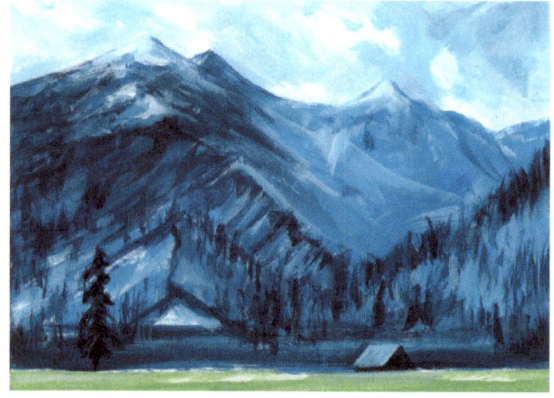

#315 Acrylic on Paper   11/11/2007

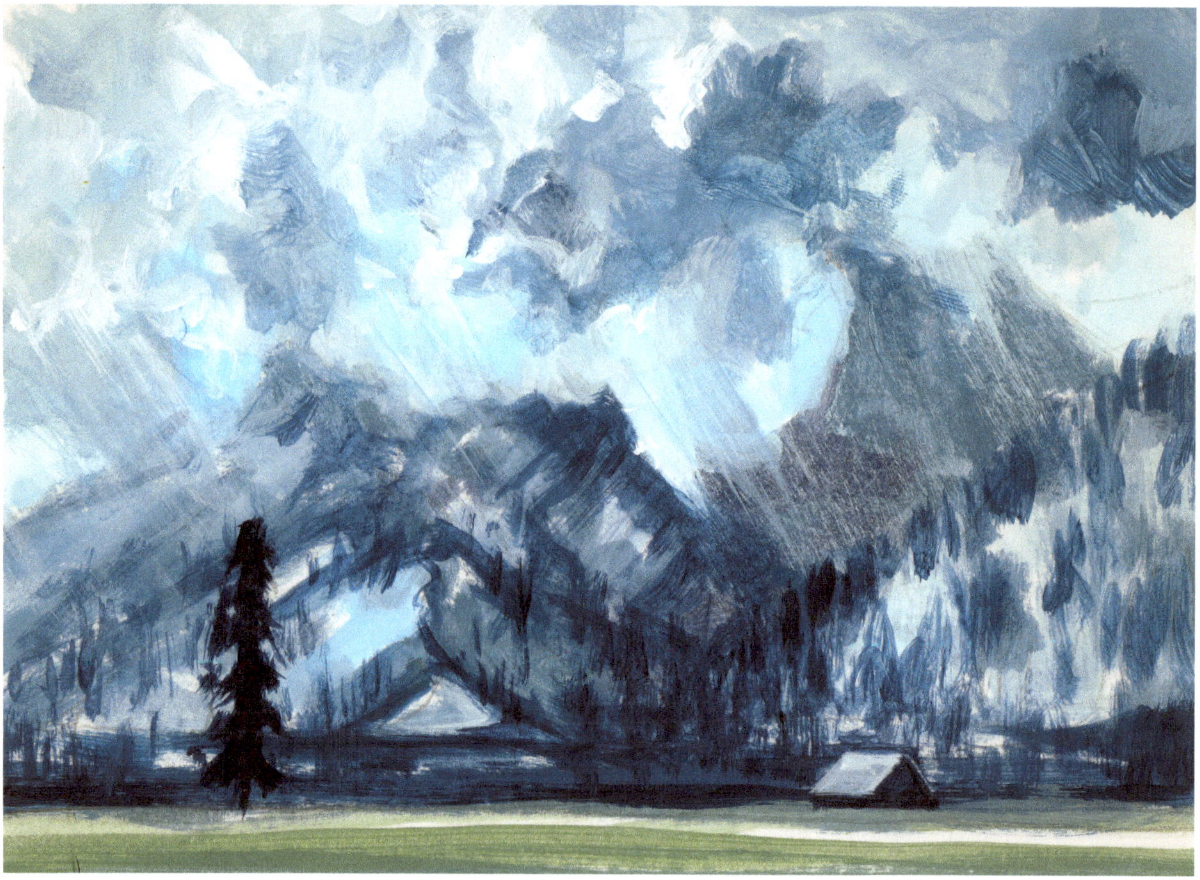

#316 Acrylic on Paper   11/12/2007

COUGAR PEAK-A-BOO
- The Art of Jared Shear -

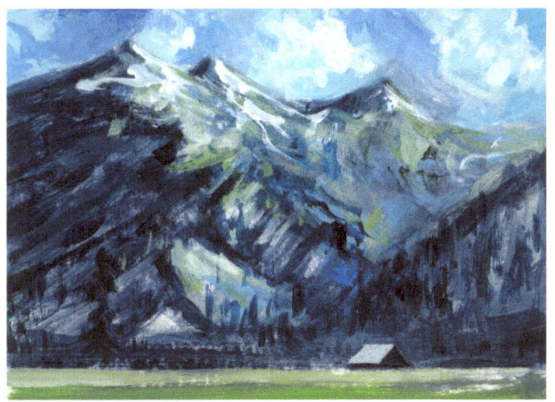

#317 Acrylic on Paper   11/13/2007

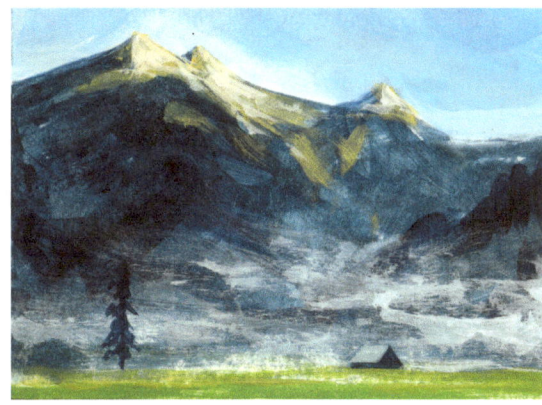

#318 Acrylic on Paper   11/14/2007

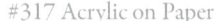

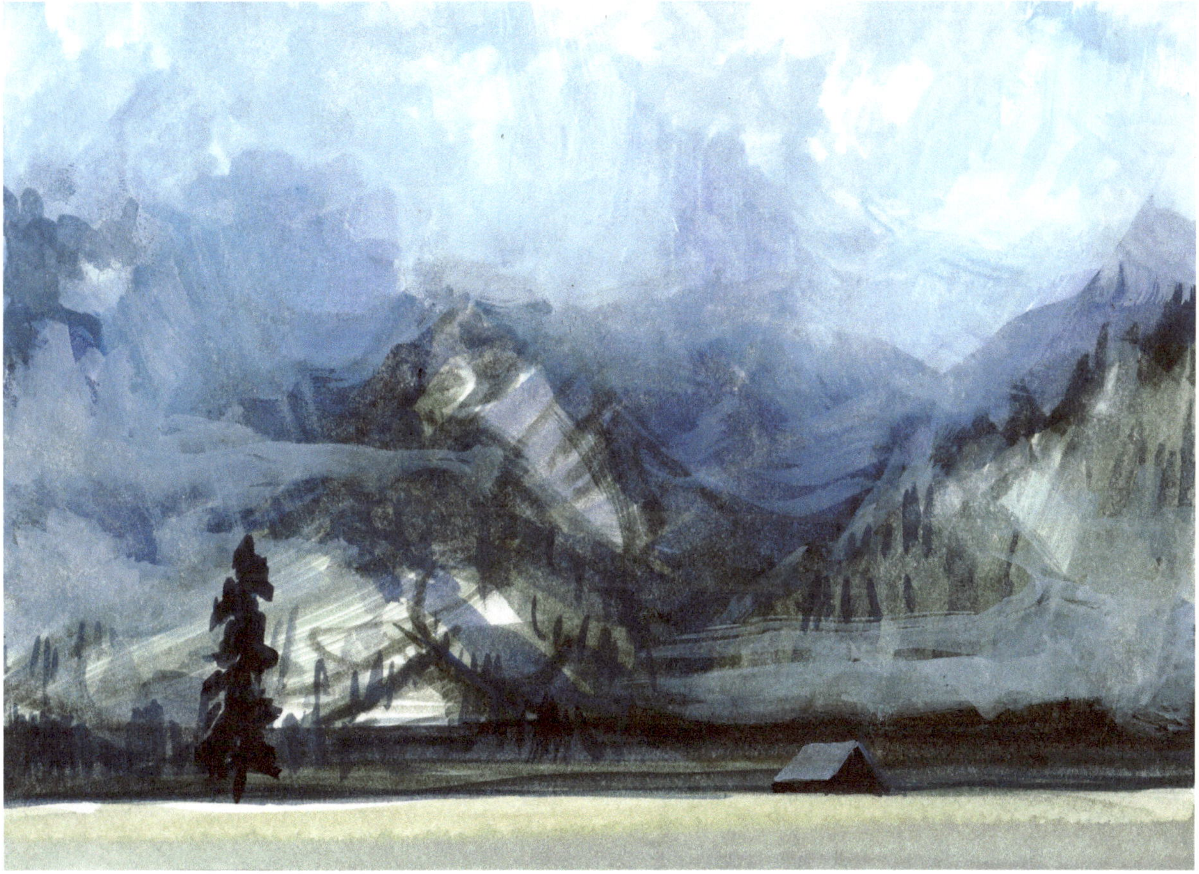

#319 Gouache on Paper   11/15/2007

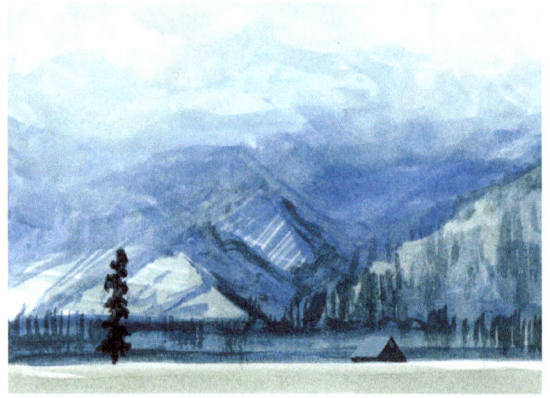

#320 Gouache on Paper   11/16/2007

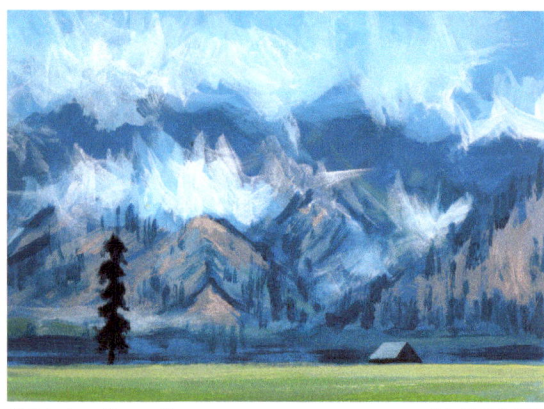

#321 Acrylic on Paper   11/17/2007

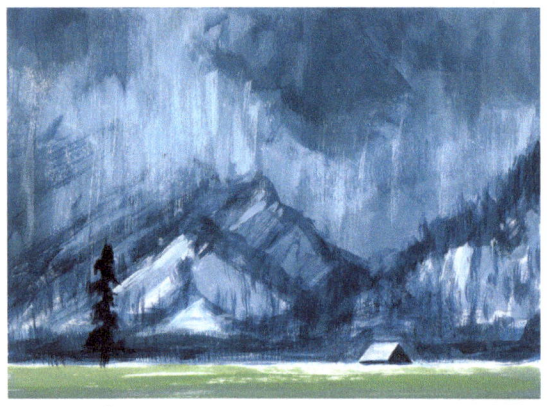

#322 Acrylic on Paper   11/18/2007

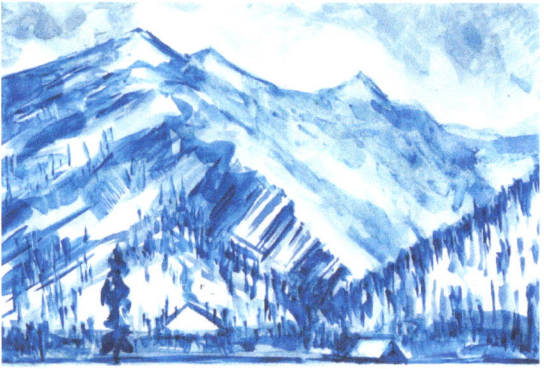

#323 Watercolor on Paper   11/19/2007

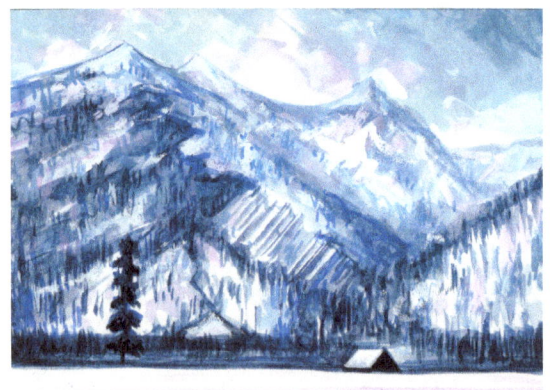

#324 Gouache on Paper   11/20/2007

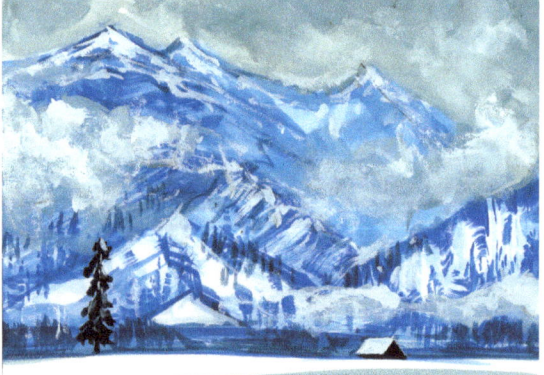

#325 Gouache on Paper   11/21/2007

COUGAR PEAK-A-BOO
- The Art of Jared Shear -

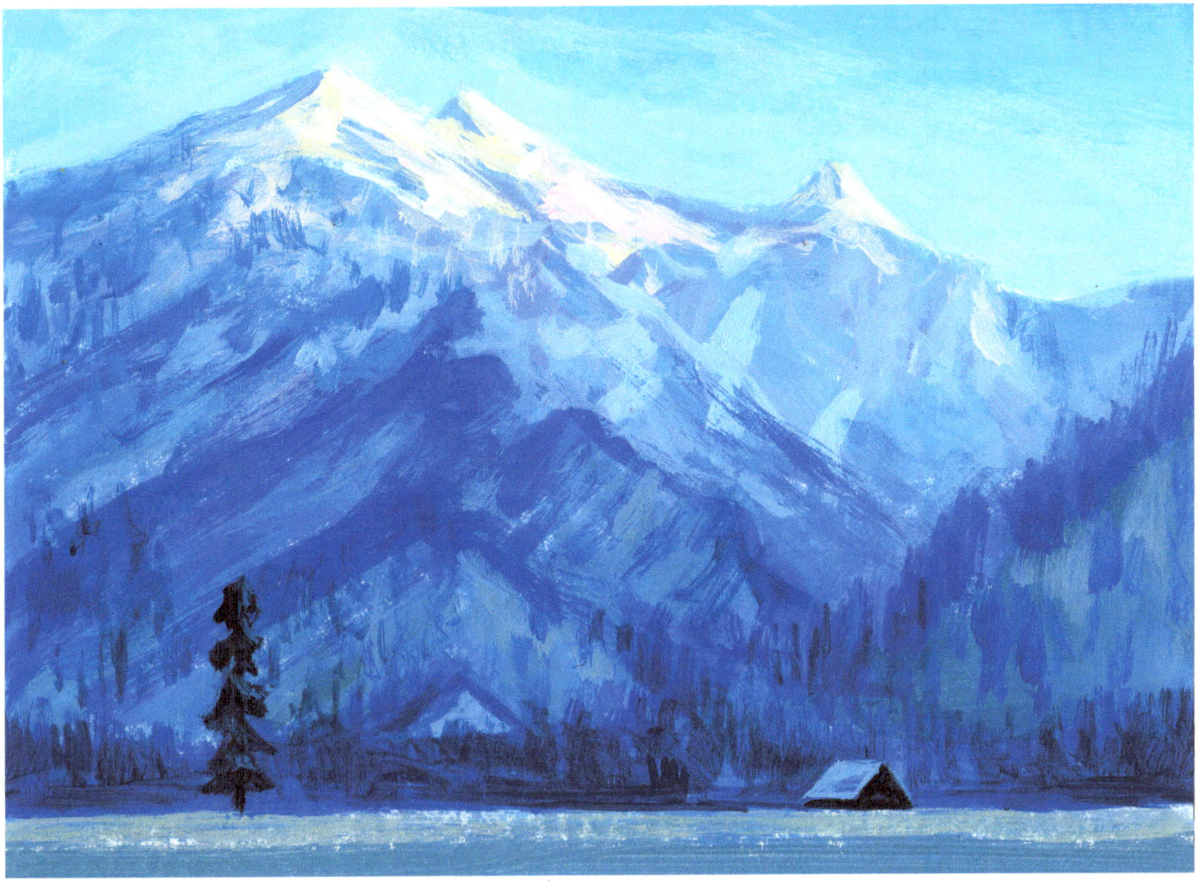

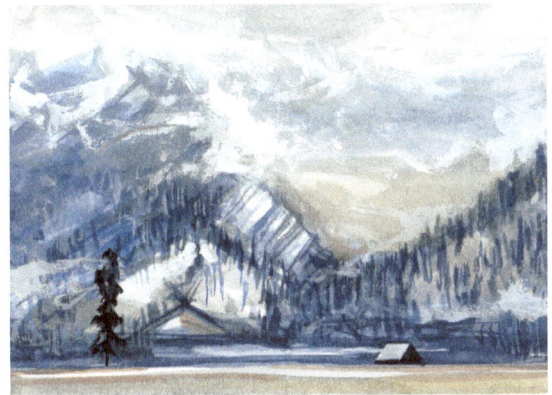

#326 Acrylic on Paper   11/22/2007

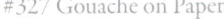

#327 Gouache on Paper   11/23/2007

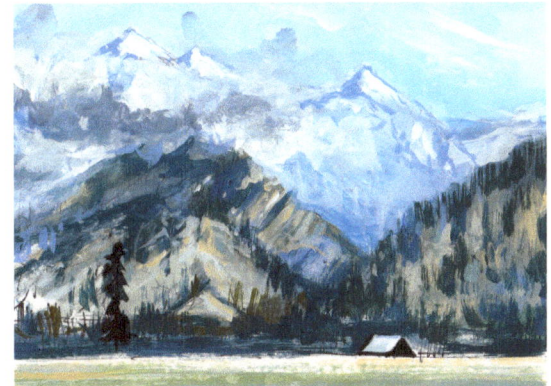

#328 Acrylic on Paper   11/24/2007

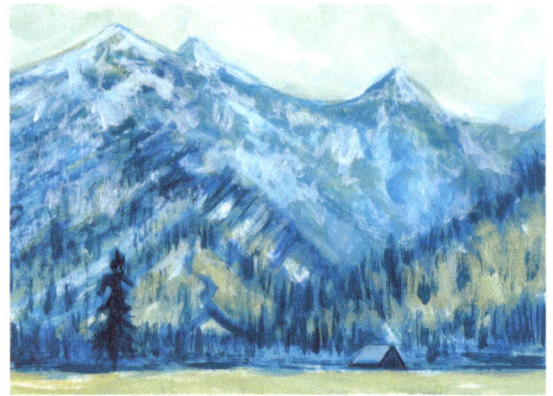

#329 Acrylic on Paper   11/25/2007

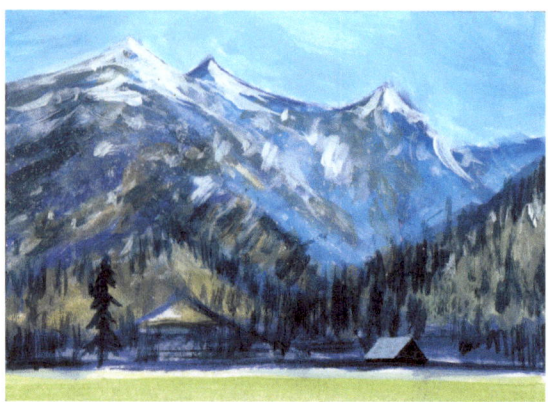

#330 Acrylic on Paper   11/26/2007

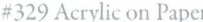

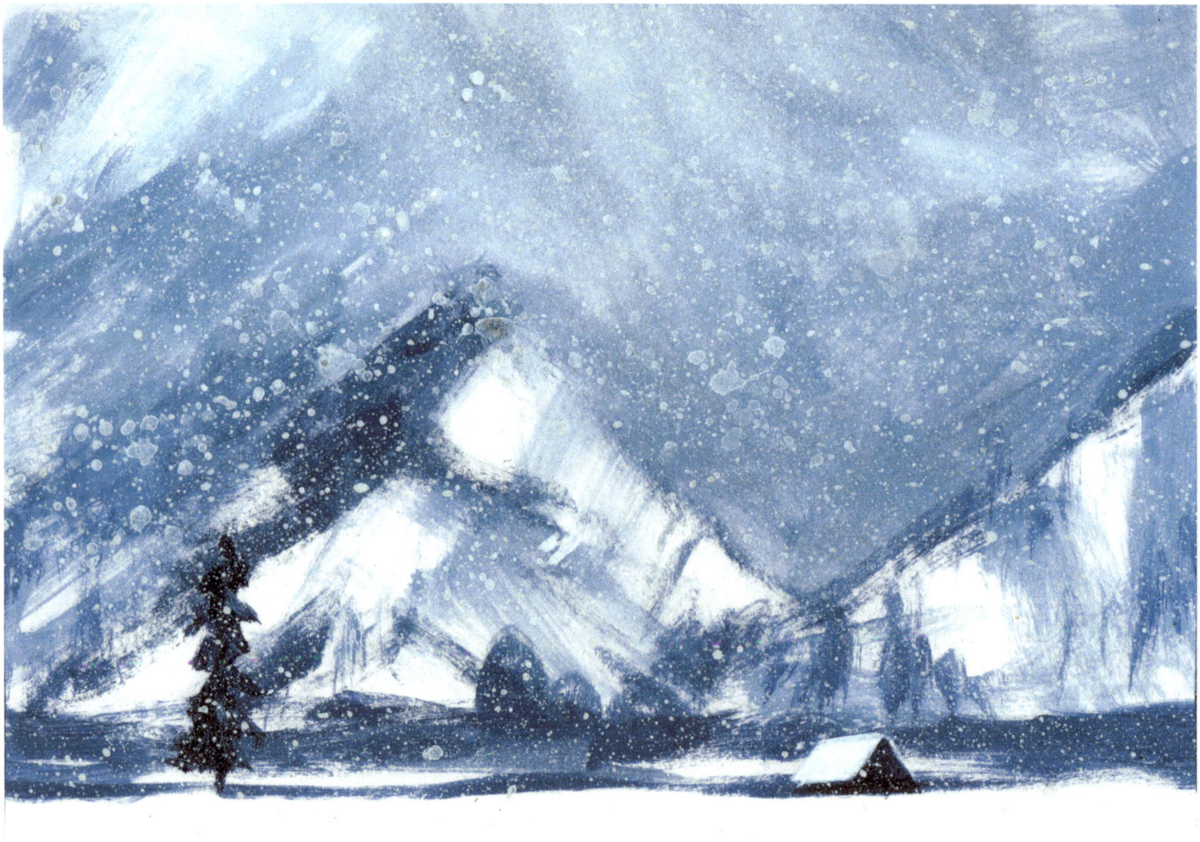

#331 Acrylic on Paper   11/27/2007

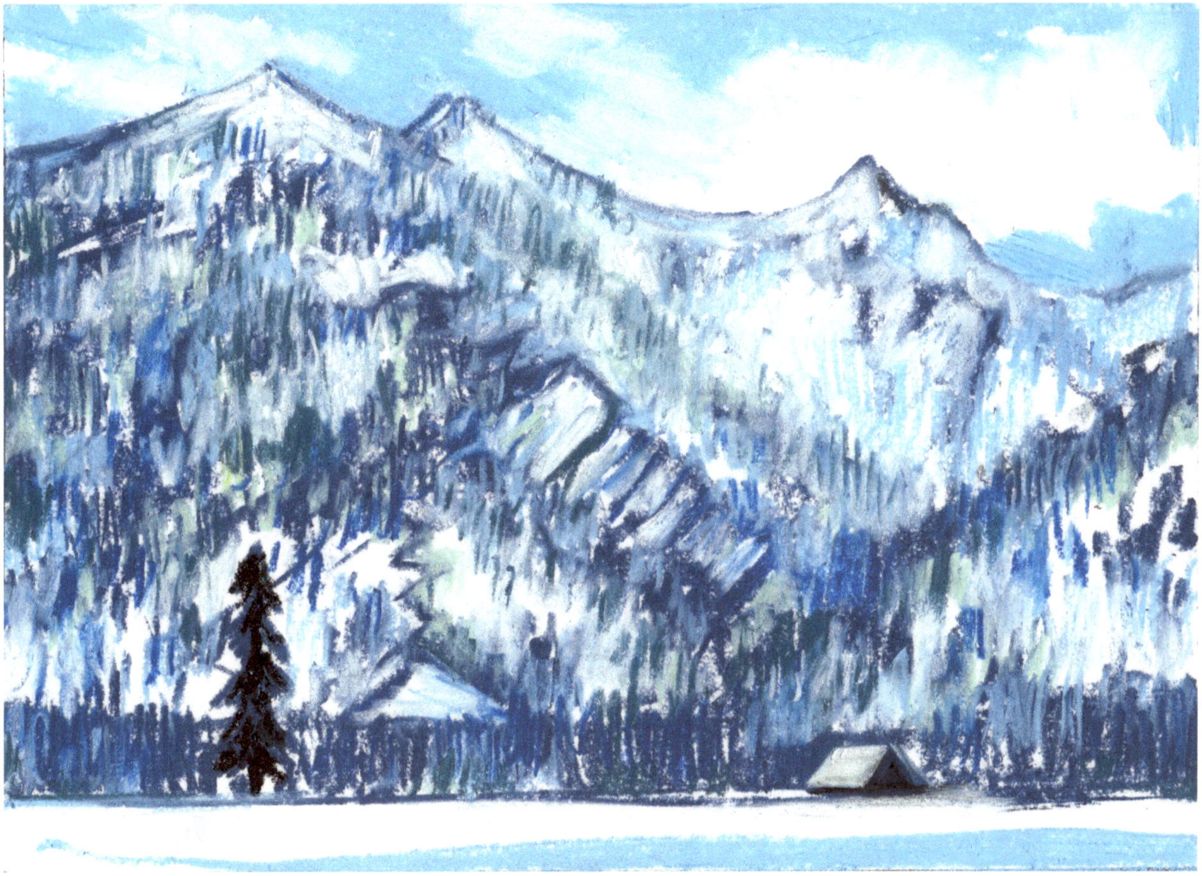

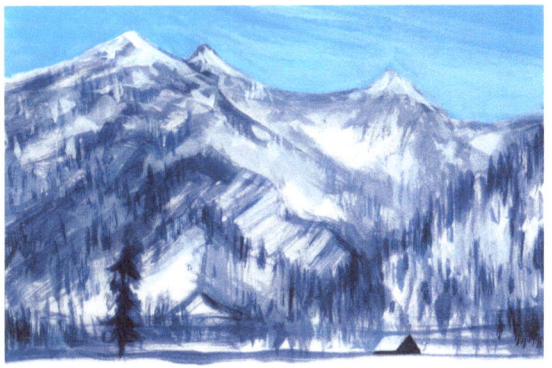

#332 Pastel on Paper   11/28/2007

#333 Acrylic on Paper   11/29/2007   #334 Acrylic on Paper   11/30/2007

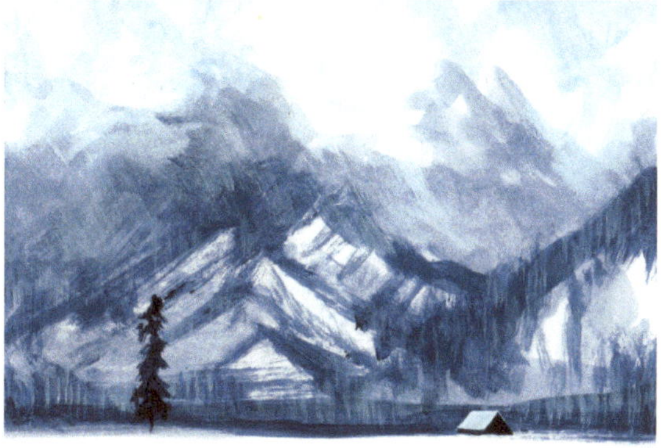

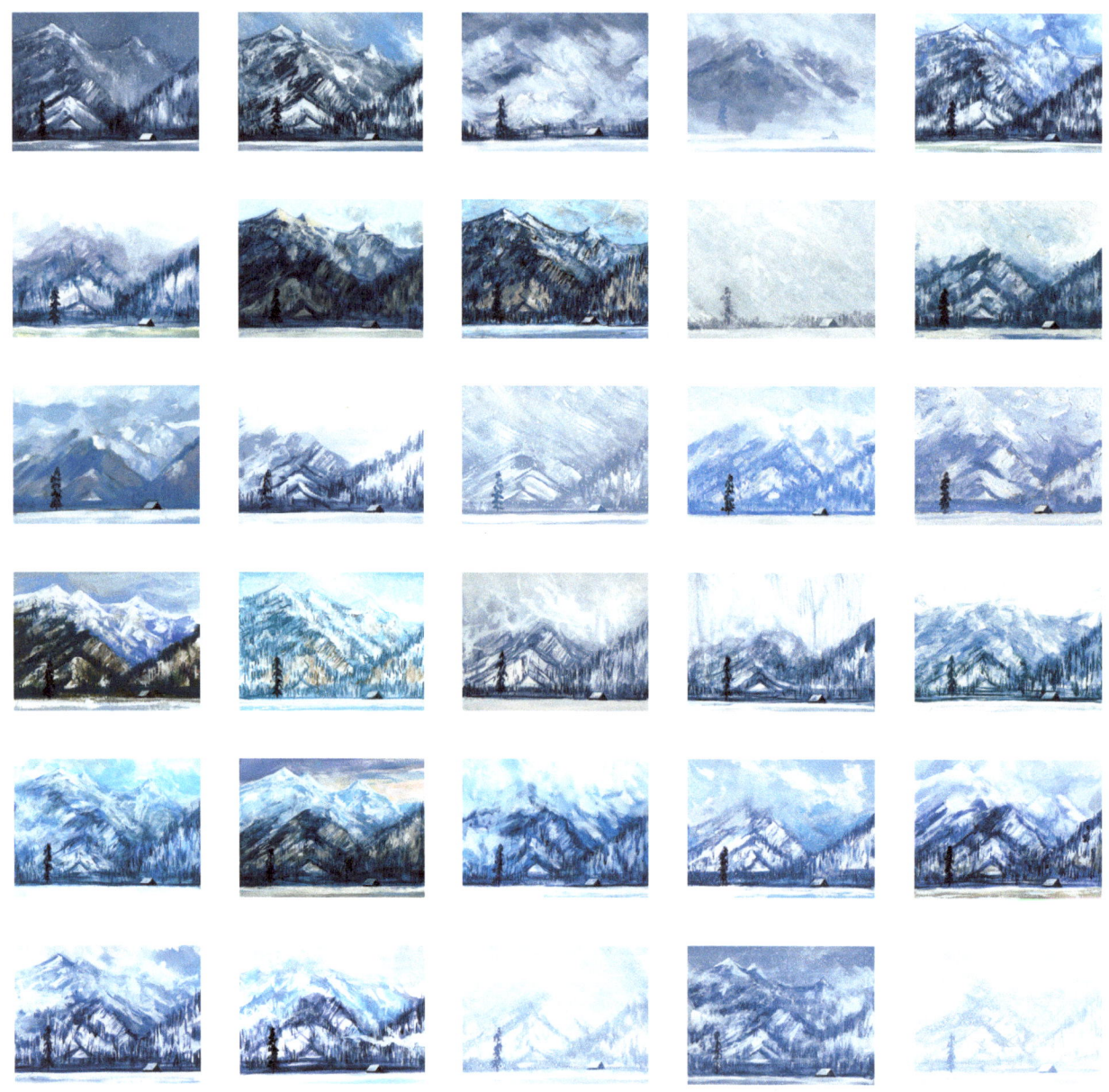

COUGAR PEAK-A-BOO
- The Art of Jared Shear -

DECEMBER

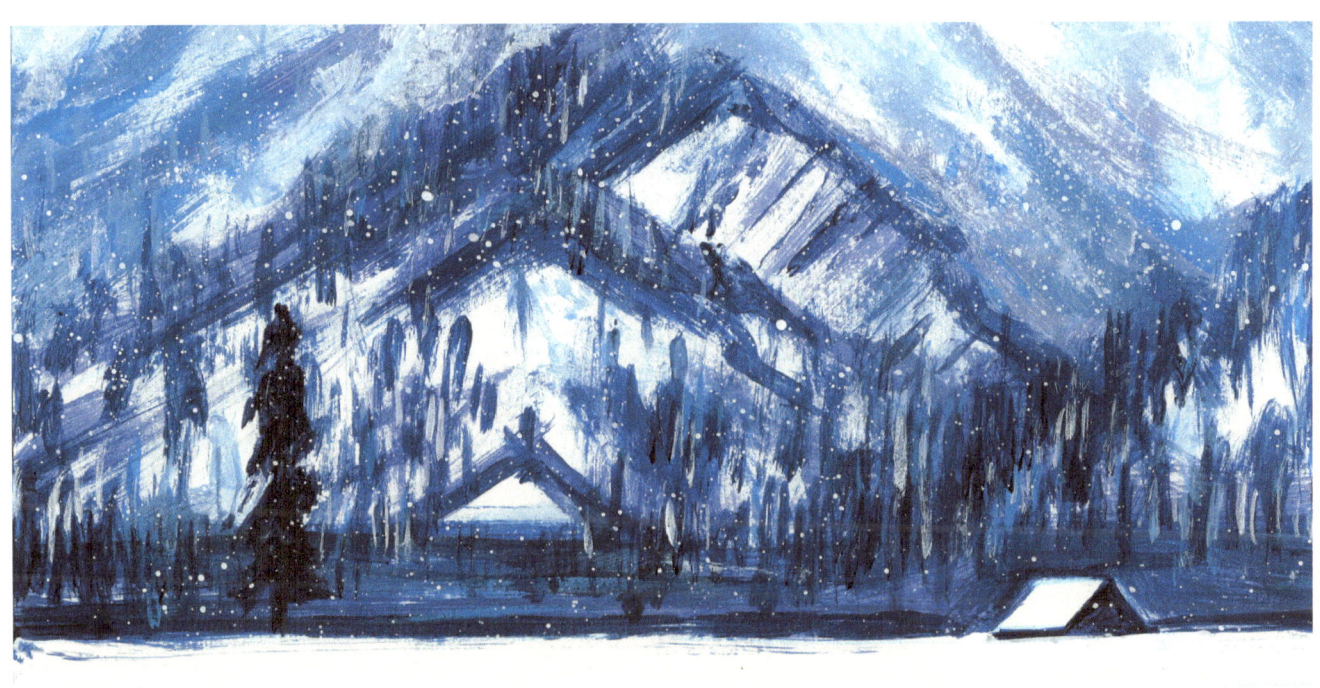

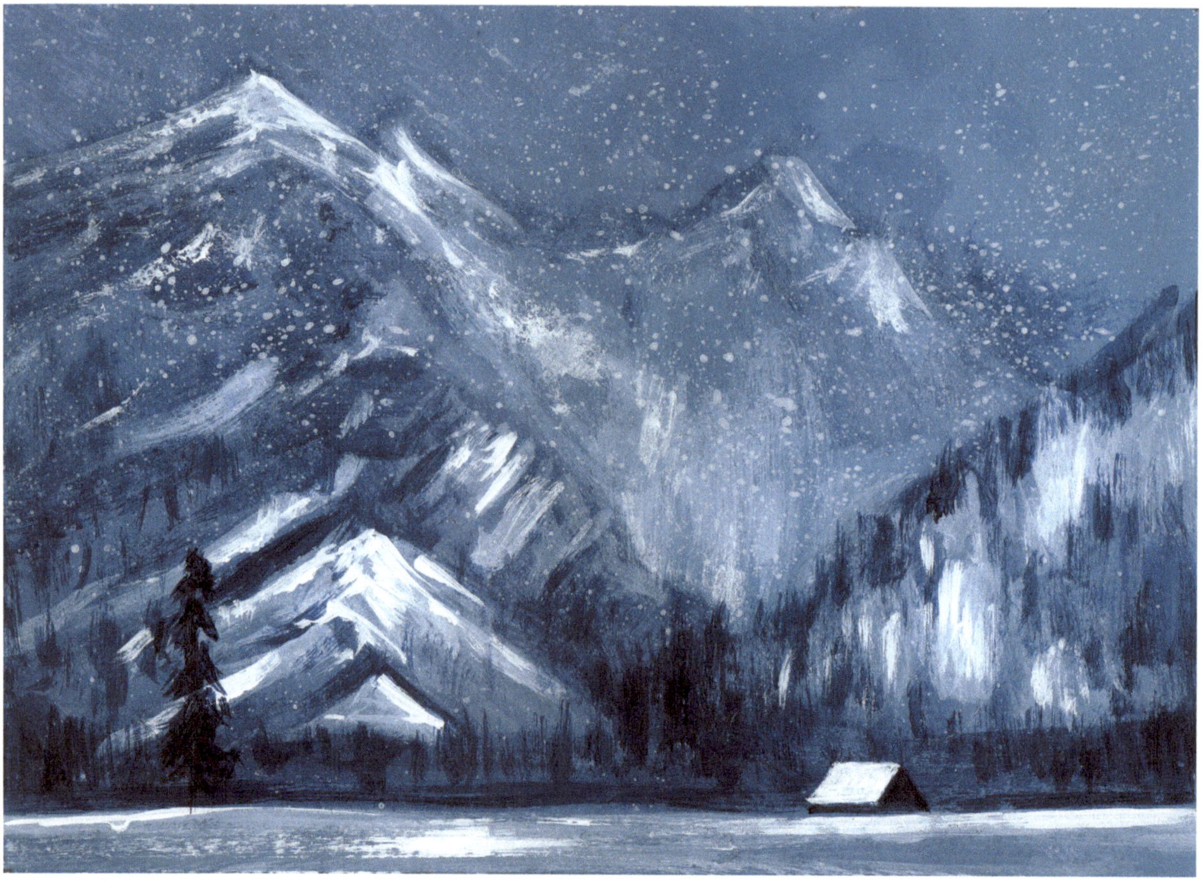

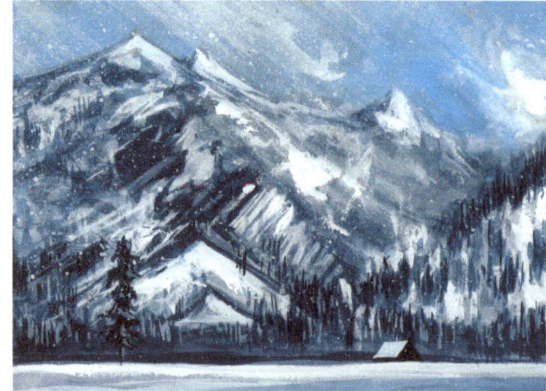

#335 Acrylic on Paper

12/01/2007

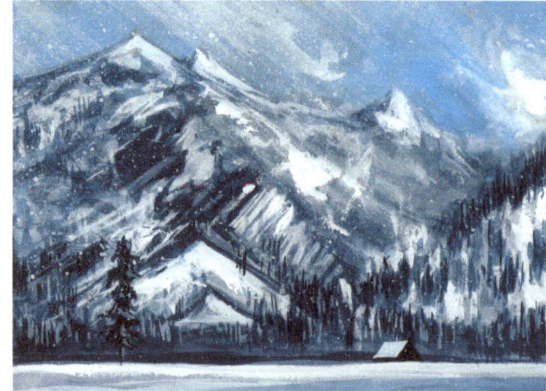

#336 Gouache on Paper 12/02/2007

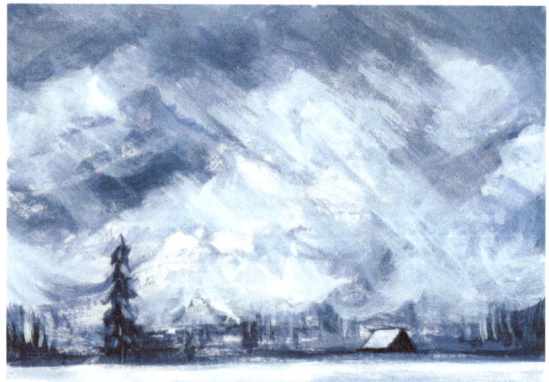

#337 Acrylic on Paper 12/03/2007

COUGAR PEAK-A-BOO
- The Art of Jared Shear -

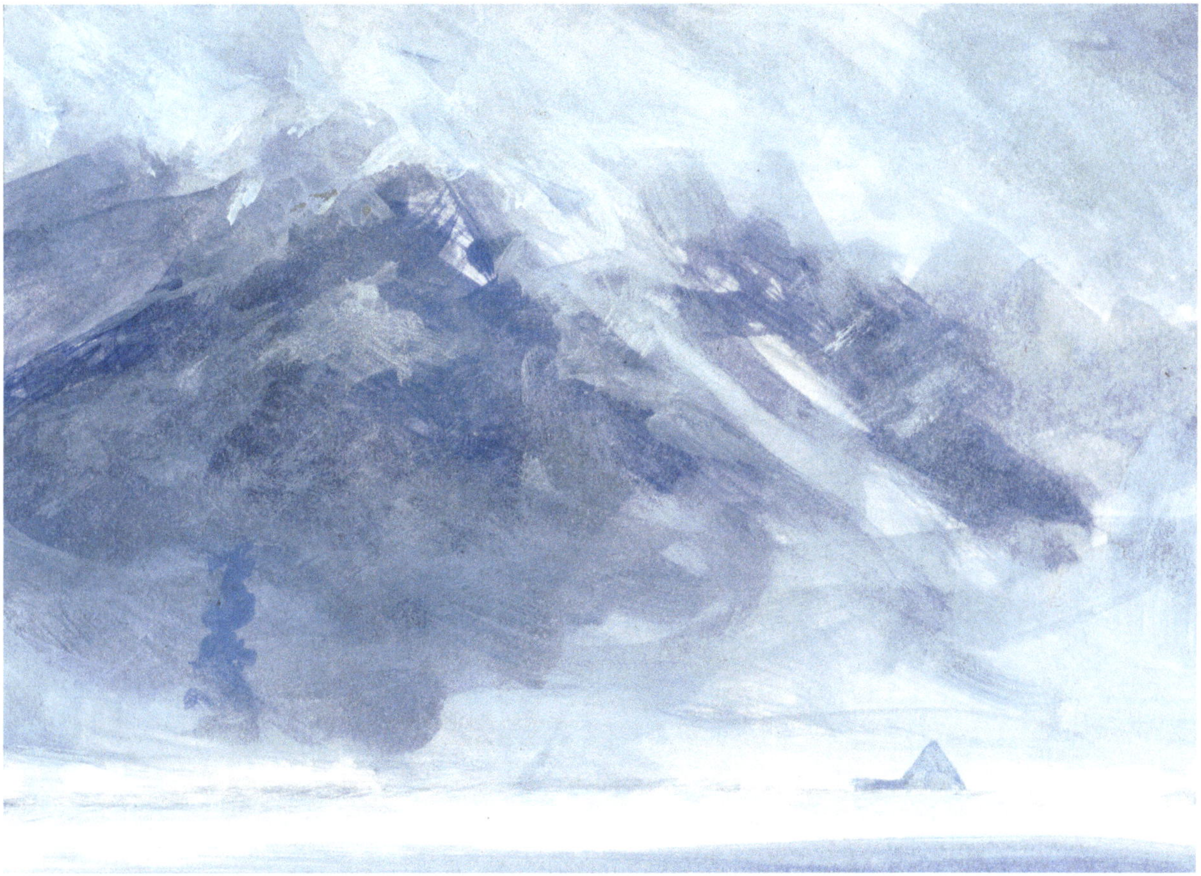

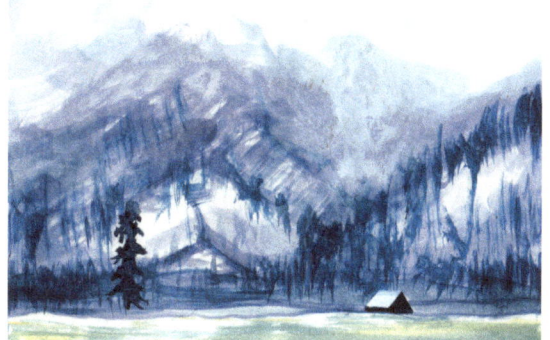

#338 Acrylic on Paper   12/04/2007

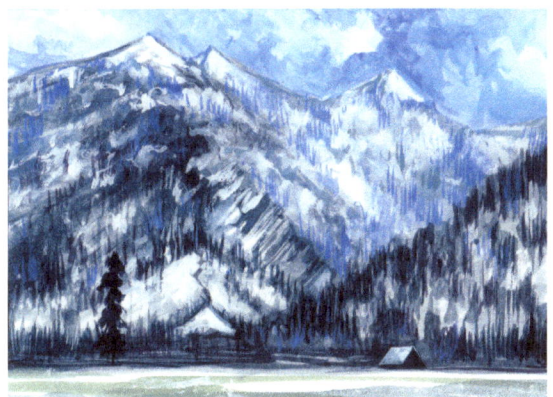

#339 Gouache on Paper   12/05/2007

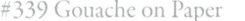

#340 Acrylic on Paper   12/06/2007

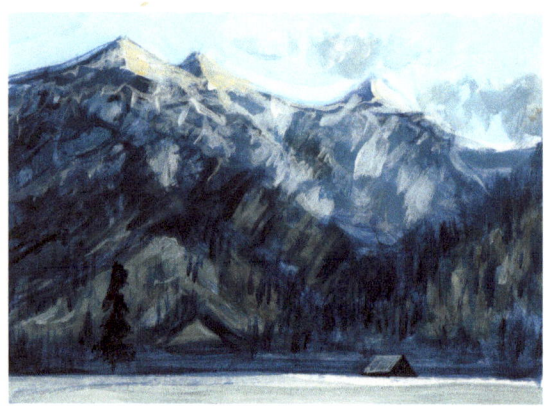

#341 Acrylic on Paper   12/07/2007

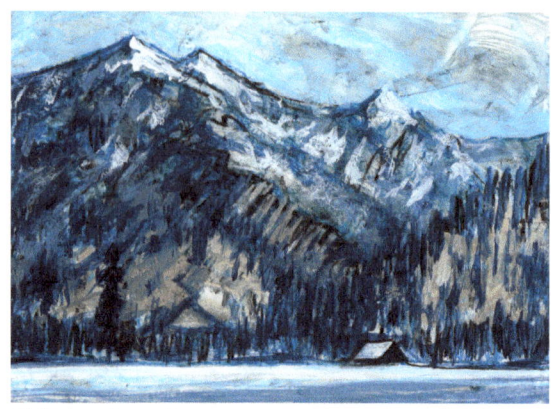

#342 Acrylic on Paper   12/08/2007

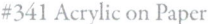

#343 Oil on Paper   12/09/2007

COUGAR PEAK-A-BOO
- The Art of Jared Shear -

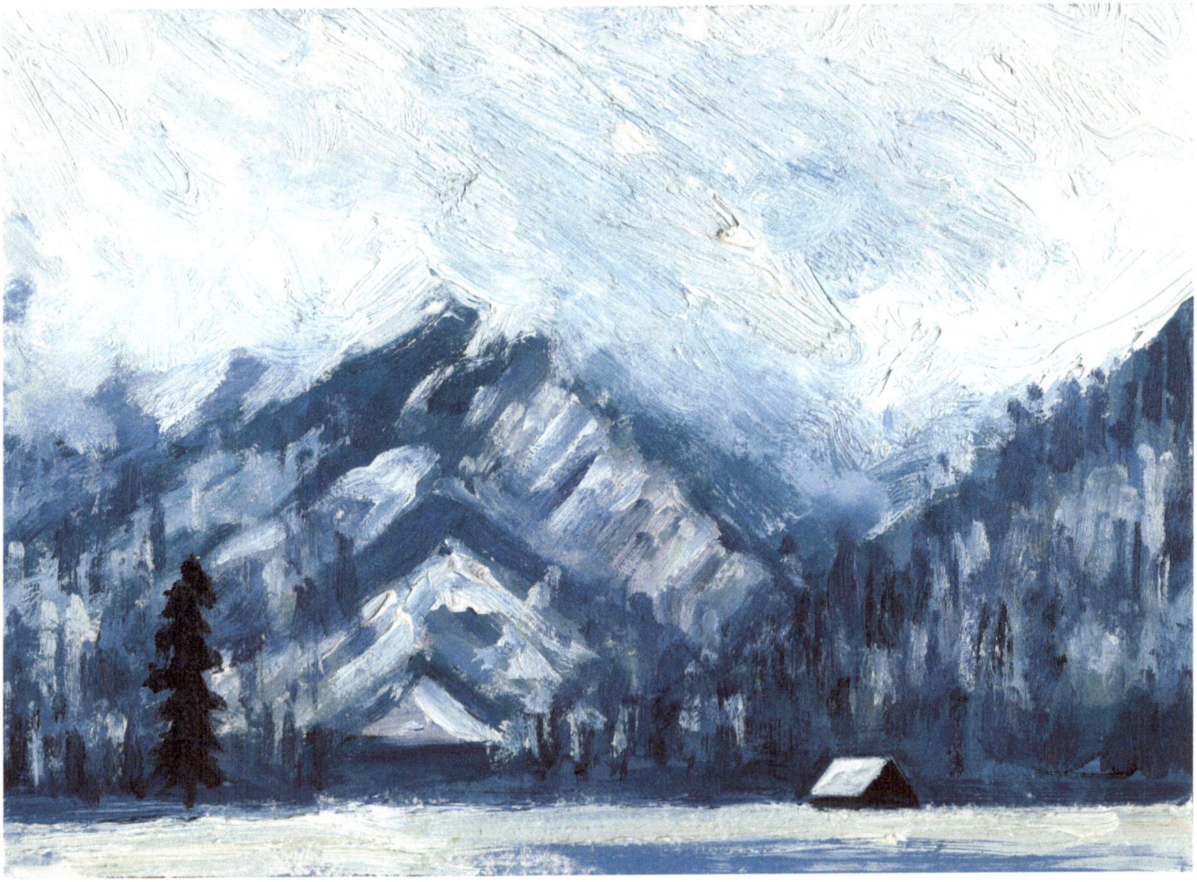

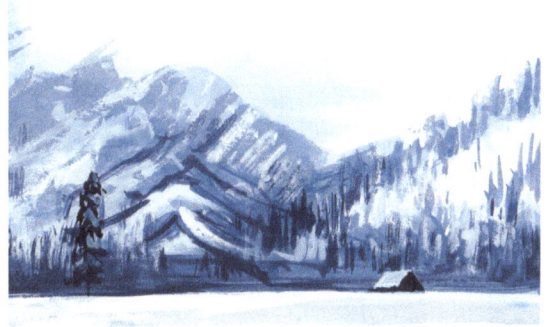

#344 Oil on Paper   12/10/2007

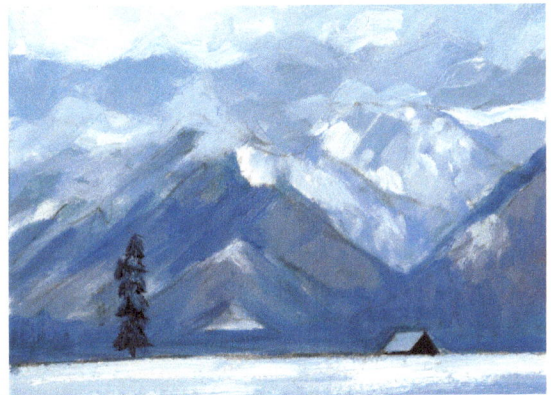

#345 Oil on Paper   12/11/2007

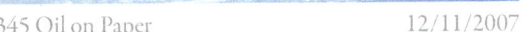

#346 Gouache on Paper   12/12/2007

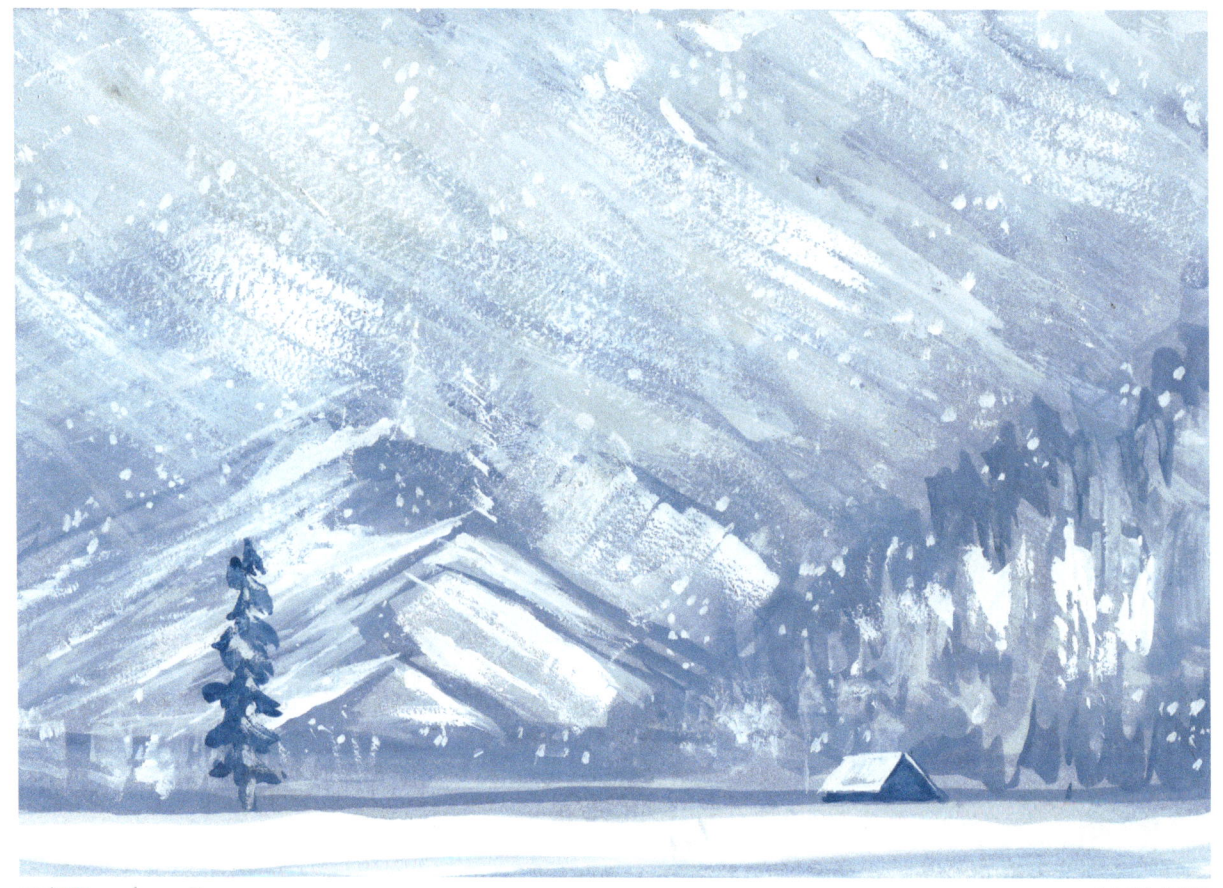

#347 Gouache on Paper   12/13/2007

COUGAR PEAK-A-BOO
- The Art of Jared Shear -

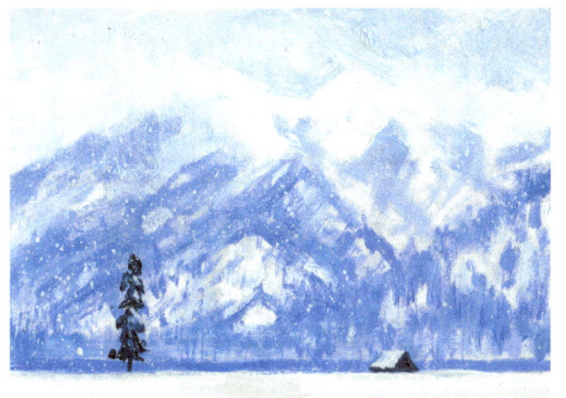

#348 Oil on Paper 12/14/2007

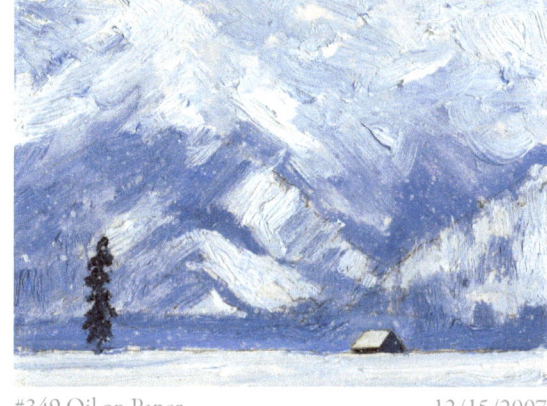

#349 Oil on Paper 12/15/2007

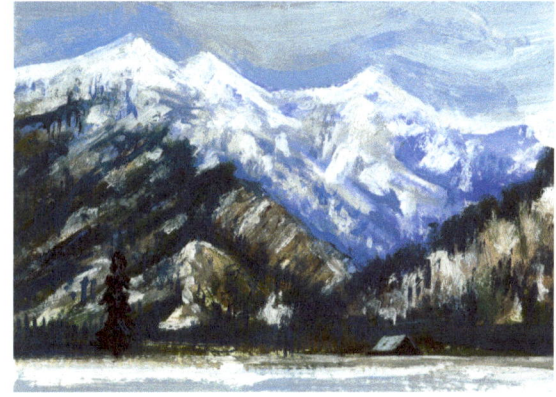

#350 Oil on Paper 12/16/2007

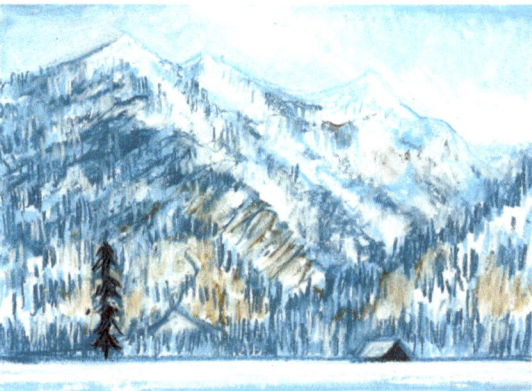

#351 Pastel on Paper 12/17/2007

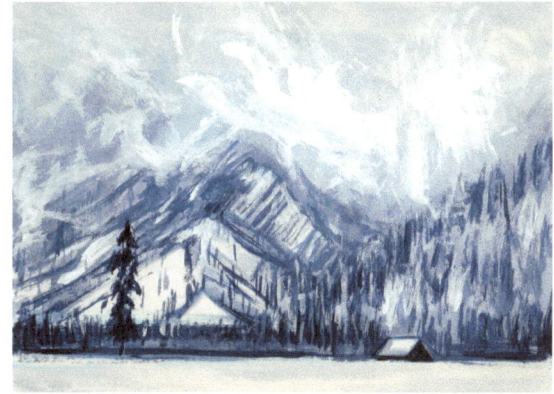

#352 Acrylic on Paper 12/18/2007

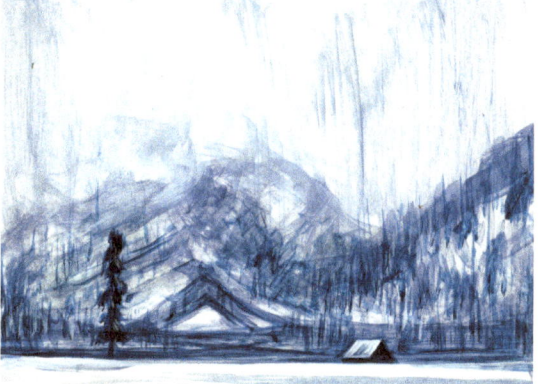

#353 Acrylic on Paper 12/19/2007

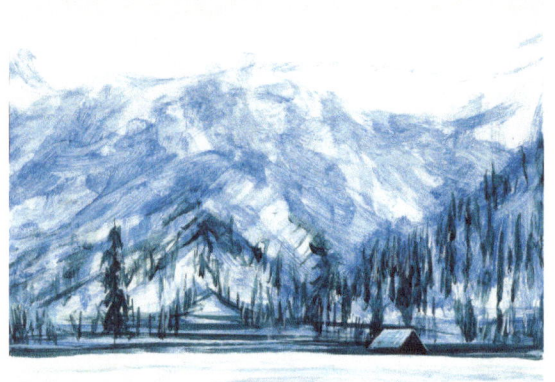

#354 Acrylic on Paper   12/20/2007

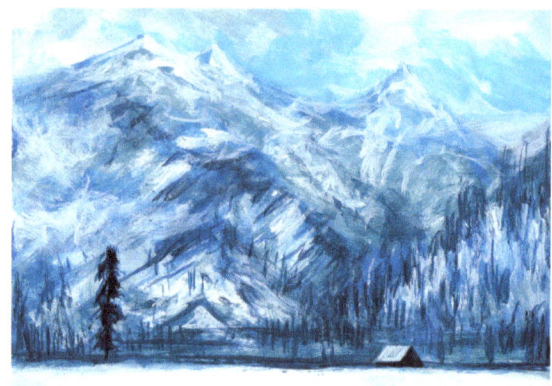

#355 Acrylic on Paper   12/21/2007

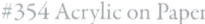

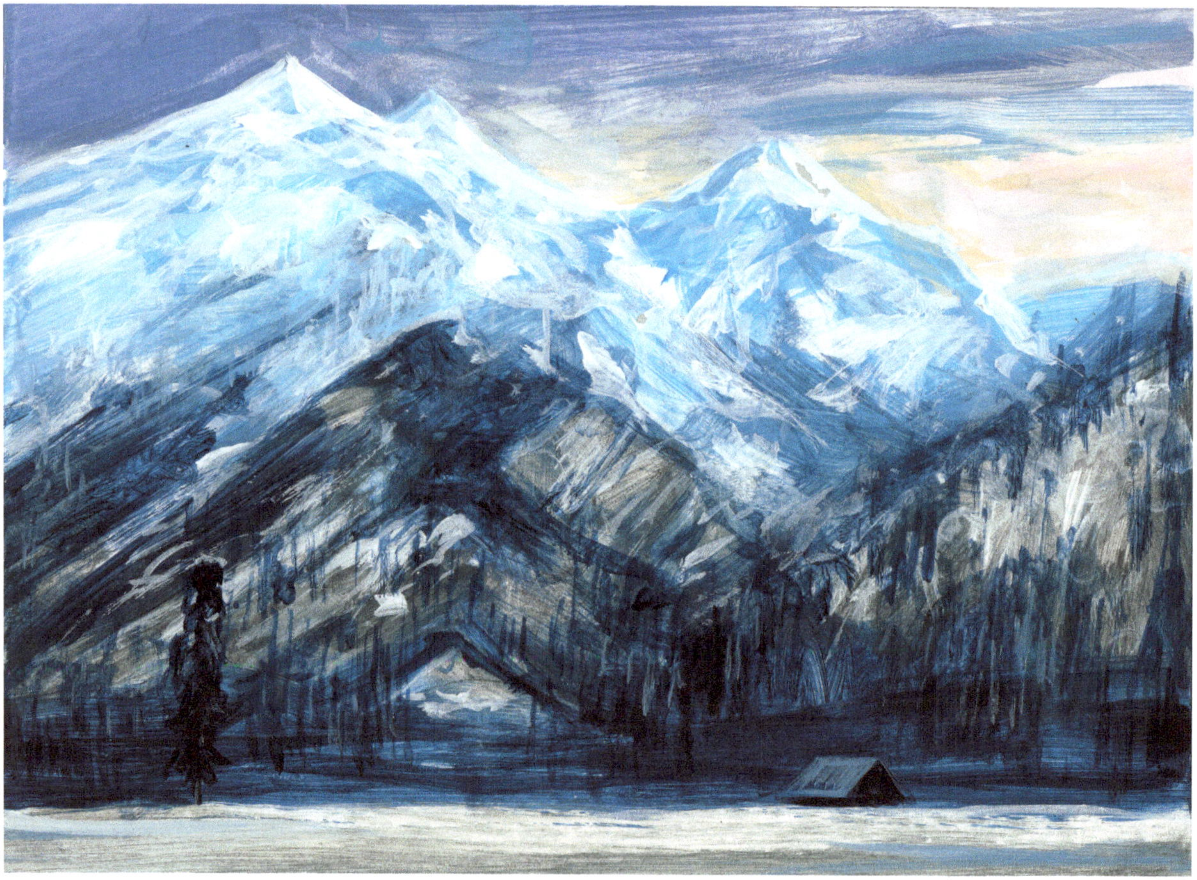

#356 Acrylic on Paper   12/22/2007

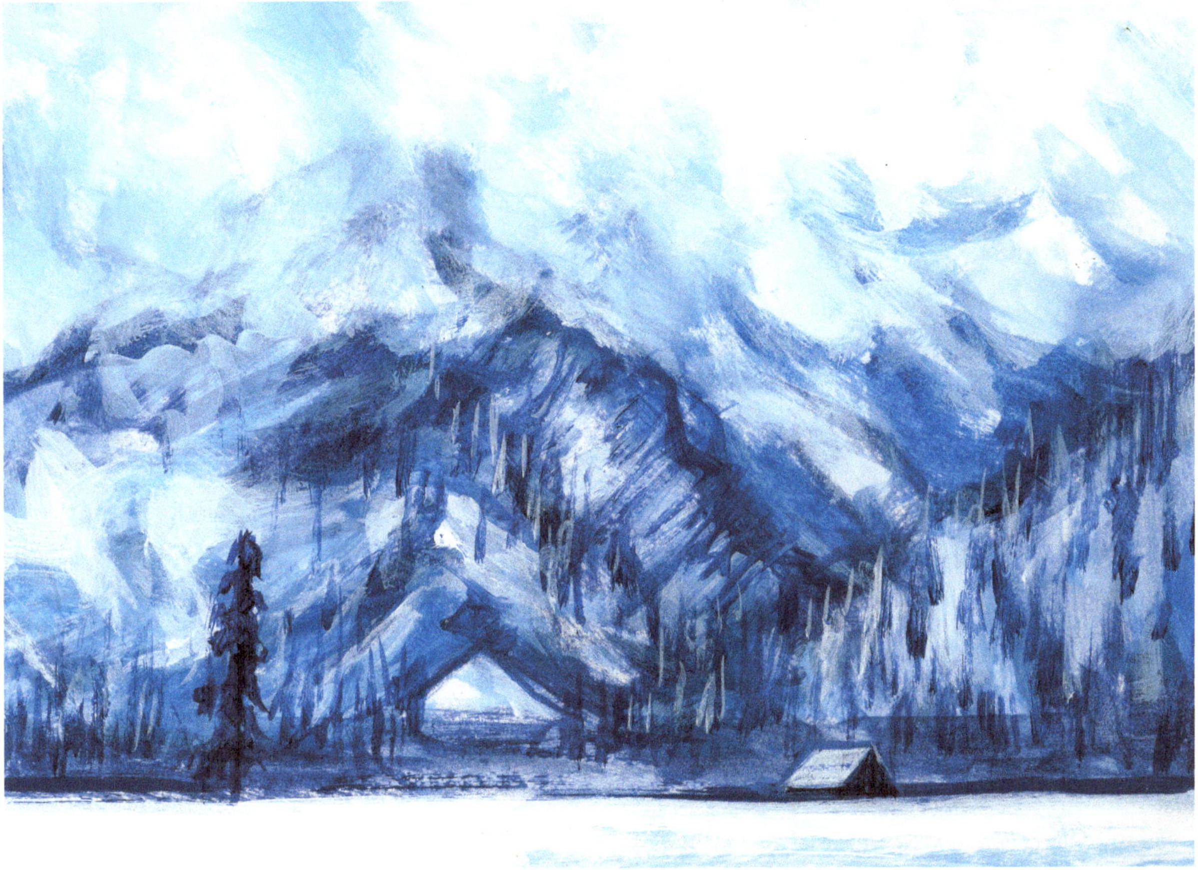

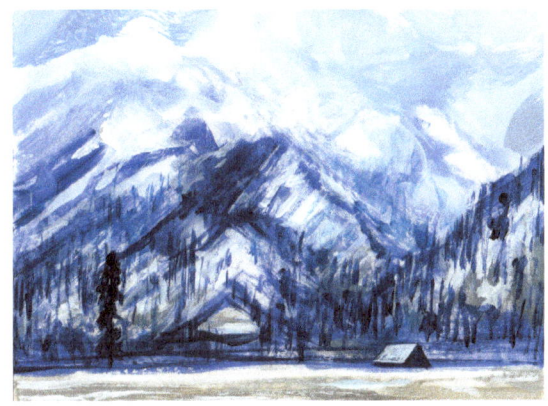

#357 Acrylic on Paper   12/23/2007

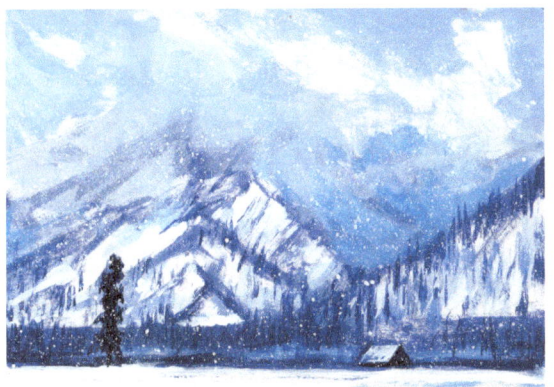

#358 Acrylic on Paper   12/24/2007

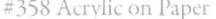

#359 Acrylic on Paper   12/25/2007

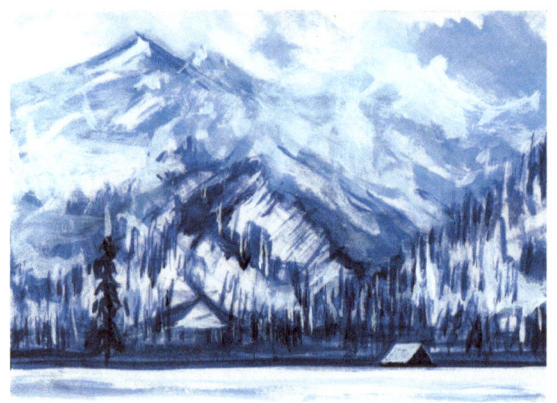

#360 Acrylic on Paper   12/26/2007

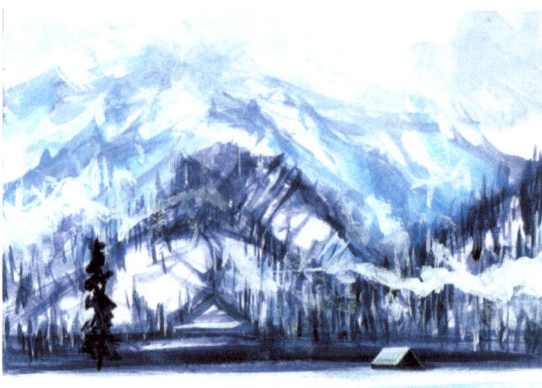

#361 Acrylic on Paper   12/27/2007

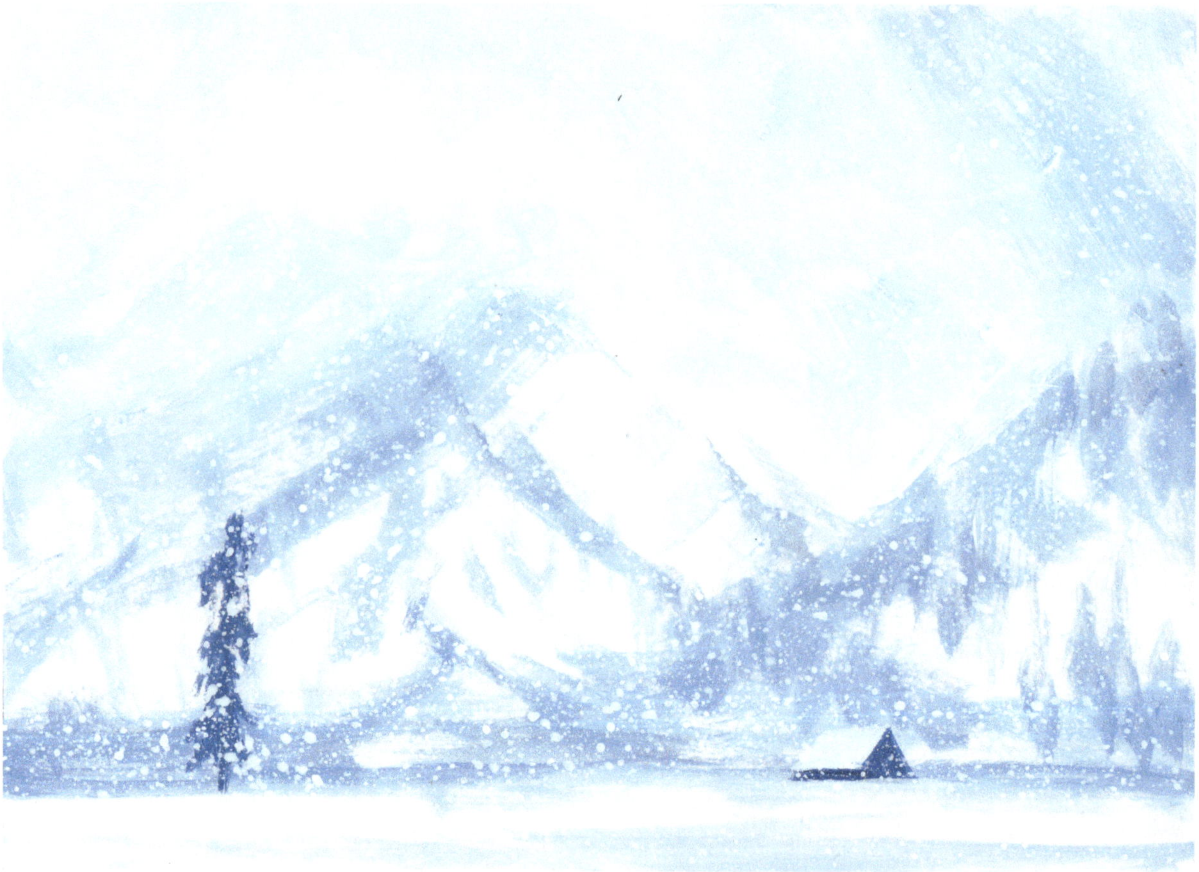

#362 Acrylic on Paper   12/28/2007

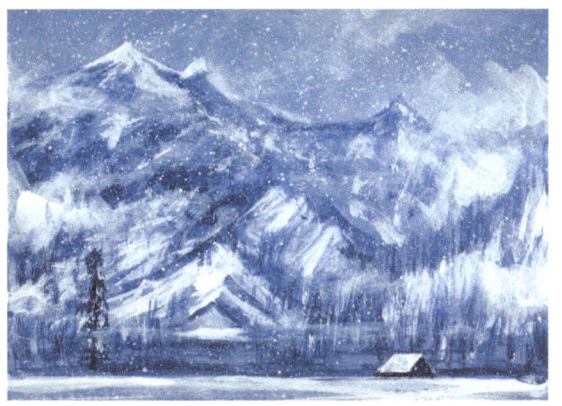

#363 Acrylic on Paper   12/29/2007

#364 Acrylic on Paper   12/30/2007

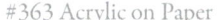

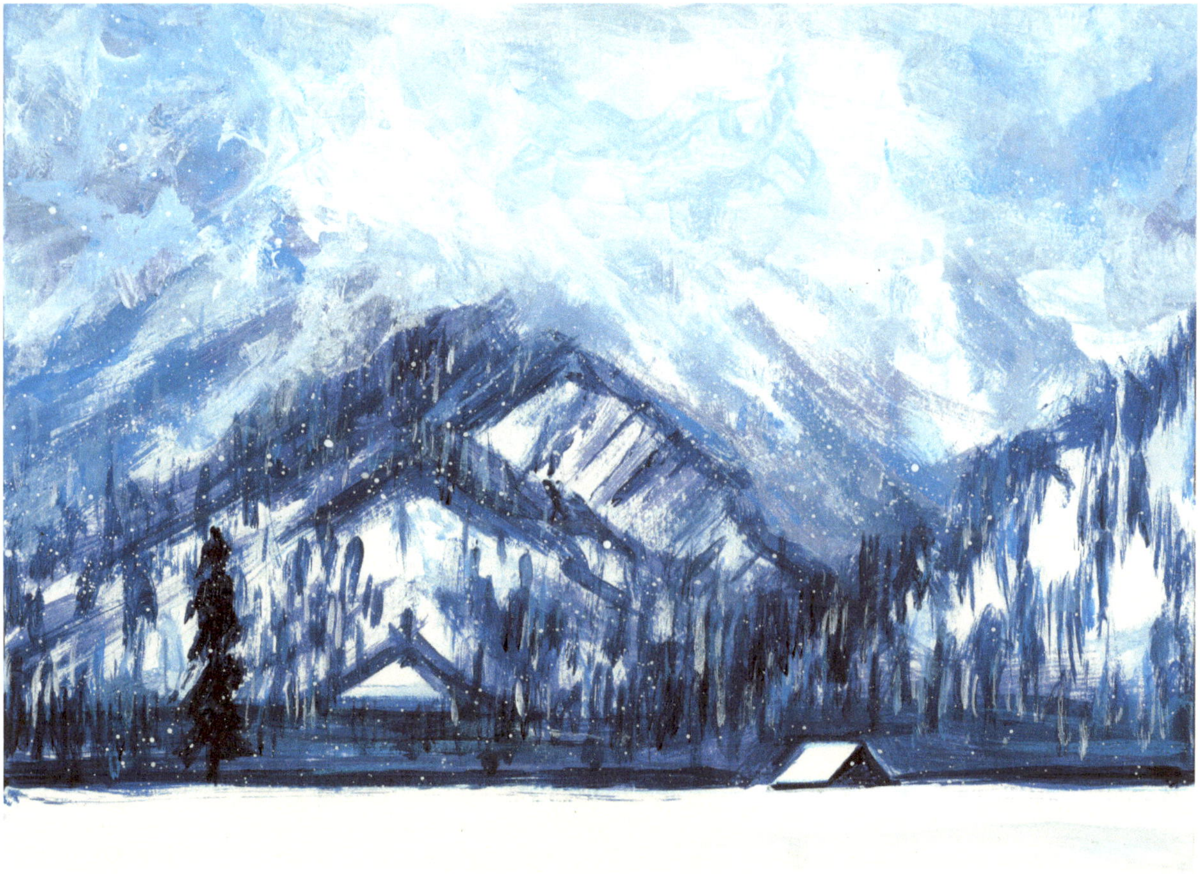

#365 Acrylic on Paper   12/31/2007

acknowledgments

I would to thank everyone who supported me during the creation of this series. I seriously could not have made it to the finish line without the interest, encouragement, and enthusiasm for these paintings that everyone showed me.

Thank you Jennifer my wife for you steadfast support!

To my parents......thank you for everything! I am indebted forever to the both of you.

I would like to extend a big thank you to all of my internet peeps that followed along on the blog while I was creating the series. You guys kept me going!

Nathan Fowkes thank you. You are a huge inspiration.

I also want to thank Kally Thurman for pushing me to display this body of work.

Of course, I would be remiss as to not credit the Creator of Heaven and Earth for forming such an amazing mountain, creating color and light to wrap around it, and giving me eyes, limbs and a mind to then capture it all with paints.

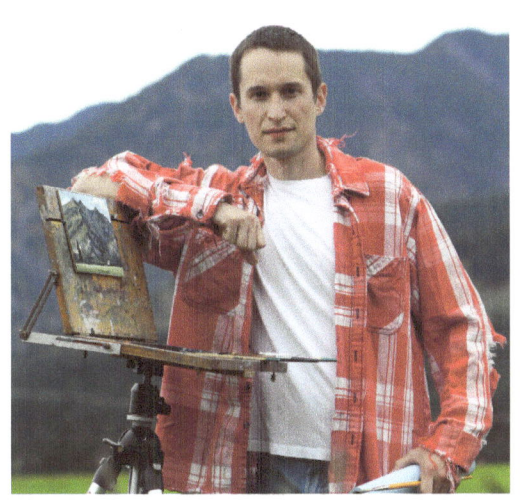

Jared Shear is a native of Montana. Currently he resides in the town of Thompson Falls with his wife and children. He studied computer animation at the Art Institute of Seattle, and received a degree in 1997. After working in the animation industry on various commercials and television properties, he returned to Montana. Jared is an avid plein air painter. His work has been shown in various galleries and museums throughout the northwest. Most days you will find him outdoors with paints, and brush in hand, capturing the landscape around him.

www.ingramcontent.com/pod-product-compliance
Lightning Source LLC
Chambersburg PA
CBHW050719180526
45159CB00003B/1077